AT WORK IN
THE FIELDS
OF
THE BOMB

1. Model of the Uranium Atom   Uranium is the basic element from which nuclear explosives are made. *American Museum of Science and Energy, Oak Ridge, Tennessee. June 11, 1982.*

AT WORK IN THE FIELDS OF THE BOMB

PHOTOGRAPHS AND TEXT BY
ROBERT DEL TREDICI

INTRODUCTION BY JONATHAN SCHELL

PERENNIAL LIBRARY

HARPER & ROW, PUBLISHERS, NEW YORK
CAMBRIDGE, PHILADELPHIA, SAN FRANCISCO, WASHINGTON
LONDON, MEXICO CITY, SÃO PAULO, SINGAPORE, SYDNEY

2. The Amount of Plutonium in the Nagasaki Bomb This glass ball, 3.2 inches across, is the size of the plutonium core in the bomb that exploded over Nagasaki with a force equivalent to 22,000 tons of TNT. *Kansas City, Missouri. September 22, 1983.*

FIRST EDITION

Library of Congress Cataloging-in-Publication Data

Del Tredici, Robert.
  At work in the fields of the bomb.

1. Nuclear weapons—United States.
2. Nuclear weapons—United States—
Pictorial works. I. Title.
U264.D445 1987   355.8′25119′0973
87-45041
ISBN 0-06-055059-7
87 88 89 90 91 10 9 8 7 6 5 4 3 2 1
ISBN 0-06-096164-3 (pbk.)
87 88 89 90 91 10 9 8 7 6 5 4 3 2 1

ACKNOWLEDGMENTS

Thanks are due here to Sidney Peterson, a guide from before the beginning; to Howard Morland, who got me started; and to Dr. Thomas Mancuso, who held me to the straight and narrow.

I am deeply indebted to the Canada Council, whose funding over the years enabled me to make my vision real; and to the United States Department of Energy and the Department of Defense, whose consistent, long-term, ongoing cooperation has made the reality of that vision meaningful.

Special thanks are due to my agent, Joseph Spieler, for his faith in the work and his production concepts; to my editor, Carol Cohen; and to Marty Moskof. All worked beyond the call of duty to help bring out this book.

I wish to thank Sarah Butterfield for her inspired assistance in putting the main images in sequence; to Merilly Weisbord, writer, for her peerless and unstinting aid on the captions and Field Notes; and to Peter Kadelbach, photographer and printer, for working with my negatives to produce all the positives for the plates. Thanks are also due to David Albright for reviewing the technical material; I hold myself responsible for what inaccuracies may remain.

My mentors in the atomic realm throughout this project include Dr. Ernest Sternglass, Robert Alvarez, Dr. Gordon Edwards, Stan Norris, Albert Bates, Ferenc Szasz, Keiko Ogura, Ichiro Kawamoto, Jane Lee, Vince Leo, Richard Elias.

I also wish to thank a network of people who made my journeys through the Fields of the Bomb especially meaningful: Helen Del Tredici, Kitty Boniske, Cooper and Namomi Brown, Gaye Devoss, Art and Maxine Dexter, Naomi Diamond, Mary Ann Flood, Bernd and Lesley Franke, John and Joan Harris, Sebia Hawkins, Gan Ishikawa, Brenda Keesal, Patsy Kottmeier, Susan Lambert, Diane Langmuir, Dorothy Legaretta, Jim Lerager, Bernie Lucht, Evelyn McConeghy, Greg Mitchell, Naoko Naganuma, Chester and Brenda Pelkey, Joan Price, Paul Schaeffer, Geoff Sea, Beth Seberger, Reed Smith, Michael Stewart of Lighthawk, Mary Stuckey, David Swain, Tom Tarbet, Linda Taylor, Ann Thomas, the late Chögyam Trungpa, Kitty Tucker, Mary Watkins, and Bob and Margaret Wyatt.

Finally, my heartfelt gratitude to Mark Achbar, who applied his unique combination of talents and technological skills to every aspect of the project, and whose unwavering support, especially in the final hours, helped bring this book in under the wire.

for Setsumi
with love

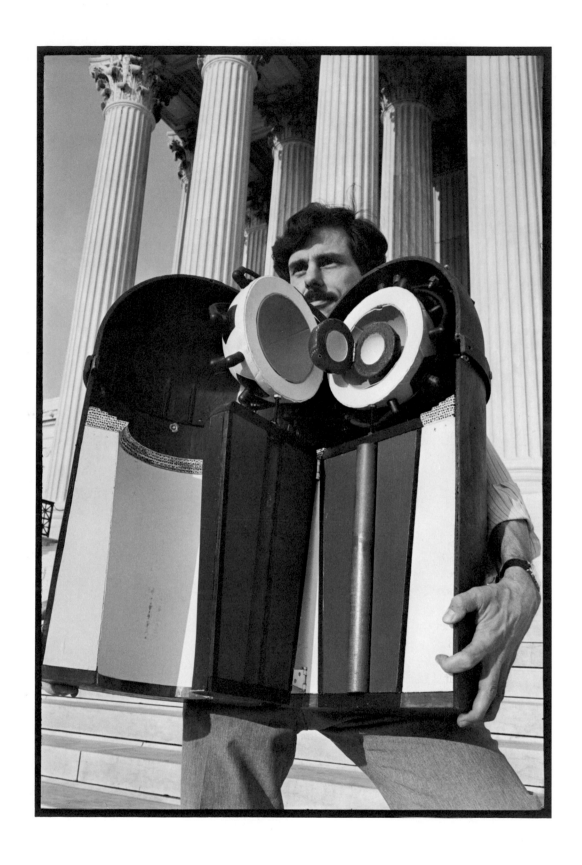

3. Howard Morland's Model of a Modern H-bomb Warhead   A warhead this size produces an explosion about 20 times more powerful than the Hiroshima bomb. Such warheads are carried by MX, Trident, Minuteman, and Cruise missiles. *Washington, D.C. July 10, 1983.*

TABLE OF CONTENTS

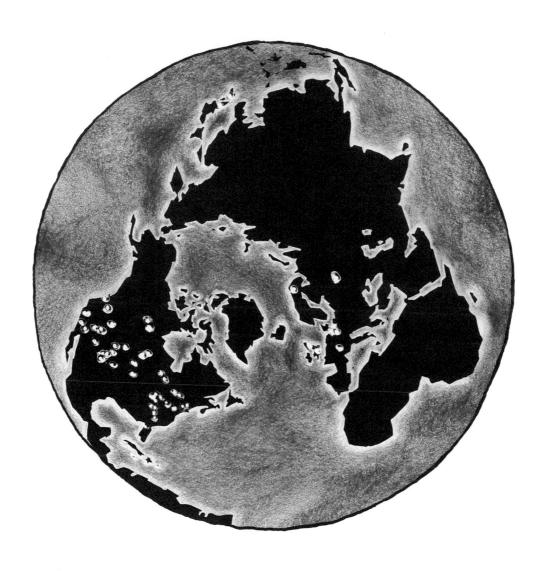

Global View All the sites depicted in this book.
These sites include about one-third of the world's nuclear weapons production facilities.

PREFACE

At Work in the Fields of the Bomb began the day it dawned on me I'd never seen an H-bomb factory. I knew that nuclear weapons didn't grow on trees, but I couldn't tell you how they did grow. I soon learned that there are thirteen plants across America mass-producing materials and parts for the Bomb's explosive warhead—a vast assembly line of factories with a single final assembly point in Texas. I also learned that these facilities, while contributing toward an end product that is highly classified, have public relations personnel to handle media requests. Finally, I discovered that the airspace directly over these plants is zoned the same as space above civilian industry. This meant that at 2,000 feet I could legally photograph the H-bomb factories through the open window of a rented single-engine plane.

These facts led me to believe I had a fighting chance to meet the Bomb on its home ground. I began from the United States, where the apparatus of democracy still allowed an outside observer like me passage through its weapons complex. I finished the project while it was still possible—through the eyes of living witnesses—to see back to day one of the nuclear age. More than once in my encounters with atomic pioneers and on expeditions to America's aging bomb factories I felt I was coming from some future time-machine back to that legendary era when nuclear weapons ruled the earth.

When the U.S. bombed Hiroshima and Nagasaki, one reason given was that the power of atomic weapons had to be seen to be believed. But news of the Bomb's aftereffects quickly vanished, censored in Japan by the Occupation's Press Code. For seven years people in Japan and abroad were kept from seeing survivors' stories, medical reports, news articles, poems, and private letters depicting the Bomb's ongoing impact. So the drama of survival in those first atomic cities was eclipsed by the Bomb as an idea: a breakthrough in physics, a device for ending war, it was, in the minds of some, even a way of saving lives.

Ever since that time nuclear weapons have been seen chiefly from the victor's point of view. Our mental picture of the Bomb includes the distant mushroom cloud, a city turned to ash, rockets in the atmosphere, the tapered cone—icons worn smooth by time and use.

This book represents six years' work on a body of basic words and images designed to shed new light on the Bomb. I am aiming to close the gap between our icons and reality in the matter of these weapons by showing the nuclear arsenal at its source—and the people of the Bomb on their own terms. I want to give the collective imagination something accurate and graphic to hang onto as it tries to come to grips with the Bomb's reality.

—*Robert Del Tredici*
July 1987

INTRODUCTION

One of the most important photographs in this very important book of photographs is one that was not taken. The act of not taking it is described to Robert Del Tredici by Yoshito Matsushige, who, in the hours immediately after the atomic bombing of Hiroshima, on August 6, 1945, wandered through the city with camera in hand, sometimes managing to take pictures but at other times refraining. Matsushige, who was a photographer for the Hiroshima newspaper *Chugoku Shimbun*, found himself confronted at one point in his wanderings with a streetcar full of dead people. "I went up to it and looked inside," he told Del Tredici. "It was jammed with people. They were all in normal positions, holding onto streetcar straps, sitting down or standing still, just the way they would have been before the bomb went off. Except that all of them were leaning in the same direction— away from the blast. And they were all burned black, a reddish black, and they were stiff." Matsushige put one foot up on the streetcar, raised his camera to his eye, and put his finger on the shutter, but he found that he could not take the picture. Seeking to account for his paralysis, he explained: "Before I became a professional cameraman I had been just an ordinary person."

No story I know of illustrates more starkly the immense, unique difficulties that have faced all of us in trying to grasp the reality of the nuclear peril—to penetrate what Robert Del Tredici has called the "amazing invisibility" of the bomb. Matsushige stood face to face with the truth of the nuclear age. He was a professional photographer. Yet he could not take the picture.

Matsushige's story shows that the invisibility of the bomb has deep psychological and spiritual causes, yet this invisibility also has what might be called a structural cause. The ultimate peril posed by nuclear weapons is the extinction of mankind, but that event, in its very nature, must always remain invisible to us—not because there won't be a great deal to see but because, by definition, when the last act is played there will be no one left to see it. Every human catastrophe short of extinction leaves behind witnesses who can record what has happened, permitting the rest of us to write about it, raise monuments to the victims, or otherwise seek to express its meaning. The opportunity to look back on catastrophes and learn from them is like a second chance—a sort of forgiveness that is built into the very nature of human events. But in the case of extinction, the second chance is repealed and forgiveness withdrawn. The verdict is eternal. Therefore, in the matter of this one peril any wisdom we might seek to bring to bear must come before the fact. We need to find in the present some equivalent of the processes that usually occur through recollection: we are asked to "remember" what hasn't yet happened, to "mourn" for victims who have not yet died, to learn from "experience" that we have not had and can never have.

Robert Del Tredici's photographs and interviews are addressd to this task. He has pitted his camera against all the forms of the bomb's invisibility. He had the idea, as original as it was simple, of traveling through the United States to photograph the H-bomb factories. A plant at which uranium salt crystals are converted into metal is no doubt a less exciting sight than the destruction of the world. But precisely because we can't see the destruction of the world, the preparations for bringing it about deserve our special attention.

This view of the nuclear peril is necessarily an oblique one, but Del Tredici has the qualities needed for oblique observation: quiet attention to detail, the ability to find meaning in "ordinary" sights, a feel for "the spirit of a place." The photographs reward our attention. They offer, for the first time, a basic visual vocabulary for the processes by which we are preparing our self-destruction. The very actuality of the factories, strangely, comes as a kind of surprise—as if, having learned to think of the nuclear peril as "unthinkable," we find it startling to see the actual machinery being run by actual people in actual communities. Missing here, of course, is the drama and spectacle of "doom." Also missing is any feeling of romantic grandeur in connection with the bomb—a feeling best represented, perhaps, by Robert Oppenheimer's grandiose thought (derived from a line in the *Bhagavad Gita*) upon seeing the first explosion of an atomic weapon, in Alamogordo, New Mexico: "I am become death, the destroyer of worlds." Instead, almost half a century later, the note that is repeatedly struck is one of blankness.

That note is struck, for example, in the words of Del Tredici's interview with Paul Wagner, public relations manager for the Department of Energy at Pantex, near Amarillo, Texas. Wagner describes the nuclear peril as "the biggest non-issue of the twentieth century" and says that for him handling nuclear weapons is "just like pickin' up a box of Silly Putty in a dime store." A note of blankness is present also in the photograph of, and interview with, the two stalwart young men whose job it is to stand ready to launch Minuteman missiles. Asked to rehearse a missile launch, they perform in perfect clockwork, but when asked what they would do after the missiles have been released, they falter: "Well, um—then we have other, uh, procedures to go through. . . . We'd remain on alert until, well, um, basically until we're told not to be." All of this is a far cry from the dramatic renderings on television and elsewhere that are sometimes offered to rouse us to the peril of nuclear war, but it may offer a more authentic clue to the nature of the peril, whose direst consequence, after all, is eternal nothingness. In *The Waves* by Virginia Woolf, there is the recurring line "a fin in a waste of waters," which the reader can interpret as a portent of death. The scenes shown in Robert Del Tredici's photographs are the fin of mankind's death breaking the waters of our world. We cannot be witnesses to our own extinction. Del Tredici invites us to look at what we can see. There will never be anything more.

——*Jonathan Schell*

4. The Hiroshima Bomb   This is a duplicate outer shell of the first atomic bomb used on a civilian population. Ten and a half feet long, 9,700 pounds, nicknamed "Little Boy," it completely destroyed the city of Hiroshima. *Smithsonian Air and Space Museum exhibit: "The Social Impact of Flight," Washington, D.C. June 25, 1981.*

5. Dr. Karl Z. Morgan, the Father of Health Physics *Atlanta, Georgia. August 8, 1983.* The Manhattan Project hired Dr. Morgan to be director of Health Physics at the Oak Ridge National Laboratory. He helped determine the radiation limits for workers who produced the first atomic bombs. Dr. Morgan went on to serve as director of Health Physics at Oak Ridge for 29 years.

"There is no safe level of radiation exposure. So the question is not: What is a safe level? The question is: How great is the risk?"

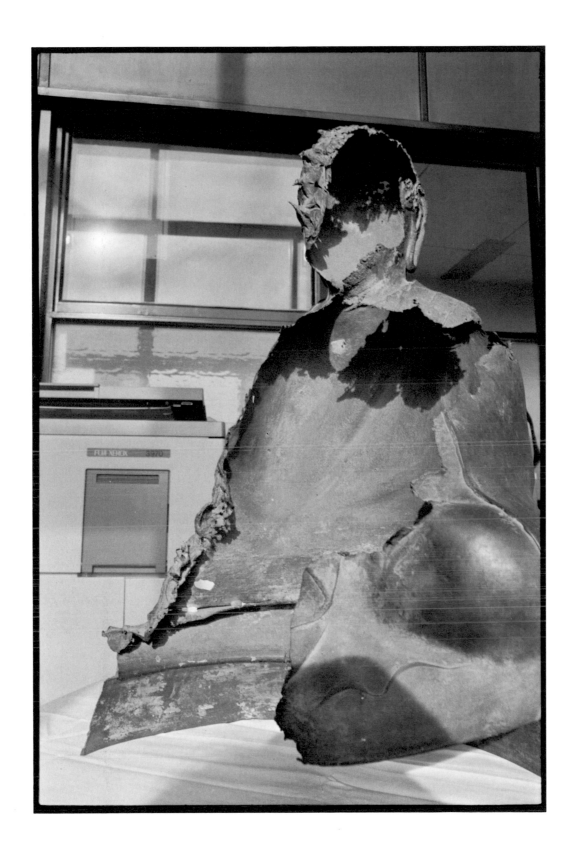

6. Hiroshima Buddha   This bronze Buddha was melted by heat from the Hiroshima bomb. Bronze melts at around 1600 degrees F. The temperature on the ground beneath the exploding Hiroshima bomb reached about 7000 degrees. *Hiroshima Peace Museum, Hiroshima, Japan. November 13, 1984.*

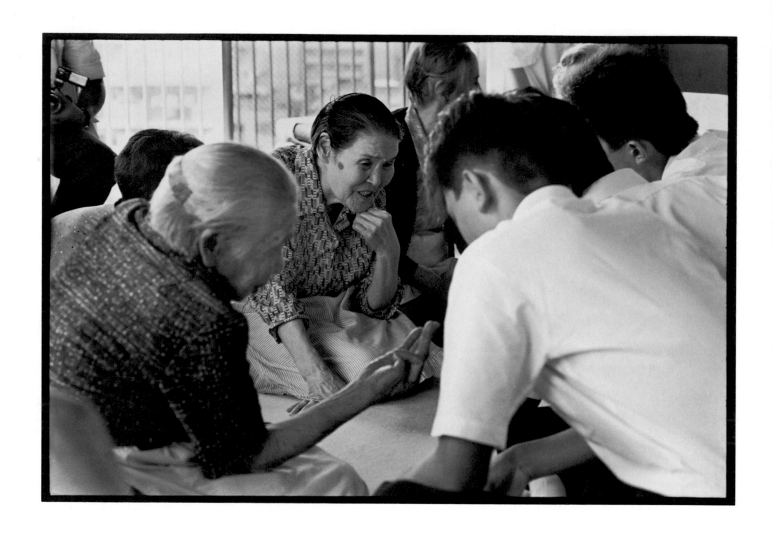

7. Aged *Hibakusha* Victims of the Hiroshima bomb pass on their experience of nuclear war. In Japan the word *hibakusha* was specially created to describe atomic bomb survivors. *Hibakusha* means "those who have received the bomb." *Home for Aged Hibakusha, Funairi, Hiroshima, Japan. September 8, 1984.*

8. Pathological Atomic Bomb Materials Storage Room   This room contains 2,000 jars of human organs from people irradiated by the Nagasaki bomb. The organs are saved in hopes that scientists will one day learn how to glean information from them about radiation damage. *Nagasaki Medical School, Japan. September 24, 1984.*

9. **Duplicate "Fat Man"**   Nicknamed "Fat Man," the plutonium bomb that destroyed Nagasaki used a different technology from the Hiroshima uranium bomb. Fat Man's trigger mechanism became the prototype for modern nuclear warheads. Paul Wagner, left, is public relations officer for the Department of Energy at Pantex, and Charles Poole, right, is plant manager for Mason & Hanger-Silas Mason. *Administration Building, Pantex Nuclear Weapons Final Assembly Plant, Carson County, Texas. August 10, 1982.*

10. **The First Droppable H-bomb**   This is a duplicate outer casing of the Mark 17, America's first droppable hydrogen bomb. Measuring 24 feet, 6 inches and weighing approximately 21 tons, it was exploded from a steel tower on Bikini Island, March 1, 1954, in a test code-named "Bravo." Its 15-megaton yield was equivalent to 1,200 Hiroshimas, making it the most powerful H-bomb explosion in U.S. history. Fallout from the test covered 7,000 square miles. *Strategic Air Command Museum, Offutt Air Force Base, Omaha, Nebraska. November 13, 1984.*

11. Terminal Guidance A Goodyear sales representative displays Goodyear's contribution to the Pershing II missile system: the terminal-guidance all-weather gyroscopic radar/video synchronization unit. Pershing II is a medium-range missile; it can strike Soviet targets from bases in West Germany within 10 minutes. Terminal guidance enables the Pershing II to correct its flight path up to the moment of final impact. *U.S. Army Weapons Bazaar, Sheraton Hotel, Washington, D.C. October 15, 1986.*

12. Pantex Nuclear Weapons Final Assembly Plant   Pantex, America's only nuclear weapons final-assembly plant, receives parts from facilities throughout the U.S., in some 120 subassemblies made up of about 2,000 separate pieces. Pantex provides 2,700 jobs. It is Amarillo's largest employer. *Carson County, Texas. August 19, 1982.*

13. The Richest Uranium Mine on Earth   The Gaertner pit at the Key Lake Mine is the most productive uranium mine in the world. Uranium rock here is richest where the earth is blackest. At a nearby mill, the ore is crushed, refined, and turned into a powdered concentrate called yellowcake. Radiation in this pit can be 7,000 times higher than normal background levels. *Gaertner Pit, Key Lake Mine, Northern Saskatchewan, Canada, September 17, 1986.*

14. Uranium Green Salt Ten-gallon drums of uranium green salt line the floor of the Fernald Green Salt Plant. Uranium green salt, the product of a long chain of chemical transformations, is the base element for the transformation of uranium into metal. *Building 4, Feed Materials Production Center, Fernald, Ohio. December 16, 1985.*

15. Fernald Feed Materials Production Center

Owner: United States Department of Energy
Managing contractor: National Lead of Ohio, 1951–1986. Westinghouse, 1986–
Area of plant: 136 acres; total site area: 1,050 acres
Structures: 9 plants, 73 buildings
Employees: 1,000
Principal product: Uranium metal forms: derbies, ingots, rods, and tubes for nuclear weapons factories

The Fernald facility is called a "feed materials production center" because it produces uranium materials which it feeds to the rest of the nuclear weapons complex. *Fernald, 20 miles northwest of Cincinnati, Ohio. May 22, 1984.*

16. Walking the Derby A metals production worker walks a hot cylinder away from a bank of furnaces into the cooling zone. At the bottom of this cylinder sits a lump of uranium "derby" metal about the size of a birthday cake, created by "cooking" a mixture of green salt crystals and magnesium granules. After 4 hours at 1300 degrees F, the magnesium flashes into an explosion, raising

temperatures to 3000 degrees and reducing the green salt crystals to metal. The new metal is called a derby because it is shaped more or less like the top of a derby hat. *Building 5, Metals Production Plant, Feed Materials Production Center, Fernald, Ohio. December 16, 1985.*

17. Cooling the Derby   The hot cylinder containing new uranium derby metal is lowered into water for cooling.

18. Sampling the Derby   This woman drills holes in new derbies and sends the uranium metal shavings to a lab that measures their radioactivity. The metal gives off alpha, beta, and gamma radiation. At the surface of the derby, the radiation levels are 260 millirem/hr of beta and 10 millirem/hr of gamma. The woman wears a flower in her hair because it is the week before Christmas.

Feed Materials Production Center, Fernald, Ohio. December 17, 1985.

19. **Ingots of Fernald at Ashtabula**   These ingots, made at Fernald by remelting uranium metal derbies, have been trucked 300 miles northeast to Ashtabula, Ohio, for further processing. Here they will be submerged in molten salt until they reach a red-hot 1100°F. Then they will be inserted into the Ashtabula uranium metal extrusion press. The sign in the background reads "Caution: Radioactive Materials."

20. **Ashtabula Uranium Metal Extrusion Press**   This press squeezes red-hot uranium ingots into long tubes. The uranium tubes are cut into 14-inch lengths at Fernald. These segments are then sent to South Carolina to be bombarded with neutrons and transformed into plutonium.

Reactive Metals, Incorporated, Ashtabula, Ohio. June 19, 1984.

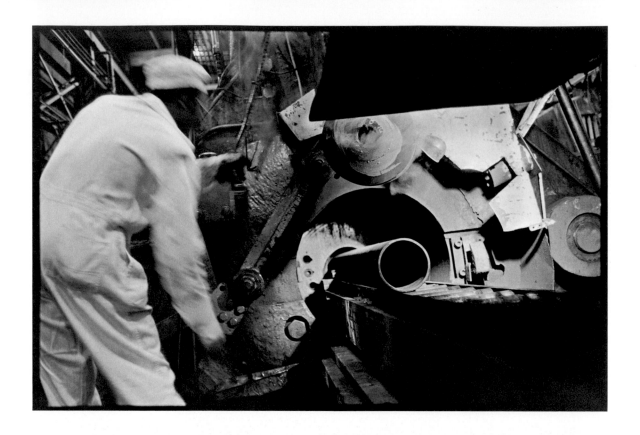

21. The Back End of the Ashtabula Press A worker waits for an extrusion of uranium metal to exit from the press.

22. Pickled Extrusion Inspection An inspector okays the new extrusion. It has been cooled in air, quenched in water, and given a bath in acid. At this point it is referred to as a "pickled extrusion."

Reactive Metals, Incorporated, Ashtabula, Ohio. June 19, 1984.

23. Ashtabula Quench   The newly extruded uranium metal, hot out of the press, is cooled in air for 6 minutes, then dunked in a quench tank. Quenching sends clouds of steam mixed with uranium oxide into the factory air. *Reactive Metals, Incorporated, Ashtabula, Ohio. June 19, 1984.*

24. Back to Fernald   Ashtabula returns uranium metal, in the form of long tubes, to Fernald. A worker stands by while a blanking machine cuts the metal into 14-inch segments, each weighing 28 pounds. These are Fernald's top product: Mark 31 Target Element Cores. They are called target element cores because at Department of Energy reactors elsewhere they will be bombarded with neutrons and transformed into weapons-grade plutonium. *Feed Materials Production Center, Fernald, Ohio. December 17, 1985.*

25. Laundry   Each day Fernald's on-site laundry washes all the protective cotton work-suits of its 1,000 employees to rid the clothing of uranium dust. Laundry water must be specially treated because of its uranium content. In December 1984, a special Oak Ridge Task Force reported to the U.S. Congress that the Fernald Feed Materials Production Center had, during its more than 30 years of process operations, released a total of 374,000 pounds of uranium dust into the air and water around the site, and that another 720,000 pounds of uranium remained unaccounted for. *Feed Materials Production Center, Fernald, Ohio. December 16, 1985.*

26. Dr. Thomas Mancuso *Pittsburgh. August 16, 1982.* In 1965, the U.S. government hired Dr. Mancuso to study the radiation exposure records of over 225,000 atomic workers in America's nuclear weapons industry. After 15 years Mancuso concluded that "low-level" exposures over a long period significantly increased workers' chances of developing cancer and that levels considered safe by industry standards were at least 10 times too high. When Mancuso published his findings, the government cut his funds, removed him from the study, and confiscated his data.

"Radiation is the most important subject in the world, and it will be forever, because of the thousands of nuclear weapons and bombs, and the constant threat to civilization and the world. Unfortunately there is no way to continue to study and make known the full range of effects without large sums of independent funding."

27. L-Reactor, Savannah River Plant   It is into this reactor that the Mark 31
Target Element Cores from Fernald are inserted. Here they are bombarded
with neutrons and transformed into plutonium. The three dark pools in front of

the reactor hold water for cooling. Like the Chernobyl reactor, the L-Reactor has no containment vessel. A total of five such reactors were built on the Savannah River Plant site. *Aiken County, South Carolina. August 6, 1983.*

28. William Lawless   *Augusta, Georgia. October 18, 1986.* From 1979 to 1983, William Lawless oversaw nuclear waste disposal at the Savannah River Plant for the Department of Energy. He criticized duPont's waste-disposal practices, particularly its use of cardboard boxes to bury plutonium and other radioactive wastes, and its use of "seepage basins" to dump billions of gallons of contaminated water into the environment. Prevented from releasing his report, Lawless resigned.

"It's a closed system. The secrecy aspect of it has made people feel that if they question what's going on, they're traitors. Somehow we've got to get people in there who really care about what's going on."

29. DuPont Administration Building, Savannah River Plant   Harry Truman signed the Savannah River Plant into existence in 1950. Its mission: to produce plutonium and tritium for America's H-bomb program. The prime contractor was duPont, which cleared 312 square miles and moved four communities to build five plutonium reactors, a tritium facility, two chemicals-separations plants, a heavy-water plant, high-level waste tanks, a low-level radiation dump, a Navy submarine reactor fuels materials facility (1986), and, by 1989, a defense waste-processing plant for turning high-level nuclear waste into glass logs. The plant employs 15,000 people. *Aiken County, South Carolina. August 6, 1983.*

30. Hanford Ditch 216-B (B-2-3)   This ditch is used to dispose of large quantities of contaminated water from plutonium production operations. The water contains radioactive and toxic chemical contaminants. Sandy soil is meant to act as a natural filter for the water as it percolates down to the water table. *200 Area, Hanford Reservation, Richland, Washington. November 16, 1984.*

31. J. S. "Steve" McMillan   *Allendale, South Carolina. August 4, 1983.* Steve McMillan raises hogs, soybeans, corn, watermelons, canteloupes, and pickle cucumbers on a 2,000-acre farm in Allendale, South Carolina. He inherited the land from his father. The Savannah River Plant's plutonium reactors are 20 miles upwind.

"The money goes north," McMillan says, "and the radiation comes south."

32. George Couch *Aiken Community Hospital, South Carolina. August 5, 1983.* George Couch was a maintenance worker at the Savannah River Plant for over 22 years. Shortly before retirement, he contracted *polycythemia vera*, a rare form of blood cancer associated with radiation exposure. He was fired without compensation.

"There is no way of telling how many people have already died from *polycythemia vera*. The only way to know would be to check your people while they're living, except they say it's very expensive. But what is the price of death? How much is a person's life worth?"

33. Test Blast: Official Portrait A public relations officer for the Defense Nuclear Agency (DNA) offers a free 8″ × 10″ glossy of "Minor Scale," a simulated nuclear explosion which took place one hour earlier in the Alamogordo Desert. Journalists were permitted to observe the event but not to photograph it because of the sensitive nature of test apparatus at the base of the explosion. According to the DNA, "Minor Scale was the largest planned conventional explosion in the history of the free world." *White Sands Missile Range, Jornada del Muerto, Alamogordo Desert, New Mexico. June 27, 1985.*

34. Minor Scale: Unofficial Portrait   This photograph of the Minor Scale explosion was taken from inside the press bus 4 minutes after the blast. The Defense Nuclear Agency spent $1 million to set up the test and $37 million to recover data from it. The Minor Scale detonation simulated blast and heat effects of a battlefield nuclear weapon chiefly to test Hardened Mobile Launchers for the new intercontinental Midgetman missile. *White Sands Missile Range, Jornada del Muerto, Alamogordo Desert, New Mexico, June 27, 1985.*

35. St. George, Utah   St. George, sometimes referred to as "Fallout City," is located 135 miles east of the Nevada Test Site. Throughout the '50s and early '60s the Nevada Test Site exploded 100 nuclear weapons in the atmosphere—on average, nearly one bomb a month for 10 years. Testing policy determined that explosions take place when winds shifted away from highly populated areas like Las Vegas and toward sparsely populated areas like St. George. In St. George and southern Utah between 1958 and 1963, the incidence of childhood leukemia was 2.5 times higher than the national average. *St. George, Utah. November 10, 1982.*

36. Sedan Crater

Detonation: 9:00 A.M., July 6, 1962, Nevada Test Site
Yield: 110 kilotons (thermonuclear)
Crater: 600 feet deep, 1,200 feet wide; 179 million cubic feet in volume
Purpose: Earth-moving experiment to determine the feasibility of national-crisis engineering projects, such as the creation of an alternate Panama Canal should the existing waterway become obstructed

Area 10, Nevada Test Site, Nye County, Nevada. October 29, 1984.

37. Judge A. Sherman Christensen *Salt Lake City, Utah, April 26, 1987.* Judge Christensen was the "sheep case" judge. In 1955 Utah ranchers sued the government for the loss of thousands of sheep that died after above-ground atomic tests. On the basis of the evidence presented at the 1956 trial, Judge Christensen ruled that radiation did not cause the deaths. Twenty-five years later he reopened the case and concluded that fraud had been perpetrated on the court at the earlier trial and that the ranchers were entitled to a new trial.

"I set aside the earlier judgment because I was convinced that fraud was practiced by the withholding of evidence and that this was of transcendent importance from the standpoint of judicial administration, trial advocacy, and the integrity of judicial proceedings."

38. Irma Thomas   *St. George, Utah. November 7, 1982.* It took Irma Thomas 18 years to realize that the illness in her neighborhood might be connected to atomic fallout. She was one of the first residents of St. George to publicly question government assurances about the safety of its atomic testing program. Since she first spoke out, many have come forward with their concerns and are suing the government for negligence.

"Psychologists call it mass hysteria. But why wouldn't it be, when it's been mass murder?"

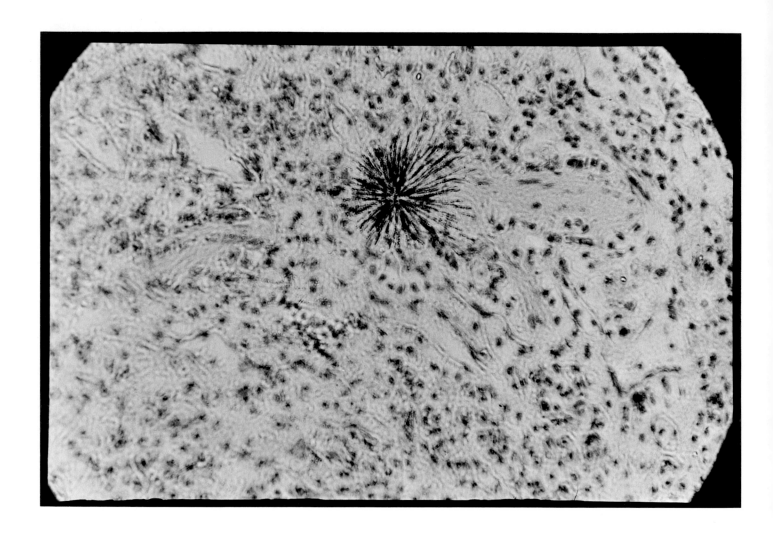

39. Particle of Plutonium   The black star in the middle of the picture shows the tracks made by alpha rays emitted from a particle of plutonium-239 in the lung tissue of an ape. The alpha rays do not travel very far, but once inside the body, they can penetrate more than 10,000 cells within their range. This set of alpha tracks (magnified 500 times) occurred over a 48-hour period. The plutonium particle that emitted them has a half-life of 24,400 years. *Lawrence Radiation Laboratory, Berkeley, California. September 20, 1982.*

40. Dr. Alice Stewart *Birmingham Regional Cancer Registry, England. September 13, 1981.* Dr. Stewart is a world authority on the health hazards of low-level radiation. It was she who determined, in 1956, that a single diagnostic X ray of a pregnant woman increased the risk of cancer in the child by 50–100%. She has gone on to study uranium miners, Japanese A-bomb survivors, and atomic workers. Her new work concentrates on the health effects of naturally occurring background radiation.

"Single-celled organisms could not exist until background radiation fell to present levels millennia ago. And it requires just as delicate an environment for us to survive. Yet today, in the arrogance of humankind, we are raising the levels of background radiation and setting back the evolutionary clock."

41. The Parents of Sadako *Kasuga City, Fukuoka, Japan. October 14, 1984.* Fujiko Sasaki, beside her husband, Shigeo, holds a portrait of Sadako, their 12-year-old daughter. Sadako and her mother were in Hiroshima when the atomic bomb exploded. Sadako was 2 years old at the time. The words under the photograph read:

Sadako Sasaki
First year, Nobori-machi Junior High School
Sub-acute lymphatic leukemia
Died: October 25, 1955

42. Sadako's Paper Cranes These are the handiwork of Sadako Sasaki. When she was 12 years old Sadako contracted leukemia from earlier exposure to the atomic bomb. She did not wish to die. She refused all painkilling medication and took literally a Japanese proverb that says, "If you fold 1,000 paper cranes, you will get whatever you wish." She folded 645 of the tiny birds before she died. *Kasuga City, Fukuoka, Japan. October 14, 1984.*

43. Tapered Line-of-Sight Pipe, "N" Tunnel This 875-foot steel pipe is dug into the side of Rainier Mesa in Area 12 of the Nevada Test Site. The tunnel tests the impact of radiation from a nuclear warhead on other nuclear warheads and on military communications equipment. At the far end of the tunnel is the "Zero

Room," which contains the warhead that will be detonated. When it explodes, radiation comes down the pipe at the speed of light, followed by its expanding shock wave. But within 16 milliseconds, huge blast doors explode shut, trapping the shock wave in the Zero Room so that only radiation hits test equipment in the pipe. The pipe is being readied for the test code-named "Misty Rain." *Area 12, Nevada Test Site, Nye County, Nevada. October 29, 1984.*

44. Tending to "Misty Rain"   This is the front end of the line-of-sight pipe, 875 feet from the Zero Room. The Misty Rain test explosion took place inside this pipe on April 6, 1985. Once the proper equipment was in place, the large, round steel door was welded shut and the line-of-sight pipe was made into a vacuum simulating conditions 300,000 feet above the surface of the earth. Data from the test were used to evaluate the hardness of MX reentry vehicles and the vulnerability of satellites. X-ray laser lethality testing was also conducted. *Area 12, Nevada Test Site, Nye County, Nevada. October 29, 1984.*

45. Trestle EMP   This is the largest wood-and-glue laminated structure in the world. Aircraft placed on top of this trestle are hit with up to 10 million volts of electromagnetic pulse (EMP) energy to simulate the effects of a nuclear explosion on planes in flight. A tiny figure, lower left center, indicates scale. *Kirtland Air Force Base, Albuquerque, New Mexico. July 13, 1983.*

46. MX/Peacekeeper   Shown here are three of the four stages of the MX rocket delivery system. *MX Integrated Test Facility, Vandenberg Air Force Base, Lompoc, California. January 16, 1986.*

47. Sam Cohen, Father of the Neutron Bomb *Beverly Hills, California, December 6, 1984.* Sam Cohen designed the neutron bomb to produce a minimum of explosive blast and a maximum of radiation.

"On a surface level, I've rationalized my fascination with nuclear weapons by saying it's important for the security of my country, and so there are no qualms to be had. If I went down another level in my psyche, I wouldn't know what to say—I've done it because I wanted to."

48. Inside Cheyenne Mountain The NORAD Command and Control Center lies deep within a granite mountain in Colorado. Military personnel enter through 30-ton blast doors. Twenty-four hours a day, Canadian and American crews scan all objects in orbit around the earth. Their job is to phone the president of the United States should a missile be observed. *Colorado Springs, Colorado. August 3, 1982.*

CRISIS RELOCATION PLANNING

49. Russel B. Clanahan *Washington, D.C. October 27, 1982*. Russel B. Clanahan, public relations officer for the Federal Emergency Management Agency, displays a diagram of America's Crisis Relocation Plan for 408 U.S. metropolitan centers.

"This is the Crisis Relocation Plan. To get people out of the hazard areas and into a host area in advance of a nuclear detonation means you're talking about fallout protection rather than blast and fire protection, and this is something that can be done with the technology and resources available. And the protection that would be gained would be substantial."

50. General Paul Tibbets   *Columbus, Ohio. February 20, 1985.* Paul Tibbets was Commander of the 509th Airborne Division, whose mission was to air-drop America's first atomic bombs. Tibbets himself piloted *Enola Gay*, the B-29 that bombed Hiroshima.

"I would like to believe that nuclear weapons as such will never be used again, but I'm not that naive. I think they will be, just because we have them. The question is, how to use them?"

51. Minuteman II Missileers Lieutenants Lamb and Goetz   *Ellsworth Air Force Base, Rapid City, South Dakota. November 21, 1984.* These Strategic Air Command missileers work together in a capsule 60 feet underground. Each is provided with a pistol. Missile duty lasts four years, during which silo operators are required to put in two 24-hour shifts per week for 12 to 16 weeks a year. On November 21, 1984, the activating launch code for a simulated key-turn exercise was "Lima, Alpha, Uniform, November, Charlie, Hotel, Echo, November, Alpha, Bravo, Lima, Echo, Papa, Lima, Charlie, Alpha, Zero, One. Acknowledge. Out." Lieutenant Goetz explains the procedure for launching a group of missiles:

"It takes two launch votes. One is transmitted by two men from this capsule, and another control center does the same thing. So there are quite a few safeguards that we have to go through before we can launch a sortie."

Plates 52, 53, and 54 depict the three components—land, air, and sea—of America's strategic nuclear triad.

52. Down the Hatch A missile silo operator enters the Personnel Access Hatch for maintenance of a Minuteman III missile. *Vandenberg Air Force Base, Lompoc, California. January 17, 1986.*

53. The "Scramble" Members of a strategic bombing crew run to their bomber. *Ellsworth Air Force Base, Rapid City, South Dakota. November 21, 1984.*

54. Trident This submarine, coming up the Hood Canal into Puget Sound, is America's largest underwater strategic weapons launching system. It is powered by a nuclear reactor and carries up to 192 independently targetable nuclear warheads. *Naval Submarine Base Bangor, Hood Canal, Puget Sound, Washington. November 2, 1984.*

55. Admiral Hyman Rickover *New York City. May 9, 1982.* Hyman Rickover was the longest-serving individual in the history of the U.S. Navy. He invented the nuclear submarine and is known as "the Father of the Nuclear Navy." His submarine reactor was so successful it became the basis for America's commercial nuclear power reactors.

"Every time you produce radiation, you produce something that has a certain half-life, in some cases for billions of years. I think the human race is going to wreck itself, and it's important that we get control of this horrible force and try to eliminate it."

56. Strategic Weapons Facility Pacific   There are two types of bunkers in this strategic weapons facility: 64 closely spaced bunkers, which store fuel propellant for Trident missiles, and 21 bunkers spaced wider apart, which store the Trident warheads themselves. *Naval Submarine Base Bangor, Hood Canal, Puget Sound, Washington. November 2, 1984.*

57. Trident Christening   Low in the water to the left of the tent sits the Trident USS *Henry Jackson*. Above it, in dry dock, is the Trident *Alabama*. Each Trident is approximately two football fields long. Missile portals are visible on the *Alabama* above the "EB" (Electric Boat) logo. In the lower right corner of the picture, a lone canoeist is being arrested by harbor police converging on him in three patrol boats. *Electric Boat Company, Groton, Connecticut. October 15, 1983.*

58. Theodore B. Taylor   *Damascus, Maryland. October 13, 1986.* Ted Taylor is the man who miniaturized the U.S. nuclear arsenal. Miniaturization led to a whole new generation of weapons systems. His experience in the Department of Defense left him disillusioned and alarmed.

"The real driving force in the nuclear arms race is the weaponeers, the people who come up with the concepts. It all starts with that devilishly creative act of imagining something which is infinitely destructive. Then they go to Franklin Roosevelt or Harry Truman or Ronald Reagan and say, 'Here's this thing. Do you want that?' The answer is invariably, 'You bet we do!'"

59. The Davy Crockett Battlefield Missile   Front and center stands the smallest A-bomb ever deployed by the U.S. military. Its yield: one-quarter of a kiloton. This miniature bomb weighs 51 pounds and can fit inside a bowling bag. The concept for its design was developed by Ted Taylor. *National Atomic Museum, Kirtland Air Force Base, Albuquerque, New Mexico. July 17, 1985.*

60. The White Train The white train waits on the Pantex grounds. Its ATMX safe/
secure rail cars will soon be loaded with nuclear warheads for delivery to submarine bases on the Atlantic and Pacific. The train will cross America east from

Amarillo to Charleston, and northwest from the Texas Panhandle to Puget Sound. *Pantex Nuclear Weapons Final Assembly Plant, Carson County, Texas. August 7, 1982.*

61. Nuclear-Powered Jet Airplane Engines (1957–1961)   In front of the technician with a Geiger counter stands a vertical nuclear reactor made into a jet airplane engine. Behind it is a second, horizontal reactor engine. Nuclear-powered jet airplanes were intended to carry nuclear bombs and fly a pattern around the Soviet Union. The program was rendered obsolete by long-range missile technology. These are the only two nuclear jet airplane engines in existence. *Idaho National Engineering Laboratory, Idaho Falls, Idaho. November 9, 1984.*

62. Nuclear Jet Airplane Initial Engine-Test Facility The two nuclear-powered jet engines were transported by rail to the distant stack, hooked up, and test-fired. The stack channeled the engines' exhaust, heat, and radiation away from the ground into the air. *Idaho National Engineering Laboratory, Idaho Falls, Idaho. November 9, 1984.*

63. Perimeter Acquisition Radar Characterization System   This is the Space Command's PARCS early-warning radar facility in Concrete, North Dakota. It assesses data from incoming missiles and calculates their target trajectories minutes before impact, and relays pre-impact data to the Cheyenne Mountain complex. *Cavalier Army Base, Concrete, North Dakota. April 24, 1987.*

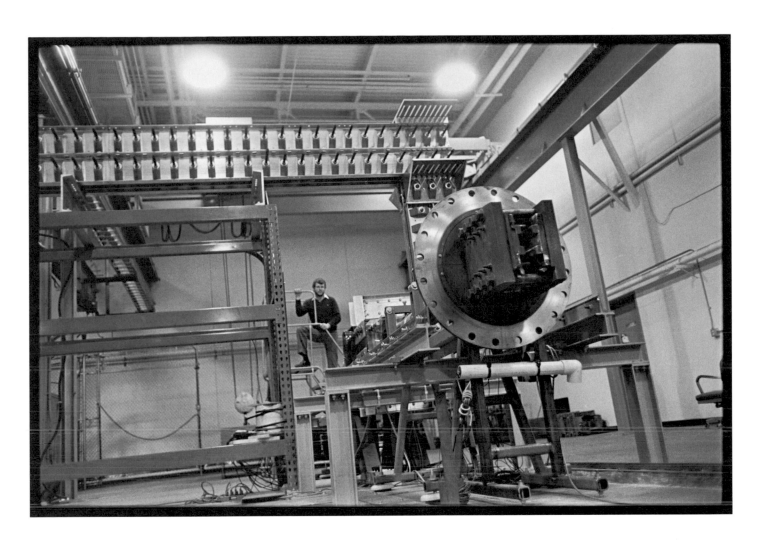

64. "Star Wars" Rail Gun   The rail gun is designed to shoot down incoming missiles by puncturing them with small high-speed projectiles. It uses electromagnetic energy instead of gunpowder. In its current state of development, the rail gun can shoot a single 180-gram projectile at 2,000 meters a second. *GA Technologies, San Diego, California. January 6, 1987.*

51. Minuteman II Missileers Lieutenants Lamb and Goetz *Ellsworth Air Force Base, Rapid City, South Dakota. November 21, 1984.* These Strategic Air Command missileers work together in a capsule 60 feet underground. Each is provided with a pistol. Missile duty lasts four years, during which silo operators are required to put in two 24-hour shifts per week for 12 to 16 weeks a year. On November 21, 1984, the activating launch code for a simulated key-turn exercise was "Lima, Alpha, Uniform, November, Charlie, Hotel, Echo, November, Alpha, Bravo, Lima, Echo, Papa, Lima, Charlie, Alpha, Zero, One. Acknowledge. Out." Lieutenant Goetz explains the procedure for launching a group of missiles:

"It takes two launch votes. One is transmitted by two men from this capsule, and another control center does the same thing. So there are quite a few safeguards that we have to go through before we can launch a sortie."

Plates 52, 53, and 54 depict the three components—land, air, and sea—of America's strategic nuclear triad.

52. Down the Hatch   A missile silo operator enters the Personnel Access Hatch for maintenance of a Minuteman III missile. *Vandenberg Air Force Base, Lompoc, California. January 17, 1986.*

53. The "Scramble"   Members of a strategic bombing crew run to their bomber. *Ellsworth Air Force Base, Rapid City, South Dakota. November 21, 1984.*

54. Trident   This submarine, coming up the Hood Canal into Puget Sound, is America's largest underwater strategic weapons launching system. It is powered by a nuclear reactor and carries up to 192 independently targetable nuclear warheads. *Naval Submarine Base Bangor, Hood Canal, Puget Sound, Washington. November 2, 1984.*

55. Admiral Hyman Rickover *New York City. May 9, 1982.* Hyman Rickover was the longest-serving individual in the history of the U.S. Navy. He invented the nuclear submarine and is known as "the Father of the Nuclear Navy." His submarine reactor was so successful it became the basis for America's commercial nuclear power reactors.

"Every time you produce radiation, you produce something that has a certain half-life, in some cases for billions of years. I think the human race is going to wreck itself, and it's important that we get control of this horrible force and try to eliminate it."

56. Strategic Weapons Facility Pacific   There are two types of bunkers in this strategic weapons facility: 64 closely spaced bunkers, which store fuel propellant for Trident missiles, and 21 bunkers spaced wider apart, which store the Trident warheads themselves. *Naval Submarine Base Bangor, Hood Canal, Puget Sound, Washington. November 2, 1984.*

57. Trident Christening   Low in the water to the left of the tent sits the Trident USS *Henry Jackson*. Above it, in dry dock, is the Trident *Alabama*. Each Trident is approximately two football fields long. Missile portals are visible on the *Alabama* above the "EB" (Electric Boat) logo. In the lower right corner of the picture, a lone canoeist is being arrested by harbor police converging on him in three patrol boats. *Electric Boat Company, Groton, Connecticut. October 15, 1983.*

58. Theodore B. Taylor   *Damascus, Maryland. October 13, 1986.* Ted Taylor is the man who miniaturized the U.S. nuclear arsenal. Miniaturization led to a whole new generation of weapons systems. His experience in the Department of Defense left him disillusioned and alarmed.

"The real driving force in the nuclear arms race is the weaponeers, the people who come up with the concepts. It all starts with that devilishly creative act of imagining something which is infinitely destructive. Then they go to Franklin Roosevelt or Harry Truman or Ronald Reagan and say, 'Here's this thing. Do you want that?' The answer is invariably, 'You bet we do!'"

59. The Davy Crockett Battlefield Missile   Front and center stands the smallest A-bomb ever deployed by the U.S. military. Its yield: one-quarter of a kiloton. This miniature bomb weighs 51 pounds and can fit inside a bowling bag. The concept for its design was developed by Ted Taylor. *National Atomic Museum, Kirtland Air Force Base, Albuquerque, New Mexico. July 17, 1985.*

60. The White Train The white train waits on the Pantex grounds. Its ATMX safe/secure rail cars will soon be loaded with nuclear warheads for delivery to submarine bases on the Atlantic and Pacific. The train will cross America east from

Amarillo to Charleston, and northwest from the Texas Panhandle to Puget Sound. *Pantex Nuclear Weapons Final Assembly Plant, Carson County, Texas. August 7, 1982.*

61. Nuclear-Powered Jet Airplane Engines (1957–1961)   In front of the technician with a Geiger counter stands a vertical nuclear reactor made into a jet airplane engine. Behind it is a second, horizontal reactor engine. Nuclear-powered jet airplanes were intended to carry nuclear bombs and fly a pattern around the Soviet Union. The program was rendered obsolete by long-range missile technology. These are the only two nuclear jet airplane engines in existence. *Idaho National Engineering Laboratory, Idaho Falls, Idaho. November 9, 1984.*

62. Nuclear Jet Airplane Initial Engine-Test Facility   The two nuclear-powered jet engines were transported by rail to the distant stack, hooked up, and test-fired. The stack channeled the engines' exhaust, heat, and radiation away from the ground into the air. *Idaho National Engineering Laboratory, Idaho Falls, Idaho. November 9, 1984.*

63. Perimeter Acquisition Radar Characterization System   This is the Space Command's PARCS early-warning radar facility in Concrete, North Dakota. It assesses data from incoming missiles and calculates their target trajectories minutes before impact, and relays pre-impact data to the Cheyenne Mountain complex. *Cavalier Army Base, Concrete, North Dakota. April 24, 1987.*

64. "Star Wars" Rail Gun   The rail gun is designed to shoot down incoming missiles by puncturing them with small high-speed projectiles. It uses electromagnetic energy instead of gunpowder. In its current state of development, the rail gun can shoot a single 180-gram projectile at 2,000 meters a second. *GA Technologies, San Diego, California. January 6, 1987.*

83. Kay Gable *Arvada, Colorado. July 16, 1983.* Kay Gable's husband, Don, was a plutonium worker at Rocky Flats. After 9 years and 4 months on the job, he developed a brain tumor and died at age 32. Los Alamos Laboratory did an autopsy of Don's brain. When Kay Gable asked for the plutonium content report, Los Alamos stated it had lost the brain. Kay Gable then sued Rocky Flats to hand over part of the radioactive pipe that had been 6 inches from her husband's head at work. After many delays, Rocky Flats said that it had lost the pipe.

"Los Alamos called me within an hour of Don's death to do tests on his brain. What really gets me, though, is how did they know he died? I mean, it was within an hour of his death and I get this phone call. There was no doctor there. The family and I are the only ones that knew."

84. John Smitherman *Mulberry, Tennessee, July 31, 1983.* John Smitherman was one of 42,000 servicemen who participated in Able and Baker, the first atomic bomb tests in the Pacific after World War II. The series was code-named "Operation Crossroads." Smitherman later developed lymphedema, a blockage of the lymph system that causes legs and arms to swell; he had to have both legs amputated. On September 11, 1983, he died of cancer of the colon, liver, stomach, lung, and spleen. He had claimed compensation for radiation damages. The Veterans Administration turned his claim down seven times. It is still pending.

"We watched the Baker shot from a ship about 19 miles away from the explosion, and mist from the mushroom fell on the deck of our ship and sand fell on our deck, little pieces of metal and rocks. We tried to wash off as much of it as we could. The mushroom cloud stayed in the air for almost two days—we could see that."

85. Congressional Hearing on Operation Crossroads   Lieutenant General John L. Pickitt, director of the Defense Nuclear Agency, testifies that standard safety procedures were followed during Operation Crossroads. There is an urgency to these hearings, since many of the Crossroads veterans are dying of illnesses associated with radiation. This hearing was held by the Oversight Committee on Issues Pertaining to Veterans' Exposure to Ionizing Radiation. *Russell Senate Office Building, Room SR-418, Washington, D.C. December 11, 1985.*

86. Marshallese in Washington, D.C. This delegation represents the people of the Pacific Marshall Islands. From 1946 to 1958, the U.S. tested at least 66 atomic and hydrogen bombs in their lagoons, on their islands, and in the surrounding ocean. The Bikini and Rongelap Atolls are still uninhabitable. The Marshallese are suing the U.S. government for $5 billion in radiation damages. *U.S. Court of Claims, Washington, D.C. April 23, 1987.*

87. ABCC, Hiroshima   These buildings were constructed by U.S. occupation forces five years after the end of World War II. The center was called the Atomic Bomb Casualty Commission (ABCC). Its mandate: to study the irradiated populations of Hiroshima and Nagasaki. Its method: to diagnose radiation illness but not to treat it. Eighty thousand people were chosen to be studied and are being followed until their deaths. *Hiroshima, Japan. September 13, 1984.*

88. Carl Siebentritt *Federal Emergency Management Agency, Washington, D.C., October 22, 1982.* Siebentritt coordinated the development of a small, durable, inexpensive radiation meter for civilian use in the event of nuclear war. It can read up to 200 roentgens per hour.

"These are the ranges you'll need to be monitoring when you've got real serious radiation insults happening. You're talking about life-threatening doses as a result of nuclear attack. That is the name of the game."

89. The Whey Train   The whey train sits in an out-of-the-way trainyard in the small town of Kolbermoor, outside Munich. Its cargo is 250 tons of radioactive whey powder from the Meggle milk factory in Bavaria. The powder is contaminated with cesium-137 from the Chernobyl cloud. The Bavarian government has tried to bury the powder, incinerate it, and sell it as food to Egypt. *Kolbermoor, West Germany, December 28, 1986.*

90. Stanrock Tailings Wall   The wall of white sand in back of the trees is made up of radioactive mill wastes from uranium mining in the Elliot Lake region of Ontario. More than 100 million tons of these tailings have been deposited directly into the environment. Some of them have been carried by the Serpent River System into the Great Lakes. The radioactive piles are unmarked and are not visible from the road. They will remain hazardous for hundreds of thousands of years. *Stanrock Mine, Elliot Lake, Ontario, Canada. August 25, 1986.*

91. Low-level Radioactive Burial Markers These granite markers sit at the back end of the ChemNuclear waste disposal site. Each is a headstone for a large clay trench containing metal drums, steel boxes, polyethylene containers, and carbon steel liners full of medical, industrial, and commercial radioactive waste. The "institutional control period" for the site is 100 years. *Barnwell, South Carolina, August 7, 1983.*

92. Windscale   is the complex of reactors and reprocessing facilities that produced the plutonium for Britain's nuclear weapons. In 1957 one of its military reactors burned out of control for 24 hours, spreading fission products over 200 square miles of countryside. Today, Windscale reprocesses irradiated nuclear fuel rods for Britain, Italy, and Japan. It also makes plutonium and tritium for the British military. Reprocessing generates large quantities of high-level nuclear waste. *Seascale, Cumbria, England. September 6, 1981.*

93. Windscale, Back View   Two pipes covered with cement slabs come out of the back end of the Windscale plant. The pipes extend two miles out into the Irish Sea where, at a depth of 50 feet, they discharge radioactive waste water from plutonium reprocessing operations. Windscale has been sending radioactive effluent directly into the Irish Sea for over 30 years. *Seascale, Cumbria, England. September 6, 1981.*

94. Hanford Tank Farm   These million-gallon double-walled carbon steel tanks are built to hold high-level nuclear waste from Hanford's plutonium production program. They are meant to replace Hanford's older, single-walled tanks which have, according to a November 1986 U.S. General Accounting Office report, leaked approximately 500,000 gallons of high-level radioactive waste into Hanford soil. *200 Area, Hanford Reservation, Richland, Washington. November 16, 1984.*

95. Irretrievable Nuclear Waste Disposal Test Shaft   Atomic Energy of Canada has dug this shaft deep into the Canadian Shield to test Precambrian granite as a possible repository for high-level nuclear waste. Additional funding comes from the U.S. Department of Energy. *Lac du Bonnet, Manitoba, Canada. September 15, 1986.*

96. Irradiated Reactor Fuel Rods are among the most radioactive materials on earth. These casks of irradiated fuel sit under 14 feet of water in the failed West Valley Reprocessing Plant. They are waiting to go into deep geologic storage. *West Valley, New York. June 30, 1982.*

97. Dr. Rosalie Bertell *Unitarian Church of the Messiah, Montreal, Canada. May 25, 1982.* Dr. Bertell is a doctor of mathematics and a member of the Grey Nuns of the Sacred Heart. Her life's work is the study of radiation and its effect on human health.

"It finally hit me that when it comes to building nuclear bombs, the military doesn't count the cost in human lives. And from that time on I really started to look for the people in every part of the nuclear weapons cycle, the hidden people, for whom World War III has already started."

98. A Woman of Greenham Common is arrested by British police. She was one of 3,000 women who surrounded the Greenham Common Cruise Missile Base and cut down half of its 9-mile chain-link fence. For five years, women have maintained a presence at the gates of Greenham Common to protest the establishment of American Cruise missiles in England and to register their concern about the genocidal nature of the arms race. *RAF Greenham Common, Newbury, England. October 29, 1983.*

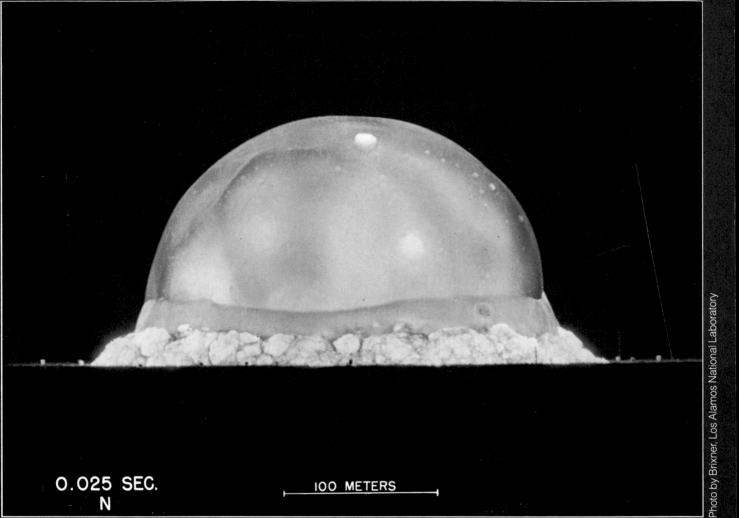

0.025 SEC.
N

|← 100 METERS →|

99. Trinity: 5:30 A.M., July 16, 1945   The Trinity atomic blast took place in the Alamogordo Desert of New Mexico. Berlyn Brixner was the official photographer for the event. This is one of his images of the world's first atomic explosion.

"There is this tremendously brilliant light that comes out of the initial part of the explosion, then the formation of a ball of fire, which becomes an immense ball of white-hot material. That's the image that persists in my mind, rather than the residue of dust and cloud that occurs afterwards."

100. Hiroshima, August 6, 1945 Three weeks after the Trinity blast, the atomic bomb was dropped on Hiroshima at 8:15 A.M. Only five photographs were taken from within the city on this day. The photographer was Yoshito Matsushige.

"Before I became a professional cameraman I had been just an ordinary person. So when I was faced with a terrible scene like this, I found it difficult to push the shutter. I was standing on the Miyuki-bashi Bridge for about 20 minutes before I could do it. Finally I t̶h̶o̶u̶g̶h̶t̶, I am a professional cameraman so I̶ ̶h̶a̶d̶ ̶t̶o̶."

101. Hiroshima Peace Park   *August 6, 1985.* This granite coffin contains the names of all who have died from the Hiroshima bomb. On August 6 each year, the lid is removed and more names are added. The inscription on the front of the coffin reads:

Rest in peace,
for the mistake
shall never be repeated.

102. Moscow Hospital Number 6   The burning Chernobyl reactor caused the evacuation of 135,000 people within a 30-kilometer radius of the plant. Some of the most heavily irradiated were brought to this hospital, where twelve people received bone marrow transplants performed by Dr. Robert Gale, who came from the United States with a team of physicians and a million dollars' worth of equipment. Two of the transplant recipients survived. *Novaya Basmanaya Street, No. 26, Moscow. December 8, 1986.*

103. Tsue Hayashi *Nagasaki, August 15, 1985.* Mrs. Hayashi is the mother of Kayoko, who at age 15 was lost in the explosion of the Nagasaki bomb. The story of Tsue Hayashi's search for her daughter has become a legend in Nagasaki.

"The morning after the bomb, and every day after that, from early morning until evening, I walked all over the city looking for Kayoko. I saw many people suffering and dying. It was very sad. I felt deeply the severe power of the A-bomb. I cannot remember seeing a single other person walking."

104. Dr. Edward Teller   *Palo Alto, California. December 21, 1984.* Dr. Teller invented the hydrogen bomb, and he is credited with having inspired Ronald Reagan with the vision of a space-based defensive shield against nuclear missiles. At a public lecture in Montreal on May 13, 1986, Dr. Teller stated in response to a question on fallout from Chernobyl:

"If you explode all the nuclear weapons in all the arsenals of the world, a large fraction of humanity will not be injured, and the damage will be more or less confined to the places where the hostilities occurred."

105. The Becquerel Reindeer   This is a freezer of radioactive reindeer meat in a slaughterhouse in Swedish Lapland. In Sweden the maximum radiation allowed in meat is 300 becquerels per kilo. Meat from reindeer feeding on lichen contaminated with cesium-137 from the Chernobyl cloud was measuring as high as 16,000 becquerels per kilo. Slaughterhouse workers refer to the radioactive carcasses as "the becquerel reindeer." *Harads Same-produktor, Harads, Lapland, Sweden. December 3, 1986.*

106. All the Warheads in the U.S. Nuclear Arsenal   This field of ceramic nose-cones represents, in miniature, all the warheads in the U.S. nuclear arsenal. Estimates set the U.S. warhead total at about 25,000. *Amber Waves of Grain* installation, Boston Science Museum, Boston, Massachusetts. February 13, 1985.

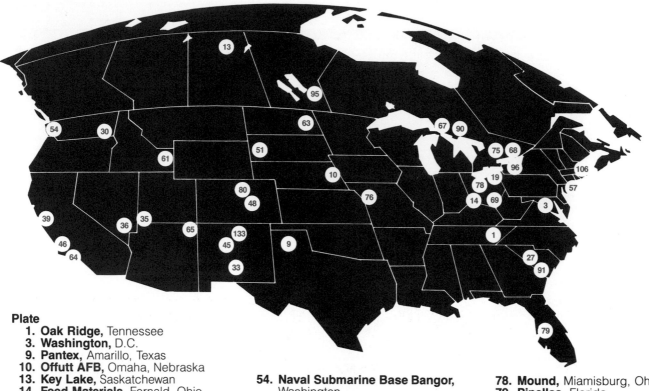

Plate
1. **Oak Ridge,** Tennessee
3. **Washington,** D.C.
9. **Pantex,** Amarillo, Texas
10. **Offutt AFB,** Omaha, Nebraska
13. **Key Lake,** Saskatchewan
14. **Feed Materials,** Fernald, Ohio
19. **Ashtabula,** Ohio
27. **Savannah River Plant,**
Aiken, South Carolina
30. **Hanford,** Washington
33. **Alamogordo,** New Mexico
35. **St. George,** Utah
36. **Nevada Test Site,** Mercury, Nevada
39. **Lawrence Radiation Lab,**
Berkeley, California
45. **Kirtland AFB,**
Albuquerque, New Mexico
46. **Vandenberg AFB,** Lompoc,
California
48. **Cheyenne Mountain,**
Colorado Springs, Colorado
51. **Ellsworth AFB,** Rapid City,
South Dakota

54. **Naval Submarine Base Bangor,**
Washington
57. **Electric Boat,** Groton, Connecticut
61. **Idaho National Engineering
Laboratory,** Idaho Falls, Idaho
63. **PARCS Radar,** Concrete,
North Dakota
64. **GA Technologies,** San Diego,
California
65. **Red Rock,** Arizona
67. **Eldorado,** Blind River, Ontario
68. **Eldorado,** Port Hope, Ontario
69. **Portsmouth,** Piketon, Ohio
75. **Candu,** Darlington, Ontario
76. **Bendix,** Kansas City, Missouri

78. **Mound,** Miamisburg, Ohio
79. **Pinellas,** Florida
80. **Rocky Flats,** Golden, Colorado
90. **Stanrock Mine,** Elliot Lake, Ontario
91. **ChemNuclear,** Barnwell,
South Carolina
95. **Test Shaft,** Lac du Bonnet,
Manitoba
96. **West Valley,** New York
106. **Science Museum,** Boston,
Massachusetts

Page
133. **Los Alamos,** New Mexico
169. **Paducah,** Kentucky

Plate
6. **Hiroshima,** Japan
8. **Nagasaki,** Japan
74. **Superphenix,** Creys-Malville,
France
89. **Whey Train,** Kolbermoor, West
Germany
92. **Windscale,** Seascale, England
98. **Greenham Common,** Newbury,
England
102. **Hospital No. 6,** Moscow, USSR
105. **Becquerel Reindeer,** Harads,
Lapland, Sweden

Page
181. **Wackersdorf,** West Germany
136. **Pershing Base,** Mutlangen,
West Germany

INTERVIEWS and FIELD NOTES

1. Model of the Uranium Atom

Uranium is one of the heaviest naturally occurring elements on earth. It can be used in nuclear weapons or it can become the base from which plutonium, a more powerful nuclear explosive, is made. Uranium is unstable; when a single uranium atom breaks apart it releases, on average, two neutrons, one of which can smash into other uranium atoms and split them apart, releasing large amounts of energy—and two more neutrons. It is this geometric progression that makes a runaway chain reaction explosion possible.

Uranium has a half-life of 4,468,000,000 years, which means that after that much time has elapsed, half of a given amount of uranium will have spontaneously decayed into other elements. Each one of these subsequent elements has its own half-life.

The Uranium-238 Decay Chain

Product in decay chain	Kind of radiation	Half-life
Uranium-238	alpha	4,468,000,000 years
Thorium-234	beta	24.1 days
Protactinium-234m	beta, gamma	1.17 minutes
Uranium-234	alpha	245,000 years
Thorium-230	alpha	80,000 years
Radium-226	alpha	1,602 years
Radon-222	alpha	3.823 days
Polonium-218	alpha	3.05 minutes
Lead-214	beta	26.8 minutes
Bismuth-214	beta	19.7 minutes
Polonium-214	alpha	.000164 seconds
Lead-210	beta	22.3 years
Bismuth-210	beta	5.01 days
Polonium-210	alpha	138.4 days
Lead-206	(stable)	non-radioactive

2. The Amount of Plutonium in the Nagasaki Bomb

The sphere of plutonium-239 in the Nagasaki bomb weighed 6,100 grams. One gram of plutonium, or one-third the weight of a penny, transformed its mass into pure energy to produce the explosion that destroyed Nagasaki's Urakami valley. The glass ball in the photograph is held by Richard Rhodes, author of *The Making of the Atomic Bomb.*

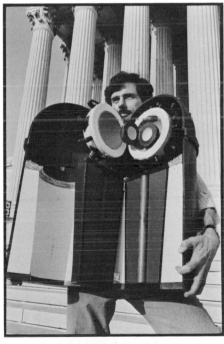

3. Howard Morland's Model of a Modern H-bomb Warhead

The modern thermonuclear warhead is termed a "physics package." This is the explosive fission-and-fusion core of a hydrogen bomb. A warhead this size would weigh about 270 pounds. Howard Morland was the first to make visible to the public the inner workings of the H-bomb. He pieced together its physics and internal design from unclassified literature and conversations with industry and government officials. In 1979 the U.S. government sued to prevent the publication of his article "The H-bomb Secret (To Know How Is to Ask Why)" in The Progressive. *Morland welcomed the lawsuit, maintaining that there are no longer any scientific secrets about H-bomb design. In court he demonstrated the public nature of his data, won the case, and published his article.*

Howard Morland—
Washington, D.C., January 12, 1984

Howard, before most people were involved in thinking about weapons, you pieced together how a thermonuclear bomb works and you made a model of its insides for all to see. How long did it take you to do that and what is it that you discovered along the way?

Well, it took six months to discover the H-bomb secret. One of the first places I looked when I began my research into thermonuclear devices was the *Encyclopedia Americana,* which is on public library shelves all over the country. In it was a very strange diagram—it showed a thermonuclear device with an atomic bomb inside one end of it, and a blob of something, lithium-6 deuteride, inside the other end. Other encyclopedias that I looked at had diagrams of H-bombs too, but this was the only one that had the stages separated, and it turns out that this "separation of stages" was the correct design concept. So in that one picture in one encyclopedia I found the essence of the H-bomb secret.

And what is that secret?

Well, the federal government, when it tried to stop the publication of my article in *The Progressive*—and succeeded in doing so for six months—said that there were three elements to the H-bomb secret that I had revealed in my manuscript. The first element was the separation of stages—the fact that within the overall casing, the atomic bomb is physically separate from the hydrogen bomb. The second element was compression of the hydrogen fuel, which basically means that if you pack any kind of material together closely, reactions will take place within it more quickly. The third element, and this was the real secret, was called "radiation coupling"—the use of electromagnetic radiation produced by the exploding atomic bomb to ignite, or trigger, the nearby hydrogen component. These three design concepts were implicit in that *Encyclopedia Americana* diagram. But I had to do a lot of digging to realize what the diagram meant.

Excerpts from Howard Morland's article "The H-bomb Secret (To Know How Is to Ask Why)," published in the November 1979 issue of The Progressive:

"Paying attention to the details is also a way of reminding ourselves that these weapons are real. The most difficult intellectual hurdle most people encounter in understanding nuclear weapons is to see them as physical devices rather than abstract expressions of good or evil. The human mind boggles at gadgets the size of surfboards that can knock down every building for miles around. But these are devices made by ordinary people in ordinary towns. The weapons are harder to believe than to understand.

"The secret of how a hydrogen bomb is made protects a more fundamental 'secret': the mechanism by which the resources of the most powerful nation on Earth have been marshalled for global catastrophe. Knowing *how* may be the key to asking *why*.

"The risks of proliferation of hydrogen weapons such as they are must be weighed against the public gain that may come from greater awareness of how and why they are already being produced.

"Whether it be the details of a multi-million-dollar plutonium production expansion program or the principles and procedures by which nature's most explosive force is being packaged in our midst, we have less to fear from knowing than from not knowing."

The following text and diagrams are Howard Morland's explanation of the inner workings of a thermonuclear bomb. Morland also traces the bomb's component parts to their corporate sources within the government-contractor system of the United States Department of Energy's nuclear weapons complex. This information updates Morland's original article published by The Progressive.

THE BOMB AND ITS MAKERS

Western Electric, a subsidiary of American Telephone & Telegraph, does general engineering for the H-bomb at its laboratory at Albuquerque, New Mexico, in cooperation with two laboratories which conduct research at Livermore, California, and Los Alamos, New Mexico, under the auspices of the University of California.

DuPont supplies small containers of tritium gas from its Savannah River, South Carolina, tritium loading facility.

Martin Marietta contributes uranium, deuterium, and lithium parts made in Oak Ridge, Tennessee.

Rockwell International fabricates plutonium and beryllium components at the Rocky Flats plant near Denver, Colorado.

Monsanto manufactures explosive detonators at its Mound laboratory near Miamisburg, Ohio.

The paper honeycomb shield and polystyrene foam which help focus pressure generated by radiation onto the H-bomb's fusion tamper are made by Bendix in Kansas City, Missouri.

General Electric builds neutron generators at its Pinellas plant near St. Petersburg, Florida.

Mason & Hanger-Silas Mason shapes the chemical explosive charges and supervises final assembly of the warhead at a plant near Amarillo, Texas.

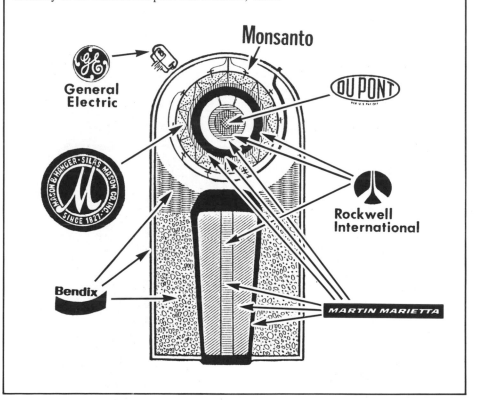

HOW AN H-BOMB WORKS

There are two discrete steps in the detonation of a modern hydrogen weapon: the explosion of the primary stage and, microseconds later, the explosion of the secondary stage. Each stage releases nuclear energy in a sequence of fission, fusion, and more fission. Although one event must follow another for the weapon to work, they happen so rapidly that a human observer would experience only a single event: an explosion of unearthly magnitude.

The "primary" is a scaled-down version of the Nagasaki plutonium implosion bomb. It has roughly the same explosive power as the World War II weapon but measures less than twelve inches across. It is called the H-bomb's "fission trigger" because energy from its initial fission explosion triggers thermonuclear fusion between tritium and deuterium, the two forms of heavy hydrogen.

This fission trigger resembles a soccer ball, with a soccer ball's pattern of twelve pentagons and twenty hexagons in a sphere. Each pentagon or hexagon is a high-explosive charge attached to a detonator; the spherical shell they form is one inch thick. A ball of plutonium and/or uranium-235 occupies the center, along with a small amount of tritium and deuterium in gaseous form.

The primary stage could level a small city by itself, but in an H-bomb its explosion merely provides the preliminary energy needed to ignite the weapon's much more powerful secondary stage. After the primary has detonated, the secondary instantly manufactures its own tritium from solid lithium-6. This tritium then fuses with the deuterium already present, and the resulting fusion energy causes, finally, large amounts of uranium-238 to undergo fission.

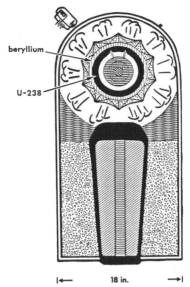

beryllium

U-238

|← 18 in. →|

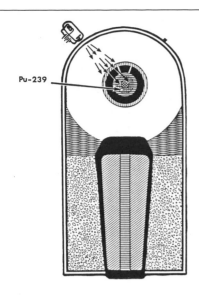

Pu-239

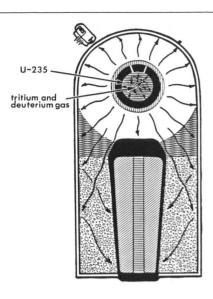

U-235

tritium and deuterium gas

1. Detonators surrounding the primary system are electrically fired. These set off the chemical high-explosive charges that surround a hollow sphere, or "tamper," made of beryllium and uranium-238. This tamper is liquefied by the implosive shock wave and driven inward toward the plutonium core of the primary, imparting the high-explosive shock wave evenly to the sphere of plutonium. This inward-moving, symmetrical shock wave is the energy of implosion that creates the conditions for a runaway chain reaction in fissionable materials. This technology was used to explode the core of the Nagasaki bomb.

2. The symmetrical shock wave created by the high explosives compresses the plutonium to about twice its normal density (from softball-size to about the size of a hardball) for approximately one-millionth of a second, at which point it is hit with a beam of neutrons produced by a high-voltage vacuum tube called a neutron generator. The stream of neutrons from this generator initiates a fission chain reaction in the sphere of plutonium-239. Because the fission chain reaction has been initiated in the mass of plutonium while it is in its densest state, it will develop with the greatest speed.

3. The chain reaction spreads outward to a layer of uranium-235 covering the surface of the plutonium sphere, and the heat and pressure of fission ignite a hydrogen fusion chain reaction in the "booster" charge of tritium and deuterium gas. Fusion adds neutrons to the fission reaction, speeding it up and raising its temperature.

The primary system of a hydrogen weapon is in effect a tiny nuclear power plant that generates 20 million kilowatt-hours' worth of thermal energy in a few millionths of a second, all inside a lump of metal compressed to the size of a hardball.

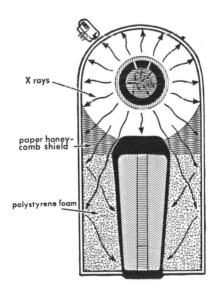

X rays

paper honeycomb shield

polystyrene foam

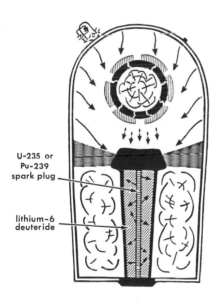

U-235 or Pu-239 spark plug

lithium-6 deuteride

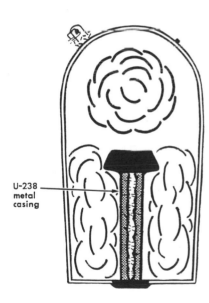

U-238 metal casing

4. The energy of the fission reaction races away from the primary system in the form of X rays traveling at the speed of light, or 100 times faster than the expanding debris of the bomb. The X rays are focused through a paper honeycomb shield and absorbed by a special polystyrene foam jacket surrounding the cylinder which makes up the "secondary." The polystyrene foam flashes into plasma that acts as a thermal explosive encasing the secondary system.

5. The exploding polystyrene foam compresses the secondary system, which is filled with lithium-6 deuteride. Running down the secondary's center is a "spark plug" of uranium-235 or plutonium-239. The exploding polystyrene foam compresses this spark plug to supercriticality, and it fissions. This fissioning, the second fission event in a thermonuclear bomb, supplies neutrons that convert the lithium fuel into tritium.

6. The fissioning spark plug and the exploding polystyrene foam form a double front of pressure which creates the conditions needed to make tritium fuse with deuterium. This tritium-deuterium fusion then showers the depleted uranium casing of the secondary system with high-energy neutrons that cause it to undergo fission and explode. This final fissioning produces most of the total energy-release of the bomb, as well as most of its deadly fallout.

4. The Hiroshima Bomb

The Hiroshima bomb contained 60,000 grams of highly enriched uranium, about 1 gram of which was converted into pure energy, giving off an explosion equivalent to 12.5 tons of TNT.

This bomb employed the "gun-assembly" method of achieving a fission explosion: a slug of highly enriched uranium metal was shot down a barrel into another piece of highly enriched uranium metal. When the two elements coupled, a runaway fission chain reaction resulted.

Nicknaming the Hiroshima bomb "Little Boy" (in reference, it is said, to Franklin Roosevelt) was the start of a long tradition of offbeat names for nuclear weapons. Other names include Genie, Honest John, Hound Dog, Snark, Mace, Condor, Sparrow, Davy Crockett, Hot Point, Walleye, and Lulu.

5. Dr. Karl Z. Morgan, the Father of Health Physics

Karl Ziegler Morgan was director of Health Physics at the Oak Ridge National Laboratory for twenty-nine years. Founder and president of the Health Physics Society, he was also the first president of the International Radiation Protection Association. He edited the Health Physics Journal *for twenty-five years and for more than forty years has participated in committees concerned with the measurement and evaluation of radiation doses to humans and animals. He has published several hundred articles on radiation safety and frequently appears in court cases as an expert witness on radiation hazards.*

Dr. Karl Z. Morgan—
Atlanta, Georgia, August 8, 1983

Prior to my becoming a health physicist I was a cosmic ray physicist. I got my doctorate at Duke University and did my dissertation on cosmic rays, which resulted in my making measurements of radiation in caves and coal mines. In this endeavor I worked at Mount Evans one summer at the laboratory of Dr. Arthur Compton of Chicago, the Nobel physicist. One day in early 1943, I received a phone call telling me I must come to Chicago, there was something exciting going on, it was secret, and it was related to my field. Well, I took the train to Chicago, and when I walked into Dr. Compton's office several people greeted me and said, "Karl, you will be in the field of Health Physics."

You mean they already had the name "Health Physics"? I've always heard you were the "father" of Health Physics.

Well, that's the point. I started to turn around for the door. I said, "There's been a bad mistake. I've never heard of Health Physics." And they said, "Hold on, Karl, we've not heard of it either." Then they

said they'd already carried through a security clearance on me so they could tell me what was going on, namely, that on December 2, 1942, the first pile of graphite and uranium went critical for the first time. They explained they were intent on making an atomic fission weapon. They felt it might have considerable bearing on our ability to win the war. At that time it appeared to some of us that our chances of winning the war were not very good. Those were very dark days. They told me they were determined to do this work safely—and it would be my job to make certain that it was done safely.

Who made up your team?

Dr. Karl Z. Morgan

H. M. Parker, C. C. Gamusfelder, and Jim Hart were some of the first health physicists with me. In addition there were medical people and radiation biologists. Sometimes it was hard to say which we were—radiation biologists, medical men, or health physicists. We all worked together very closely.

What was it like, being involved in work on the first atomic bombs?

We worked very hard in those days. We knew that Hahn, Strassmann, and Meitner had been the ones to discover fission and they were Germans, and we supposed that they were giving advice to Hitler to go hell-bent in the production of a nuclear bomb. So we worked night and day trying to develop techniques by which this work could be done safely. But we had, all of us, a serious misconception in that we adhered universally at that time to the so-

called "threshold hypothesis," meaning that if a dose were low enough, cell repair would take place as fast as the damage would accrue, and there would be no resultant damage. In other words, we believed there was a safe level of radiation.

How long did that remain a misconception?

I would say by the time of the Chalk River Conference in November of 1949 at Chalk River, Canada. It was a tripartite conference of people in this field from the United Kingdom, the U.S., and Canada. By that time I think the majority of us realized that there really wasn't a so-called safe level of exposure.

I'm surprised to hear that. I was under the impression that no early studies existed showing health hazards at extremely low levels of exposure.

That's not correct. In that early period, there were some in the Atomic Energy Commission who recognized the importance of doing basic research, so they set up large laboratories at Oak Ridge, at Hanford, at the Argonne Laboratory in Chicago, at Los Alamos, also at Savannah River and later at Brookhaven. In these laboratories they had large studies of animals, all kinds of animals, as well as plants, to see the effects of all types of ionizing radiation. They investigated the effects of dose rate, the effects of low doses, the effects of high doses, and the production of malignancies. Some of us at the Chalk River Conference had seen the results of those hundreds of early experiments on animals, and we saw no reason—at least I saw no reason—why you wouldn't anticipate the same sort of effects on man as we had found on rats and mice and dogs.

What were some of the things you found? Why is radiation dangerous at low levels?

There isn't a safe level because it's just a matter of chance that a photon or alpha particle or neutron, when it comes through your body, will come close to the nucleus of a cell, damage the cell, and disturb some of the information in the nucleus. In the nucleus of a normal cell are forty-six chromosomes; along these chromosomes we have the genes. In combination, if these genes were like letters in a book, it would take millions of books to record all the information available in every nucleus of every cell in our whole body. So when the radiation goes through, occasionally—very, very, seldom—it damages a cell in such a way that it can survive in its damaged form. These damaged cells can be likened to a library that a madman has broken into and ransacked, randomly ripping pages out of books. The damaged cells no longer have sufficient instructions as to what to do under many adverse circumstances. One of the most serious consequences happens when a cell doesn't know when to stop dividing, or how big to get, or what chemicals to produce; and eventually there are enough of these cells that you can identify as a cancer.

How does this tie in with the "linear hypothesis" about radiation levels and the cancers they can cause?

The linear hypothesis means that you can predict the amount of cancers you will get from a given amount of radiation— and it doesn't matter whether you get the radiation over a short time, in high doses, or over a longer time in smaller doses. The way it is expressed is: you can expect one fatal cancer for every 1,000 person-rems of radiation.

What does "1,000 person-rems" mean?

This refers to the total amount of radiation that can cause one cancer. It's called "person-rems" because it can be spread out among a number of people. According to the linear hypothesis it makes no difference whether 1,000 people receive one rem or whether 500 people get two rems—or whether 10,000 people get a tenth of a rem apiece. All of the standard-setting bodies at the present time assume the linear hypothesis is true, and they say that if you have twice as many person-rems of exposure you'll get twice as many cancers. And, except for the latency period in the appearance of a cancer, it doesn't matter over what period of time you receive the exposures. Radiation-induced leukemia has been known to appear in a time as short as one year, although the average latency period for leukemia is eight to ten years, and in the case of solid tumors like cancer of the breast, brain tumors, bone cancer, and thyroid carcinoma, the latency period is about thirty years.

In the past decade some of us have gone further in examining the literature, and we have concluded that instead of the linear hypothesis, there is a "supralinear" hypothesis which fits the data more appropriately. In particular, Drs. Stewart and Kneale in England and myself here, and Mancuso in Pittsburgh, and Sternglass, and maybe fifty or so other people have been publishing papers showing that down at the low doses you actually get more cancers per person-rem than you do at the high doses. Now, I'm not saying that you

get more cancers at these low doses than at high doses. I'm saying that damage per unit dose is greater at these low levels. And that's true in part because the high levels will more often kill cells outright, whereas low levels of exposure tend to injure cells rather than kill them and it is the surviving, injured cells that are cause for concern. There are of course other factors involved with high doses, and one of them is that high doses can do serious damage to the body's immune system.

So the supralinear hypothesis says there really is a difference between 500 people who get two rems each and 10,000 people who get half a rem. Will more damage occur among the 10,000 people who got the lower doses?

It looks that way, yes. This is now becoming quite a point of contention. When we first began these discussions many people thought we were crazy, because they believed that even the linear hypothesis was overconservative.

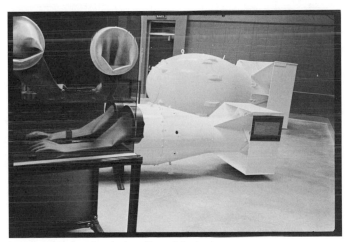

Foreground: glove box for handling plutonium
Background: Hiroshima and Nagasaki duplicate bomb casings
Bradbury Science Museum, Los Alamos, New Mexico

If the supralinear hypothesis is founded on reality, what would that mean for the commercial nuclear power industry and the nuclear weapons complex?

If it can be established that the damage per unit dose at very low levels is greater than at high levels, there's no question that the effects of fallout, the effects of handling radioactive materials, and the effects of even a small medical exposure will be much more severe than had been anticipated. This, I suppose, is one reason why we have received so much flak when we presented our case.

Can you talk a bit about plutonium? I understand you were an expert witness in the Karen Silkwood case, where you testified on the hazards of plutonium, and

you told the trial judge it was so toxic that it didn't matter how it got into her refrigerator, it still meant negligence on the part of the company. How toxic is plutonium?

For more than a quarter of century I was an active member of the International Commission on Radiological Protection and the National Council on Radiation Protection, and during that time I was chairman of the Internal Dose Committee for both these organizations. I made the earliest calculations on permissible levels of plutonium and all the radionuclides when I was at Oak Ridge. It was my committee that set the levels for all the nucleides, and these same levels are now being used by the Nuclear Regulatory Commission, the Environmental Protection Agency, and others, with essentially no modification. We set the permissible body burden for plutonium-239 as .04 millionths of a curie, that is, .04 microcuries. You never want to permit a worker to exceed that level in his body. If he ever did build up this much it would be serious because

this represents an average dose-rate to the skeleton of 30 rems per year for the rest of his life. Essentially it's there forever, and it continues to irradiate you. I've published papers in the *Journal of Industrial Hygiene* showing that this level was in fact far too high and should be reduced by a factor of 240. Those in the nuclear industry found every way they could to try to show flaws in the arguments I used. The typical response from consultants to the Department of Energy is: "Although you observe this effect in a baboon, you have no proof you would observe it in man." So they want to wait until you have human guinea pigs, I guess, to get the proof.

Just yesterday I was visiting the Chem-Nuclear waste disposal site in Barnwell, and I watched workers moving all kinds of boxes and casks of radioactive materials into huge clay trenches. I brought along my own Geiger counter and as soon as we got close to the edge of the trench, my beeper started reading thirty and forty times higher than background. I asked Jim Purvis, who was showing me around, whether men who worked over the open trenches got any special hazard pay. He told me, "No, they do not receive a hazard pay, because there is no hazard. The radiation they are subjected to is well below the acceptable level."

This employee gave you the response that you might have expected—namely, that there was no hazard, and no need for special hazard pay. They assume that as long as you don't exceed the maximum permissible exposure level of five rems per year, there's no hazard. They don't appreciate the fact that all the standard-setting bodies in the world today set these standards on the assumption that there is no safe level of radiation exposure. So the question is not: What is a safe level? The question is: How great is the risk? All exposure subjects you to some risk. The more exposure you get to radiation, the greater the risk it will cause a cancer. The cancer may derive from one single small exposure, but on the other hand, it may derive from a series of exposures, one of which sometime in the past happened to be the actual cause. On many occasions I have tried to point this out to my students by saying that when radiation passes through our bodies and comes near a particular cell, there are several things that can happen. The most likely thing is that it will go right by or right through the cell without doing anything. Number two: there's a high probability that if this radiation comes near the nucleus of the cell it will cause its destruction. I don't mean it will be evaporated, I mean it will damage it in such a way that it cannot reproduce itself, so for all purposes in a few months at most it will be dead. Number three: there's a remarkable possibility that this cell will be damaged, yet it will survive, and it will repair itself, and for all intents and purposes it will be quite normal. But number four is what we fear. Fortunately the probability of it is exceedingly low. Number four is: the radiation comes near the nucleus of this cell, it produces damage, and the cell survives, but it survives in its damaged or perturbed form. It divides, it divides again and again, and, on the average, if it's leading to a solid tumor, after thirty years it will be large enough that it will be recognized as a malignancy.

These forms of damage don't show up immediately. With exposure to radiation you don't feel the sense of pain that you do when you burn yourself. But the damage shows up in a very serious and dramatic way some years later when the results are diagnosed as cancer. That is why I think it behooves us to find out more accurately what these risks are.

Karl, there are a number of populations at risk in America from radiation: the nuclear workers at the different sites, people who bury the waste, truck drivers, the atomic veterans. Is the radiation story going to end up looking like the asbestos story when all the data are in? Do you think we should anticipate a rash of diseases related to radiation, and that eventually there will come a unanimous understanding of the real hazard?

I wish I could say yes. I have confidence in the future, provided, of course, we can prevent a nuclear war. But it takes a very long time for man to learn the lesson and for the information to filter down to where it has some effect. Back in the year 1500 it was known that miners in the cobalt mines of Bohemia and Saxony were dying of the so-called miner's disease. And yet it hasn't been long in this country since we've had many miners working underground at levels as high or higher in radium and radon as existed in these mines over 400 years ago. I think we'll be having many sad lessons more before we learn what we should already know by now.

6. Hiroshima Buddha

The temperature on the ground beneath the exploding Hiroshima bomb reached about 7000 degrees F for several seconds. The brevity of the heat pulse explains why the bronze was only partly melted.

7. Aged *Hibakusha*

The *hibakusha* in the photograph are talking to high school students. The woman in the center is Mrs. Katsuyu Matsuhashi, age eighty-two.

Hibakusha have suffered discrimination. The unpredictability of their health limits their employment opportunities, and the possibility of genetic damage disqualifies them as good marriage material. The children of *hibakusha* also experience some of this discrimination. The majority of *hibakusha* do not speak out. But within the last five years a change has been noticed among them: before, they were hesitant to describe their experiences; today the global nuclear buildup has prompted more of them to address themselves openly to the threat of nuclear war.

8. Pathological Atomic Bomb Materials Storage Room

Organs from victims of the atomic bomb are stored in both Nagasaki and Hiroshima.

9. Duplicate "Fat Man"

The Nagasaki bomb was nicknamed "Fat Man" in reference, it is said, to Winston Churchill.

The American government works with private contractors to build nuclear weapons. This is referred to as a "GO-CO" arrangement, a government-contractor agreement. The contractor working with the U.S. Department of Energy at Pantex is Mason & Hanger-Silas Mason, the Kentucky engineering firm that built New York's Holland Tunnel.

Paul Wagner, public relations manager for the Department of Energy at Pantex—Amarillo, Texas, August 10, 1982

Mr. Wagner, how would you describe the function of the Pantex plant?

Assembling nuclear weapons.

Do you make or shape or mill any parts for weapons here?

We do not manufacture any components except the chemical high explosive.

What is the chemical high explosive?

I won't say any more than that it's a necessary component in a nuclear weapons assembly.

They say you turn out three warheads a day here. Is that a fair average, or is that something you can neither confirm nor deny?

I won't even answer that.

When you assemble the warhead, does that include the missile?

That's the Defense Department's responsibility. The delivery vehicles belong to the Defense Department. They design 'em and build 'em and pay for 'em and operate 'em and shoot 'em.

Can you talk about how long it takes to assemble a warhead or how many parts are involved?

No.

Here you also disassemble outdated warheads. Can you say anything about what the average shelf-life of a nuclear weapon is?

I can. But I won't.

Then let me ask you this: When they give the number of warheads in the U.S. arsenal as around 25,000, does that include the ones assembled but removed from service, or does it mean only those ready to go?

I won't answer that.

Has there ever been more than one nuclear weapons final assembly plant?

There was another one in Burlington, Iowa. It was closed in 1975.

How do you feel about this being the only one, then, with no backup?

I have no comment. That's above and beyond any of us here.

Were there ever more than two plants like this?

The Atomic Energy Commission from 1955 until 1965 had two smaller nuclear weapons assembly facilities, but there were only two just like this.

When you say "just like this," what makes this plant unique?

The high-explosive manufacturing capability.

What goes on in that boomerang-shaped building with the circles on the roof?

Just assembly work.

Is that the building they call the "Gravel Gertie"?

Right. A Gravel Gertie is a circular structure which has a gravel roof on it. If we have an explosion in the assembly area, that roof will vent the explosion and also act as a filter for any materials that are in the structure. It lets the gases of an explosion go out into the atmosphere, but it filters and traps any particulate radioactive material that's still in there.

Is there something about the gravel coming down on everything and burying it if there's an explosion? Is that part of the filtering process?

Not really, no.

Does that happen?

That happens, but it doesn't buy anybody anything.

I heard about the chemical explosives accident here that killed three workers. Have the procedures changed since then?

Oh yeah, sure. The procedures change every time we get smart.

At Rocky Flats there's a lot of controversy about the quantities of plutonium that have escaped into the environment. Are there any problems like that here?

No. All the plutonium we have is received in a finished form with a case of some benign material around it, like stainless steel or titanium. So there's no plutonium exposure. It's always contained.

You never handle plutonium as such?

We handle it in a package. Now we take care to make sure we don't want the package to break. And there is radiation that comes through most material to some degree. But we don't have the open handling of radioactive material—none of it is cut, sawed, welded, or lathed. All of that is done at Rocky Flats.

How radioactive are the warheads?

Very low, because people handle 'em all the time. I used to sleep on top of one.

You did? Does your wife know about this?

Paul Wagner

Sure.

What were you doing, sleeping on top of one?

I was tired.

Did your senior officer know about this?

It didn't make any difference if he knew or not. I was on a ship that had nuclear weapons on it, and we had a bunk right over the top of these things. Big deal. I just say that to give you an idea of how much radiation is coming out of them.

How much is coming out of them? Did they monitor them to find out?

Not back in those days.

Do they monitor them now?

I don't know what they're doing now.

Last week I opened up Life *magazine and found a two-page spread on Bishop Leroy Matthiesen, who became famous for asking Pantex workers to examine their consciences; and on the next page was a picture of Eloy Ramos, the worker who quit Pantex for reasons of conscience after sixteen years on the job. How does this publicity affect workers here?*

It doesn't. The only people it affects are Mr. Poole and me.

How does it affect Mr. Poole and you?

We get people like you asking questions like that. It's a non-problem as far as we're concerned. As somebody said on television last week, it's the biggest non-issue of the twentieth century.

But when it brings a million people out to Central Park, isn't that a pretty big non-issue?

It's still a non-issue. People go to Central Park for no reason at all.

I think they had a reason for going on June 12.

Charles Poole: Well, anyway, it doesn't bother us. We're speaking in terms of us, you know. There might be reactions in New York or West Germany, I don't know . . . but it doesn't really affect Amarillo."

I'd like to conclude by asking you a personal question. Do you ever get used to seeing the warheads? Do you have any particular feelings when you see them coming down the assembly line one after another?

Wagner: Just like pickin' up a box of Silly Putty in a dime store. Hell, there's nothing to it. I don't react, and I've been in the business for years and years.

You don't think of the awesome forces?

I've seen nuclear explosions in Nevada, and I've seen 'em in the Pacific. . . .

And what was your reaction?

Big deal.

You mean, not such a big deal?

Yeah. Sure, it's an awesome sight, but it didn't change my life. I'm very blasé about the whole thing. There's no hazard to it that particularly affects me. But you've got to realize, you know, where people are coming from. If they've been living a protected and uneventful and nonadventurous life, it might be a big deal. But I've done a helluva lot more dangerous things in my life than screwing around with nuclear weapons.

Name two.

I was a deep-sea diver, for one thing. And I was an explosives demolition man in World War II. I had to defuse sea mines, and when that thing is right in front of you with 300 pounds of explosives, if you make one mistake you're gone. After that, this work at Pantex doesn't bother me a bit. And I'm fairly characteristic of people who have been in the business as long as the people around here have been around it.

10. The First Droppable H-Bomb

About 90 minutes after the Bravo explosion, a gritty white ash fell on twenty-three Japanese fishermen aboard the *Lucky Dragon Number Five*. Their total external radiation dose was estimated to be 170 to 600 rems. (The maximum permissible radiation limit for a worker in a nuclear power plant is 5 rems.) The fishermen suffered from radiation sickness. Four to six hours after the blast, white, powdery radioactive material fell from the sky and blanketed the island of Rongelap. The average total gamma dose on Rongelap was 175 rems.

11. Terminal Guidance

Medium-range ballistic missiles are propelled into the upper atmosphere by booster rockets. After the rocket burns out, they fall down through the atmosphere, pulled by gravity to their target. The Pershing II is America's only medium-range ballistic missile. It was first deployed in Germany at the Mutlangen base in 1983 as a replacement for the short-range Pershing Ia.

Pershing II has a range of over 1,000 miles. It delivers one warhead, which can vary in its yield from .3 to 80 kilotons. Terminal guidance makes the Pershing II ten times more accurate than the Pershing Ia. Because of its heightened accuracy Pershing II is perceived to be a first-strike weapon.

Pershing base, Mutlangen, West Germany

12. Pantex Nuclear Weapons Final Assembly Plant
Annual Budget: $198,100,000 (1986)

The mission of the Pantex plant is to assemble new nuclear warheads (approximately three to five a day); disassemble retired nuclear warheads; and fabricate the plastic high explosive that surrounds the plutonium in the fission "trigger" of a nuclear weapon.

Assemblers of nuclear warheads work in pairs in thick-walled rooms called cells or bays. They wear blue coveralls, hard hats, safety shoes with rubber slip-over covers, and gloves of cotton or soft leather. One worker does the assembly; the other checks the proper procedure step by step in the Pantex Final Assembly Safety Manual. Assembly work goes on in thirteen bays. Assemblers constitute 15% of the Pantex work force and are among the highest-paid employees, earning in the range of $30,000 a year, compared to the average Pantex salary of $23,000.

13. The Richest Uranium Mine on Earth

Key Lake is located on the southern rim of the great Athabasca Sandstone Basin of northern Saskatchewan, Canada. In uranium circles, this region is referred to as "the Saudi Arabia of uranium mining" because it contains the richest uranium ore-bodies in the world.

The Gaertner Pit, shown in the photograph, is 1,000 meters long, 300 meters wide, and 80 meters deep. The photograph shows only one corner of the pit. In the distance two workers can be seen positioning a water pump. Ground water has to be continually pumped out of the pit, which was once Seahorse Lake. When the pit is mined out, it will be allowed to fill up with water again.

Canada is the largest producer and exporter of uranium in the world today. It was a partner in the Manhattan Project and has provided uranium to the U.S. nuclear weapons program. Today Canadian uranium exports are limited to commercial nuclear reactor fuel, but the depleted uranium left over from the enrichment process can end up in the U.S. weapons program.

14. Uranium Green Salt

15. Fernald Feed Materials Production Center
Annual Budget: $119,392,000 (1986)

16. Walking the Derby

17. Cooling the Derby

18. Sampling the Derby

19. Ingots of Fernald at Ashtabula

20. Ashtabula Uranium Metal Extrusion Press
RMI Annual Budget: $7,251,000 (1986)

21. The Back End of the Ashtabula Press

22. Pickled Extrusion Inspection

23. Ashtabula Quench

Bud Schaeffer,
extrusion plant manager,
Reactive Metals, Incorporated—
Ashtabula, Ohio, June 19, 1984

Okay. I'm plant manager at the extrusion plant. I have been with this operation since 1954, and associated with the Department of Energy contract since that time.

What goes on in this facility?

Well, this plant operates as a conversion facility. That means we take customer-supplied billet and form it by the extrusion process to whatever shape the customer requires.

What is billet?

Billet is a cylinder of solid metal, in varying diameters and lengths, which is put into the extrusion press and formed to a particular size and configuration.

What is an extrusion press?

(*Laughs*) An extrusion press, as we have it, is a horizontal piece of equipment that operates under very high pressures, that takes billets or cylinders of metal and with this pressure and temperature forces the metal through a die to form it to the shape required.

How much pressure can the extrusion press at this plant exert on a billet?

3,850 tons.

How old is this press, and how old is the kind of design that this press represents?

This particular press is a World War II–vintage Loewy hydropress. It was built in 1943. I guess extrusion presses must have come on board sometime in the twenties, and the design of extrusion presses is basically unchanged. This particular press belongs to the Department of Energy and was moved here from Adrian, Michigan, in 1961.

How does the Department of Energy figure in what you do here?

Our primary purpose here is to extrude uranium under contract to the Department of Energy. Under that contract, when we've satisfied their requirements, then we're permitted to use the press for what we call commercial work.

How is it that you can do private work on the side?

The press belongs to the government; the land and the buildings are my company; so, as part of the contract when it came down here, we were allowed to use their equipment for so-called commercial work.

Isn't this arrangement unique within the government's materials-production side of the weapons industry?

We pay them a fee for the use of this equipment, and while we're doing that, we're soaking up overheads that otherwise they would bear. So it's a benefit to them, and it's an advantage to us.

Let's talk a little bit about the primary purpose of the press, which is the extrusion of uranium. What kind of uranium are we talking about, and what happens to it?

Well, we're involved in two streams here for the Department of Energy. The first stream is the Savannah River stream, which involves depleted uranium. Basically the Savannah River flow is the ingot, or billet material, which is cast at Fernald, and the billets are shipped here, where they are extruded to a tubular product. We then ship the tubes back to Fernald, where they're machined into fuel cores and shipped from Fernald to Savannah River for further processing.

What is the other stream?

We're also involved in the N-Reactor stream at Hanford, Washington. It involves slighly enriched uranium.

When it comes out of the press here, which we'll see today, are they kind of like logs?

Yes, they're a log sixty-seven inches in length and they're hollow. All of the billets going to Hanford are hollow.

When you said the N-Reactor stream used slightly enriched uranium, what is the level of enrichment we're talking about?

It's 1.25 percent U-235. Normal is .711 U-235.

When we talk about depleted uranium, say, for the Savannah River stream, is that less than natural, then?

That's less than .711. It's .2.

Is there a concern about health hazards when you're working with this material?

Bud Schaeffer

The closest analogy I can draw is that you handle them more as a toxic material than as a radiation hazard per se. All of our employees have protective clothing, they wear film badges, and we monitor radiation. But there is no radiation hazard to our employees from this material.

You talked to me earlier this morning about something called uranium oxide. Is that a gas or vapor?

No, it's a powdery substance. When uranium is heated to the forming temperatures that we use, which is somewhere up around 1100 or 1200 degrees Fahrenheit, as it cools, uranium has a tendency to flake off in the form of this oxide.

Is this oxide a potential hazard?

It can be a problem if employees inhale enough of it. That's why housekeeping is very important here, to keep the oxides down and not let them get airborne.

How do you do that?

Vacuuming, sweeping. And we quench a lot of the materials in water to inhibit oxidation.

And the workers all wear film badges because, I guess, there's some slight possibility of exposure to the uranium?

The badges are to monitor radiation exposure. It's just good Health Physics practice to do this, and we've done it ever since I've been here. Everyone wears a film badge that works in the plant.

When we walked briefly through the plant this morning, the first things we saw were these red-hot billets in trenches of liquid salt. Why do you put the uranium into molten salt?

It heats the metal to the right temperature for extrusion, and it prevents the uranium from oxidizing while it's being heated. As long as it's in a salt bath it won't oxidize because it's not in contact with air. If you were to heat uranium metal in a furnace, eventually it would completely become oxide.

The whole thing would just . . .

You'd have a big pile of oxide.

Or a cloud of it?

(*Laughs*) It's very heavy, you don't get clouds of it.

I mentioned that only because I thought that one of the hazards was breathing it.

Yeah, that's true.

So it can become airborne?

Well, *I* can become airborne.

Okay, so it's heated up to around 1200 degrees before it goes in the press. When it comes out of the press a few moments later, is it still 1200 degrees?

It may even be a little higher than 1200 degrees at that point because of the force exerted on it.

How do you deal with these hot logs?

These particular ones are taken from the press exit, or die-head area, and pulled over onto a cooling table where the pieces revolve for four or five minutes to make sure they cool down uniformly. Then we pick the extrusion up and quench it in water to get it down to where it stops oxidizing and our inspectors can handle it.

So when it's rotating, would that be the chief oxidation point, because that's where it's the hottest and it's in air?

That's right.

Do you have fans over it?

The whole operation is ventilated, yes.

I'm just curious, is that a billet sitting on the floor?

That we would consider an ingot.

What's an ingot like that worth? What does uranium go for per pound?

There's a standard transfer value between here and Fernald, I think it's about thirty dollars a kilogram, something like that. Don't quote me on that. It's, say, fifteen dollars a pound.

There is no radiological hazard with this material?

It is radioactive, and there are very low levels of radiation involved, but not to the extent that you're talking about lead shielding and all this kind of thing. Generally the protective clothing that the workers wear is sufficient to virtually eliminate their exposures.

What is the special clothing that they wear?

Just cotton coveralls is all it is. It's very, very low level, very little radiation. Nothing there, really.

In what way is cotton a protection? I know that lead is, I wasn't sure about cotton.

It's the type of radiation that's emitted from this material. Usually when you're speaking of radiation people are thinking of gamma radiation, that's the stuff you get behind lead shields to protect yourself

Lunchroom, Reactive Metals, Incorporated, Ashtabula, Ohio

So the N-Reactor stream goes to Hanford. Where do you ship the Savannah River stream?

The Savannah River product goes back to Fernald in truckload lots, by commercial, common carrier.

Does it have to have special safeguards when you truck it?

Not really. The only thing we're doing is shipping it in sealed truckload lots. It's not at the strategic level of enrichment. I think it has to be above twenty percent U-235, then you get into all these escorted armed-guard shipments and this kind of thing.

How big a load of uranium metal can a truck take?

It's whatever the highway limits are, and that's normally around 40,000 to 42,000 pounds a gross.

from. Alpha radiation, which I think mostly—again, I'm not a radiologist—but you're talking about a different type of radiation than gamma radiation, and it is such that simple cotton clothing is sufficient to block it, given the low levels that are involved.

I remember hearing that with alpha radiation a sheet of paper can stop it.

Yes. Cotton acts the same way.

So that's nonpenetrating radiation coming off the metal?

Yes.

But the hazard with it is if you breath it in, right?

Mm-hm. And the DOE [Department of Energy] furnishes to us annually a special machine that's in a semitrailer and goes

around to all these DOE sites. It measures the total body burden of radiation a worker might have, and we generally try to count everybody.

What's the average count that comes out of a person working around this material?

I'd better not give you numbers, but there are established limits. There is a DOE requirement that you have to report anybody who's exposed at a rate of fifty percent of that limit, and we've never had to report anybody. I'd say the maximum body burden we've ever seen here is somewhere about ten percent of the acceptable limit.

And if you have ten percent you're still considered to be within the safety margin?

Well within it, yes.

Okay, I think that covers it. I guess we should go on the tour now. I haven't been into a lot of factories myself; I've been dealing mostly with public-relations people and talking to people outside the factories, so this is an opportunity for me to really see something. But when I came out from this morning's short trip out onto the floor I had a little bit of a sore throat, and I figured there's all kinds of vapors there from all sorts of things going on, and I was wondering. . . . I bought a face mask in this welder's store. Would it be all right to wear that on the site? I'd feel a little bit better about having it.

If you'd feel more comfortable, you're more than welcome to wear it.

24.   Back to Fernald

25.   Laundry

26.   Dr. Thomas Mancuso—Pittsburgh, Pennsylvania, August 16, 1982

I am a physician and a research professor at the University of Pittsburgh at the Graduate School of Public Health. I have been here since 1962. Prior to that I served as the chief of the Division of Industrial Hygiene for the state of Ohio for seventeen years. I have concentrated on the study of occupational cancer. I have designed and conducted long-term epidemiological studies to determine industrial cancer hazards of a wide range of different industries and substances such as chromate, rubber, asbestos, beryllium, benzidine, and an extensive study of radiation in the atomic energy facilities.

Before we go further, Doctor, could I ask: What is the science of epidemiology?

Well, epidemiology describes the methods used to search for the causes of diseases among populations.

When did you begin studying radiation effects?

Early in 1964, I was approached by representatives of the Atomic Energy Commission's Division of Biology and Medicine to do a feasibility study to determine whether it was possible to undertake a national study of workers exposed to radiation at AEC facilities throughout the country. I reviewed the situation in fourteen AEC facilities and determined that the necessary records systems could be developed that would make it possible to undertake the correlation of the lifetime mortality experience of the AEC contract employees with occupational radiation exposure. The research contract was then awarded to me at the University of Pittsburgh.

When you say workers in atomic energy facilities—does that mean the bomb factories?

Yes—

Which ones did you study?

The point was to include all of the AEC facilities in America, but the amount of money available was limited. I started by touching base with all the major ones—Hanford, Oak Ridge, Los Alamos—and I went to Argonne, National Lead, and Mound laboratories, and I collected worker exposure data.

Did you include Reactive Metals, Incorporated, at Ashtabula?

Yes.

Did you include Savannah River Plant?

Yes.

And Pantex Nuclear Weapons Final Assembly Plant?

Yes.

Pinellas?

Yes.

Livermore?

Yes.

Portsmouth? Bendix? Rocky Flats?

Yes. I got the rosters of their employees. I initiated the study, but I got only to a certain point. The government would fund only certain things.

How many people made up the study?

The total population that I was working with at some point in time must have been somewhere between 225,000 and 250,000 people. The overall total for the various AEC facilities was over 300,000. But when the research funds were being terminated, I had to make a decision and choose a facility for final analysis, and the only one that was far enough along was Hanford. That's the one we did the analysis on.

Dr. Thomas Mancuso

I know you have done a lot of work on all kinds of industrial health problems—but had you dealt with radiation before?

I had never done any work in radiation at all. I think they wanted someone to look at these workers who was new to the subject. They came to me primarily because of two things: my experience designing epidemiological studies, and second, I was the one who first designed and developed the use of the Social Security record system in the United States and applied that to research in the study of industrial populations over several decades. This became a real breakthrough for epidemiological methodology. Because the basic problem with the effects of radiation was that they can occur twenty or thirty or forty years after the individual has been exposed. But after the individuals have left the plant no one knows what happens to them, and they'd get sick and die years later in another state, and no one would be able to make the correlation between subsequent events and the earlier exposure which caused the disease. Using the Social

Security system was the only way to keep track of these individuals over the decades. The method has since been used by scientists and the government and everybody else all over the country.

What was unusual in this radiation assignment was the fact that the workers I would be studying weren't sick. Other researchers have attempted to do studies of sick people, but this was a long-term study of healthy workers, individuals who had exceptionally fine medical screening and first-rate medical care. In our study we had one other component: the worker had a film badge every day, every week, every month, and every year, so we knew precisely what his radiation exposure was. That made this the only study of a population of healthy workers in atomic energy facilities who were uniformly badged and monitored for radiation during the course of their work experience, and who were followed for twenty-five or thirty years or more to determine what their causes of death were, and whether the cause of death was different, not as compared to the general population, but against an internal control. Not only that, but our study also differed in that the worker population was exposed to levels of radiation that were very low over a span of years.

You said you matched the workers against an "internal control." What does that mean?

The usual pattern in doing an epidemiological analysis like this is to compare the people in your study to a control group, using the general population, which can be misleading. But we compared the workers in our study who had cancer with those with non-cancer who were within the employee study group itself. We did this because the general population includes all the sick, disabled, and hospitalized people, and the industrial population, being more fit, has an actuarial mortality experience which is twenty-five to thirty-five percent better than the general population.

So that means that the industrial population could have a serious health problem even though their death rate was less than the general population?

That's exactly right! That's why the best control is an internal control. So that's exactly what we did. This is considered the highest and the best epidemiological test in determining a health effect comparing workers within the same facility.

Can you briefly describe the scope of the Hanford study and how that fits into the much bigger study?

Our overall study of workers in all the AEC facilities was the largest study in the world of this kind; eventually it would have included over 300,000 workers in the extension of the study that we had recommended. Initially we focused on the oldest and the largest AEC facilities, the Hanford and Oak Ridge operations. The Hanford study and analysis looked at some 35,000 employees. At the Oak Ridge facilities we were getting ready to analyze another 112,000 to 115,000 workers. But in the end, it was not possible. Our research was stopped.

In the case of the Hanford study, each person was a normal, healthy individual at the time of hiring. Each was given a film badge, each was monitored uniformly. And this was the only healthy population at that time ever identified and monitored in this manner, from the first day of occupational exposure to low levels of radiation, and followed for several decades. That made our study very different from the Hiroshima/Nagasaki study, which is an extrapolation, a guess-estimate, a reconstruction—a reconstruction from high doses, and a reconstruction that didn't start until five years after the atomic bombs had dropped. I think that the radiation guidelines and standards should be based on the Hanford data on a healthy, normal population, exposed to known, uniform amounts of low levels of radiation accumulated over a span of years, in contrast to extrapolating downward from the extremely high, instantaneous bomb doses to the survivors such as occurred at Hiroshima and Nagasaki.

Now when I started in on the overall study on atomic workers for the AEC, I discovered that the past data on the workers was being systematically destroyed and only current information was being kept. They told me that this was being done to save file space. I told them this was wrong, that they must keep a chronological record. I got them to stop. A tremendous amount of money and years of time were then required to abstract and reconstruct millions of pieces of information from the original, raw data sources in the various AEC facilities. By the time we were though, we had developed a basic electronic data-processing system of uniform information that went back to day one for each employee for each facility. That made it possible to determine for a series of workers, in a matter of seconds, the complete chronological work history and radiation measurement exposures with all the related data, whereas before it took about six months to reconstruct what happened to just one individual.

And when you focused on the Hanford worker population, how did it turn out?

Let me put it this way: if one was to design the ideal human experiment for trying to determine the effects of low levels of radiation, that's the way you would do it. I don't like to compare humans with animals, but if you think of this in terms of comparable animal experiments, you will see what I mean. Basically, you start with a healthy population that has been carefully screened, and you know that they have no medical problems. You put them in a closed environment, exposed periodically to a specific agent, in this instance radiation, and you carefully monitor them and the exposure and you follow them through their life-span. Now in the case of the Hanford worker with radiation exposure, he's monitored daily, so you know exactly what he was exposed to. He's from a normal, healthy population and you know his age and health status, and you know exactly when he was hired and each time he was exposed, and the exact amount and type of radiation that he got, together with the job assignments. Then you follow these people for several decades. Nobody had ever done that for atomic workers, for both the current and the former employees. No one ever had the opportunity to do that.

How long did you work on the Hanford study?

I worked on the radiation research project for about fourteen years to develop the necessary data systems and to obtain the necessary information from the Social Security system and the death certificates. I knew that I had to allow for the long latency period for cancer effects. A good deal of pressure was put on me to publish preliminary findings. But I would not do so.

And what was it that you did find after fourteen years?

Well, the findings were that low-level radiation does cause cancer, and that's definite, and the risk is anywhere from ten to twenty times greater than had been estimated. That is the essence of our findings. It's a very controversial finding. It means the lower levels of radiation, the so-called "safe" levels, are not safe at all. We wanted to continue the study and apply our analysis to another, much larger group of 115,000 workers at Oak Ridge, and beyond that to many thousands more in the other AEC facilities. The government refused to continue our research project. I said to them, "If you really want to know the truth, let us continue the project, since we designed the study and developed and

know the data best."

And they said . . . ?

They refused. Basically, they had their own reasons, but their reasons were not in the interests of the public. The interests of the public would require that we continue the study, since we knew more about the data than anyone else to determine the full range and extent of the health effects of radiation.

At a certain point you brought in Dr. Alice Stewart from England.

Yes, she was the one who did the pioneering Oxford Child Survey in which she identified the cancer effects of children born to mothers who were X-rayed during pregnancy. I brought her in because I wanted an independent scientist to review my data. I felt it was extremely important that my data be verified by a scientist independent of me and independent of the people working for me. What happened was, Alice became my primary consultant, along with George Kneale, and I think this was the most important step that I took on the study.

How was Dr. Stewart helpful?

She has an experience in radiation epidemiology that no other person in the world has. She brought with her over twenty years' experience in studying the radiation effects relative to children. She was able to apply her basic knowledge as a physician and clinician, as well as her knowledge of radiation and statistics to adult populations. What Alice Stewart has is a little difficult to explain—but she's like a musician who has a rare gift of sound. She has that rare gift of medical insight and objectiveness which only comes from experience. And she provided very rigorous tests to the data. And I remember sitting with her here on this sofa, we were talking about the project, and she said it was a very formidable undertaking to be able to detect this, because only a small percentage of the study population was affected at that time.

The point of the matter is, she's been able to determine and establish the effects of low-level radiation. She did that with children in her Oxford studies, and she identified it in the Hanford study. Now the reason the Hanford analysis was done and everybody keeps referring to the Hanford study is that it was the only one in which we could do the analysis before the money ran out and our research project terminated.

After we completed the Hanford analysis we asked for the Oak Ridge data, but they wouldn't give me a copy of my own research data—and here I was, the project director who designed, developed, and accumulated the data. Naturally, I'm furious about it because there's a scientific principle here, as well as a moral one.

I think it's scientifically outrageous. They knew that I had developed positive findings with the Hanford study and they were absolutely scared that if I kept on delving deeper I'd come up with other significant problems in the AEC facilities.

I think that there's a political equation, Bob, which has not been expressed in all this, and that is, our government has played down the radiation effects relative to Hiroshima and Nagasaki. Alice Stewart, when she did her study, independently found out that they had substantially underestimated the risk in Japan.

In the United States, basically, it's a question of officials introducing a political/economic equation to deny and delay the scientific facts to avoid payment of compensation to the atomic veterans. In this matter the government officials have also used a very misleading approach, saying that atomic veterans were exposed only to low-level radiation. This is actually a diversion because, if you look at the total radiation that they got, it would also include the dangerous radioactive fallout, and fallout is inhaled and ingested and provides doses of internal radiation.

I think that radiation is the most important subject in the world, and it will be forever, because of the thousands of nuclear weapons and bombs, and the constant threat to civilization and the world. Unfortunately there is no way to continue to study and make known the full range of effects without large sums of independent funding, and there's nobody coming up with any funds that are independent. From my experience, radiation research should be independent from government influence. I have felt the pressures. Basically the government itself does not want to know, and it does not want anybody else to know, that we are right, because if we are right, this nonsense about a limited nuclear war having very little effect is not only asinine, but unfortunately a real tragedy of huge proportions. Why, the impact of the fallout would be absolutely devastating. So that's the way it is. I think that we are right.

27. L-Reactor, Savannah River Plant

Two of the Savannah River Plant's five plutonium production reactors have been shut down. After the Chernobyl accident, regulators reviewed the condition of the remaining Savannah River reactors and ordered them cut back to 40% capacity.

James Gaver, public relations officer for the Department of Energy at the Savannah River Plant—Aiken County, South Carolina, August 3, 1983

The mission of the Savannah River Plant has not changed from the conception that originated its being in the early 1950s, and that is the production of plutonium and

James Gaver

tritium for the nation's nuclear defense program. Fundamentally we receive, from off-site, raw materials, if you will, and in one of our facilities we form these materials into fuel and targets which will be placed into plutonium and tritium production reactors. For the production of plutonium, we use both enriched uranium (U-235) and depleted uranium (U-238) in metallic form. We receive enriched uranium-235 from Oak Ridge. It is then alloyed with aluminum here, and that material is then put through a press to form fuel tubes—they're about fifteen feet long—and that is the fuel or the driver or the neutron source for the reactor process.

For the target materials, there are two separate processes. One type of target material produces tritium, another type produces plutonium. For the production of plutonium, we receive depleted uranium-238 slugs from Fernald, Ohio. They come here in their basic shape that will be used in the reactor. What we do here is to clean them up and to clad them in aluminum, and that aluminum-cladding process is what occurs at the Savannah River Plant. The aluminum provides a housing, if you will, and a form of holding the material in such a configuration that it can be used in the reactor. So we get the materials in as I have described, and then they are taken down to one of the reactors. And very simply, to produce plutonium, we irradiate depleted uranium-238 in the reactors, using enriched uranium-235 as a

fuel or a driver for the reactor process. And to produce tritium, we irradiate lithium. There were originally five nuclear materials production reactors at Savannah River, and let me say right off the top that these reactors are just that—they have no other purpose, there is no generation of electricity or other use. As of this day, Savannah River is the only facility that is producing weapons-grade plutonium to the defense programs. It is also the sole source of tritium.

But we don't have anything to do here with the actual fabrication of weapons. And from my perspective, I make a very conscious effort to know as little about that end of the nuclear defense programs as possible. I don't have a *need to know* about weapons design or quantities, or anything like that. That's not material that's available to me.

28. William Lawless—
Augusta, Georgia, October 18, 1986

I was hired by the Department of Energy at the Savannah River Plant to oversee duPont's waste: low-level waste, high-level waste, airborne waste—radioactive waste of all sorts, and hazardous chemical wastes. I oversaw the research end of it, plus some of the operational ends of it. My background was in solar energy and energy conservation.

For me, one of the most stunning things was finding out that after a couple of months on the job I had become the final stopping point for all the technical reports in my area. I became the one ultimately responsible to make the judgment for the American people. I couldn't believe it.

How long were you there?

In nuclear waste, four and a half years. Today I'm recognized as an expert in that area, but I find it bothersome because it wasn't that difficult to get to be an expert. If I'm an expert at all it's only because I've been able to ask hard questions and refuse to give up on those questions. The problems I addressed have been going on for years. It's just that they've never gotten out in public before.

So the public record has been sterling. . . .

Yes, up until about 1984–1985. But we're only talking about the public record. In actuality the performance at each one of these facilities is very, very poor. There isn't a Department of Energy facility in the country that could operate under comparable commercial regulation. What we really need are small peer review groups. Scientists and engineers can make some very bad mistakes working by themselves. Peer review groups drawn from the local community should be formed, made up of people with a vested interest in making sure that the environment around that facility is maintained properly.

So what's going on out there? Is there a way to describe it in broad terms?

The Department of Energy did just that recently. It has finally gone on the record and said that it will take at least one century before the plant grounds can be turned back over to the public. I was glad to hear them admit that, although I think that one century is being overly optimistic. The attitude was, up until this recent admission, that as soon as the plant's mission was over, we could turn it off and walk away from it. That's the story we've been telling the public for thirty years. Once the manager of the plant had a hearing before Senator Strom Thurmond. They were talking about the contamination in the river, and the manager said, "Senator, you'd have to drink 50,000 glasses of water before you would receive any dangerous contamination whatsoever." My reaction to that was, yes, if you pulled swiftly moving water from the middle of the river, but you'd have to watch where you were standing, because we've got 7.5 kilometers of very hot territory just off the site. The river swamp system is grossly contaminated with cesium-137.

Where?

It's at the plant boundary on the river, downstream—in the swamp area known as Steel Creek. Over the years there have been a lot of fuel failures in the reactors, and the reactors have been flushed out through the system, so it ends up off-site. I think the contamination got off-site through seepage basins.

What's a seepage basin?

The Savannah River Plant's seepage basins are like huge ponds or swimming pools. They've got four sides, but no liner on the bottom. The bottom is soil.

And the water goes through the soil?

That's right. At the Savannah River Plant this is the exclusive means of releasing liquids into the soil.

And what kind of liquids are these?

The water is a combination of steam condensates, wash water, cooling water—the full spectrum of waste water that any large industry would be running through. This is all waste water from the plutonium production process. It contains radioactive and toxic material.

William Lawless

How much water do the basins release in a day?

The basins vary in size, and the flow rates vary from day to day, but on average, each basin would process about one million gallons per day.

How many seepage basins are there at the Savannah River Plant?

There are sixty-eight. Cleanup is in progress at one—the infamous M-Area seepage basin. The M-Area is the Manufacturing Area. That's where they finish manufacturing the fuel and target rods for the plutonium production reactors.

Does Hanford have seepage basins for its plutonium production program?

Hanford does have a few seepage basins, but it has many more natural soil columns.

Soil columns?

"Natural soil columns" is a euphemism for all these different types of releases into the soil. "Natural" means "untreated," "soil" means "soil," and "column" means a place in the earth where chemicals filter down. So "natural soil column" is just a fancy term for a hole in the ground. At Hanford the main soil column release-mechanism is something called a "crib," which does pretty much the same thing as a seepage basin except it is not a pond, it's a long, narrow ditch, often covered with a cement top. Crib releases are made via a long perforated pipe inside the ditch—it's like a garden hose sprinkler with holes punched in it. If you were to flip that sprinkler upside down you'd have the basic crib soil-release mechanism. Mostly radioactive material was released this way at Hanford—it was pumped in through the pipe, forced out through the holes, it filled up the crib, then dripped down through the bottom of the crib into the column of soil. I know that at Hanford, up through 1984, soil column liquid releases amounted to 210 billion—that's *b* as in "boy," billion—gallons. All of it was radioactive, but there were many hazardous chemicals mixed in as well.

And at the Savannah River Plant?

Let's see . . . The M-Area basin received a million gallons of waste water a day, times 365, times maybe twenty years. That puts it at about . . . seven billion gallons, if they used it every day, 24 hours a day, and I think that they may have done that. Now multiplying that figure by 68, if they all received the same amount of effluent—which they did not, because some basins were much bigger, and some were smaller—that would come to . . . 500 billion gallons. That may not be accurate, but it looks like the Savannah River Plant had probably the same order of magnitude of releases as Hanford. The interesting thing about the Hanford number is that the 210 billion gallons only concerned the 200 Area, which is the reprocessing area. It doesn't take into consideration any of the outlying systems. If you factor in the water from Hanford's outlying systems, that would almost double that figure. At the Savannah River Plant, on the other hand, the 500 billion gallons would include everything.

Bill, in order to get some distance on this, let me ask you: How would you describe the Savannah River Plant to a child who was going to grow up to become an ecologist a hundred years from now?

Well, we know there is significant contamination on the surface of the soil throughout the 300 square miles of the Savannah River Plant, and we know there is contamination off-site as well. Right now if you looked at levels of radioactive tritium in public and private drinking-water systems around the plant, you can see it decrease up to 50 miles away, and there is tritium as far as 100 miles away in the pine needles. But it's at levels that are very low and, supposedly, it's absolutely no health hazard. But it's there; it's part of who we are in this area.

What would he or she see in 100 years? It's hard to say. With our wind patterns you could expect some sort of a smear in the soil going northeast and southwest.

The people exposed to the greatest concentrations are the workers. It's like a small city out there—more than 15,000 people live daily on site, in the middle of contamination that is quite unacceptable. It's from toxic and from radioactive constituents—you'd be hard-pressed to decide which was worse. The Department of Energy still does not report the levels of toxic chemical waste released into the environment there, and it has no intention of producing that information. And there are many substances that we don't even know about today. We learned in 1982, for example, that we don't know anything about the chemicals we've been putting into the ground for the past thirty years—we have no records. We can only surmise what's there based on the processes that were used. And we don't know where any of the hazardous stuff is buried. So this ecologist that comes along about 100 years from now is going to be like some archaeologist looking into the Pyramids today. There's no telling what they'll find. We certainly can't tell them.

Do you think that things have gotten this way because these facilities make bombs, and bomb-building has a sense of secrecy about it?

It's connected with defense, but the moment you mention nuclear weapons the issue gets very emotional. So I limit myself to discussing my area: how waste is handled. One other thing that this is connected to is income. People make pretty good money there, and good money inspires loyalty. The trouble is, not dealing with the problems is bound to have a bad effect on engineering operations of a plant, because when you can't get the informa-

tion, you make mistakes, and when those mistakes get covered up, you make more mistakes. The use of cardboard boxes for some thirty years is a good example of that.

Cardboard boxes? What cardboard boxes?

The Savannah River Plant buries some of its plutonium-contaminated wastes in ordinary cardboard boxes. When you question this practice, the stock response from DOE or duPont is: "We take no credit for the cardboard." This means that because the cardboard deteriorates in a short period of time, we don't accept any credit for it as a protection against the environment. So we don't count it as a protection. But this doesn't recognize the major problem with cardboard: it collapses. And that causes the soil above it to subside. And when subsidence happens you lose the integrity of the burial ground, which means you can no longer guarantee it will be a coherent facility hundreds of years past the time that you walk away from it. All of the commercial burial grounds that have been shut down around the country have failed because of the use of cardboard boxes. Cardboard has now been banned for waste disposal in the commercial sector. But it has not been banned within the Department of Energy.

When I gave a talk before the State of Washington's legislature this past June, we had a debate with my counterpart at Hanford, Gerry White, and when cardboard boxes came up I said, "I know they have stopped using cardboard boxes at the Savannah River Plant, but I don't know if they've stopped anywhere else in the country. And I'm not allowed to ask. If you go for a Freedom of Information request, you have to ask for a specific publication. You cannot ask a general question." Well, one of the congressmen stopped the action at that point and said, "Wait a minute, I'm a farmer, and I don't understand anything about radioactive waste at all. But I do know what cardboard boxes are. Were these reinforced cardboard boxes, or something like that?" I told him, "No, these are typical cardboard boxes that you can get out of a grocery store." He then turned to Gerry White and said, "Are you guys still using cardboard boxes at Hanford?" Now this was a year and a half after they had quit using them at the Savannah River Plant. And Gerry says, "Yes, we are still using cardboard boxes here at Hanford." To me that struck to the heart of the problem. We were able to stop things at the Savannah River Plant because we made it public, but we could not do it

across the board.

And what else is going on that you don't know about? Why has nobody catalogued the hazardous chemicals that have gone into the ground? Why has nobody questioned the use of cardboard boxes? Why has nobody challenged the use of seepage basins or the airborne releases that go out of the Savannah River Plant? It's a closed system. The secrecy aspect of it has made people feel that if they question what's going on, they're traitors. Somehow we've got to get people in there who really care about what's going on.

Sometimes the public gets interested in these issues because of the dramatics that are associated with them. But we're dealing with the public only on surface issues, not on the real issues.

Aren't cardboard boxes and seepage basins real?

More real is the fact that this is a closed system which is primarily responsible only unto itself, not unto Congress and not unto the American people—because they don't know enough to ask the good questions.

Does the closed system look like it's going to change at all?

I don't think so. The people in it are not unusual in any sense. They love their jobs. They love their families. They believe in what they do. They think that what they do is very important. And they believe that they are doing a good job.

How many other sites have problems like the Savannah River Plant?

I think the worst problems are at Hanford, by far. The Hanford facility with its 149 failed tanks, high-level waste tanks, is probably the nation's first actual high-level waste repository. The cost to remove the contaminated soil around the leaking tanks has been estimated at about $12 billion. That's what it would cost to put it into a deep underground repository, which we promised to do in 1973. If we wanted just to cover it up it would cost $2 billion.

What does it mean when a tank fails?

It means it loses its integrity as a container. In 1980, 35 of Hanford's 149 single-walled, high-level tanks were known leakers, and the rest were in a state of continuous disintegration. So they cut the piping on all of them. They blanked them off. This made them nonoperational. They are all considered failed. I don't know if you've ever seen a model of a tank—it's got thirty or forty lines going into it, like a pot in the middle of a spider web. A tank farm could have 20 or 30 or 40 of these in

143

a single area, all interconnected so that you can move fluids and radioactive waste back and forth. These were the old-style ones. The new style are the double tanks—a tank within a tank. They're much better. But we've had some terrible problems with them too.

What problems?

Well, the new high-level waste tanks were being completed at $8 to $10 million apiece at the Savannah River Plant and at Hanford. In September 1980 we made a final inspection tour of the new tanks. We were walking around inside one of them and, quite by accident, one of the engineers discovered at his feet a blue spot. He bent over to scrape it away. As he scraped it he found a deep pit. All the tanks were then checked and some of them were described as looking like Swiss cheese: corrosion pits were everywhere. An area the size of this tabletop would have had maybe up to a thousand pits in it. The deepest pit went about thirty-five percent of the way through the tank's half-inch carbon steel shell.

What caused the pits?

Apparently during construction plywood sheets had been put down to protect the metal floor from damage, and the plywood had been there for years. When it was lifted away they found galvanic cells had been created as a result of the humidity and the tight space, and that wound up cutting into the steel. But that wasn't the sole cause, because pits were also found in the annuli of the tanks where there was no plywood flooring. And pits were found on the walls as well.

So what happened? What did people do?

They had a big meeting in May of 1981 and decided, over strenuous objections, that we would not go public with this. The objection in our branch was that we'd gone on record telling the court in 1980 that there were no problems with the tanks and we specifically mentioned corrosion pitting. We felt it was important to tell the court that what we said in 1980 was incorrect. Also, not going public meant that no official reports could go into distribution as required by law, and no scientist or engineer would be allowed to report on it in public at any conference forever, period. That was the decision in 1981.

After Hanford and the Savannah River Plant, the next worst sites are Oak Ridge, the Idaho National Engineering Laboratory, and Los Alamos. Problems at those five facilities are motivating Congress to introduce legislation to remove self-regulation from the Department of Energy. DOE was policing itself in radioactive and hazardous waste up until the mercury spill was discovered at Oak Ridge. Oak Ridge is where we had the largest mercury spill in the United States—two and a half million pounds went into the river from the Y-12 plant over a number of years, and it wasn't discovered until 1983. A lawsuit was filed, DOE lost in 1984, and it has now conceded the regulation of hazardous waste to the Environmental Protection Agency. This in turn has resulted in the State of South Carolina and the State of Washington moving onto the Savannah River Plant site and onto Hanford and those states have for the first time assessed fines against the Department of Energy. That's never happened before.

Bill, if you had to put a price tag on the cleanup of the nuclear weapons complex, what would it come to?

I had one of my duPont scientists estimate how much it would cost to pull one high-level waste tank out of the ground. The tank costs about $9 million to build, and it will cost about $40 million to remove it from the ground. And if you look at the hard structures at SRP we estimated that it would come to between $2 billion and $20 billion just to remove the things we could lay our hands on, without any cleanup of the soil or the ground water. And that's just one facility. Multiply that by ten or so to cover the major facilities, and by a few numbers more to cover the minor ones, and you could real quickly be well in excess of $100 or $200 billion. We concluded that there was no way such money could ever be gathered together. It would exceed the will of the American public to see it through. So what do you do? How do you balance this against the need to defend yourself? I don't know.

---

29. DuPont Administration Building, Savannah River Plant
SRP Annual
Budget: $1,119,000,000 (1986)

---

30. Hanford Ditch 216-B (B-2-3)

The ditch is one of three systems for discharging toxic and radioactive waste water into the ground. The other two are cement-covered ditches called "cribs," and seepage basins, large open ponds through which pass, on average, one million gallons of water a day.

The Savannah River Plant uses sixty-eight seepage basins that have been in operation for more than thirty years.

---

31. J.S. "Steve" McMillan—Allendale, South Carolina, August 4, 1983

I'm an old country boy. I'm not really brilliant, but I'm curious. And I'm interested in people and things. I'm known as a man with a vast knowledge of a lot of loose facts. I'm fifty-seven years old and I've been farming since 1950.

Something else started in 1950 around here too, didn't it?

Yeah. We had a big industry come into our fair state, and the government bought out, supposedly, the farmers and businessmen and a large area of Aiken County and Barnwell County.

What do you mean, they bought out people "supposedly"?

Well, they bought the land from the farmers, and some of them got paid what the land was worth at that time, and some of them didn't. They moved the graves, the towns disappeared, the people disappeared, and the government gave us what is known as "the Bomb Plant."

SRP Best-Ever Safety Trophy

This trophy stands in the reception area of the SRP administration building. A card at the base of the trophy reads:

"United States Atomic Energy Commission's Best-Ever Safety Trophy won by the employees of the Savannah River Plant with an accumulation of 39,345,150 man-hours during 1,774 days between June 24, 1967, and May 2, 1972, without a disabling injury."

Disabling injuries are those which cause loss of time on the job. On-the-job radiation doses are not considered disabling injuries.

I thought it was "the Savannah River National Environmental Research Park."

Well, they do a lot of research up there. I don't know if any of it is made public. Even though I suspect a lot of damage to our health and our environment, I can't prove it. I don't have any way to prove anything.

Dr. Reinig, the health officer for duPont, told me the other day this is the safest plant in the world and that no worker has ever received more than 5 rems, except once when one worker received more than 5 rems, and nobody in the population has received more than the minimal amount.

Steve McMillan

I wouldn't say that's not true. I'd just call that an outright lie. I think that eventually somebody is going to have a grudge against DOE [Department of Energy] and duPont and they are going to tell what's really going on up there. A man that is a scientist will eventually tell exactly how badly they have done by the people and by the environment in this area. And when that happens, I'm not going to say, "I told you so." It's going to be a sad day when we do find out what those super-agents have been doing.

"Super-agents"?

Yes. It's a highly top-secret outfit. They have, in my opinion, thoroughly brainwashed the workers as to how safe radiation is, and I know some of them don't completely believe the little pep talk they give them up there. I feel sorry for some of those men that are being radiated. You

know, they like to say that that plant is the safest plant in the world. It might well be as far as visible accidents go, but if it is so safe, why is it also the most monitored and most checked plant in the world?

Is it?

It is the most monitored plant in the world. And why might they be doing all that monitoring if it is so safe?

One thing Mr. Reinig told me was, "If we didn't feel it was safe, we wouldn't live in this area." He maintains that most of the people who manage the plant live in the area and that that's proof of its safety.

I think it is possible that the whole bunch has been brainwashed as to the effects and damage that radiation can do to man, the land, and the animals. I once tried to pin Dr. Reinig down about the effects of different nucleides, like, say, plutonium against cesium against tritium against uranium. And he said, "Radiation is radiation." But recently I read in the Augusta *Herald* that he's changed his story. He says now that some nucleides are more dangerous than others. Which I knew all the time. And plutonium is the most dangerous of them all.

Is plutonium released from the plant?

Well, they make it there.

I know. That's the main purpose of the plant.

If you think they can contain all of it, then why is plutonium always missing in their inventory?

Is it always missing in their inventory?

It is. They say it's in the pipes. What pipes? Your windpipe?

The plant pipes.

Yeah, okay, the plant pipes, I'll buy that. I'll buy some of that windpipe too. Listen, I think they've pushed the whole thing under the rug so long that there's no longer any room under the rug, and it's beginning to spill out, and eventually the people are going to find out what they've done up there. I'm certain of it. Radiation—you can't see it, you can't taste it, you can't smell it, you can't feel it. Who identifies it? A scientist. How many scientists do you see walking around here with Geiger counters? There's no such thing. Nobody. Nobody's checking. And the government knows full well that the Savannah River Plant is violating practically all clean air and water regulations. Now they want to reclassify the streams that they've already contaminated.

From what to what?

Well, so they can go ahead and put the scalding hot water in the streams. Or the radiation. Or both. They want to change the classification of the stream. If they do that, the state will allow them to keep right on polluting. It's not fair to us in South Carolina to let the government violate laws the other citizens in this country have to go by.

But what makes you so convinced that it's a bad place? You can't see the records, you can't see the radiation, and you have no instruments, yet you seem sure the plant is a catastrophe for the environment. What makes you so certain?

Listen, no man lives that does everything perfect. And they are no different. And they are not going to jeopardize the nuclear industry, and they are not going to jeopardize their paycheck. They are not going to buck the federal government. The way they see it, everything is perfect. But it's too perfect. *Nothing* is perfect. They make it sound like radiation is God's great

Scalding water from SRP plutonium reactor dumped into wetlands

gift to the world. But all the scientists and all your doctors agree on one point: all radiation is potentially dangerous to your health. *Any* radiation, even the radiation that God gives us.

Have they ever done a health survey of people in this area?

I think we probably have a much higher cancer rate here. But I don't have the figures, and I can't find out any figures. I've asked all the politicians to have a health study, and they turn their heads and talk about something else. Maybe we need a different political party that will represent the people in this country.

You know, the money goes north and the radiation comes south. Now I know people have got to make a living, so I'm not trying to get their jobs. What I am saying is, there will be enough work up there to clean up the mess that's accumulated to give many jobs for many years. It's going to cost many billions of dollars to decontaminate that whole site. There's thirty million gallons of radioactive waste that need to be processed and removed from the plant site, and it's sitting over the most prolific water-bearing strata in the United States: the Tuscaloosa Aquifer. The waste is about fourteen to twenty feet above the top of that strata in big tanks. And they have tanks up there right now that are leaking. You know, if they'd have picked the world over they couldn't have found a place that would have been more dangerous to put all this radioactive waste in than they have at Savannah River Plant.

But—"it's necessary for our national defense."

Well, if we decide to annihilate Russia with thousands of nuclear missiles and if Russia decides to annihilate us with thousands of missiles, yes, it's all very, very necessary. But it seems to me we should be able to reach some kind of agreement, and I don't mean one that any lawyers would draw up. We should just get a bunch of farmers together from both countries, and we'd just let them destroy one weapon and then we'd destroy one, and we'd just keep going back and forth, back and forth, until we had all the weapons destroyed. Nothing complicated about it!

I ran into a man the other day, he says, "Damn them Russians." He said, "Let's shoot that big gun over there on 'em." I said, "Man, do you know what you're talking about?" I said, "Have you ever heard one of them things crack? I'm telling you they make a loud noise." "Naw," he says, "we don't have to take that." I says, "They don't have to take it either." That is

the one thing that is hindering this country. You know, a lot of Americans think, "We'll just wipe 'em off the face of the map." They don't know that the Russians got a washrag too. They can wipe us. And we both keep getting more sophisticated, bigger, better, faster, stronger. Pretty soon we'll have some in space. Man gets smarter and smarter and smarter and smarter and weaker and weaker and weaker.

But if we don't—

Look, who built the first bomb?

America.

Who used the first bomb?

America.

Who used the other A-bomb?

America.

Who sells more weapons than any country in the world?

America?

I think the Russians are frightfully scared of American people. And maybe they have a right to be.

---

32. George Couch, maintenance worker, Savannah River Plant, and **Evelyn Couch,** his wife—Aiken Community Hospital, Aiken, South Carolina, August 5, 1983

George, how long did you work at the Savannah River Plant?

George Couch: I worked there for twenty-two years and eight months, since October 1952. Saw most of it start up. I worked in every area and in all but one building. I did not go in the vault.

What's the vault?

George: That's where they kept the product. I did go up to the gate of it. I worked in guard houses, shacks, right on up to water-pump houses and your reactor. I worked underneath the reactor and when they shut it down we'd go in and put up scaffolding. On that job we had to work in a squatting position. We were told if you stood up you'd get your full dose right then, immediately. And we'd build the scaffolding for the other people to go in and work with. I was on other jobs where they would tell you to go through and just barely stop and maybe make one-quarter of a turn on a bolt, and just keep walking right through. It would take so many men going through to just run one nut on a bolt. This is the radiation that we had at that time.

For some time I worked with a manipulator mechanic. He worked on the other side of a hot cell using remote-control armatures and he watched what the armatures were doing through three or four feet of glass that was ninety-five percent lead. I came into the picture whenever it was time to remove the remote manipulators out of the hot cell. The operators would bag them out in plastic and turn them over to us and we had a grub box that we would put them into. We'd take them out and cleanse them down and if we got the radiation count down to a certain level then we could go ahead and work on them and rebuild them and put them back into service. If we couldn't decontaminate them low enough, we'd bag 'em and bury 'em. Box 'em and bury 'em. That was in the laboratory—that was the largest laboratory in the world, as you may know.

Did you ever find out what your total exposure was for the twenty-two years that you worked there?

George: We were told different things at different times. Frankly, I haven't ever gotten a total.

In general, was it a pretty clean operation?

George: It had to be pretty clean, yes. We had to wear coveralls and sometimes we put on as many as three pair. You'd go into a place and come back out and take off these coveralls and put on clean ones. So I mean as far as actual filth, yes, it was clean, but as far as radioactivity goes, I mean, is it dirty or is it clean? It's there.

Did you ever have a meter on you so you knew?

George: We'd wear film badges. And we have what they call "Health Physics." These people monitor and see the radiation count that's coming off your body, or whatever, and keep checks on it. And they make out a job procedure when you sign in. You pick up your job procedure and that tells you what you have to do. I was on a job one night, me and this other boy, and we went and found the work procedure and got it listed out, and dressed out like it told us to, and went on in and started to work and started welding. So a man standing up on there screamed at me and I looked up and by that time something was coming at me and I caught it. He says, "Get that on quick!" So I snatched on the gas mask.

He threw down a gas mask?

George: I came out and told him, "What in devil was that for?" He said,

"You know better than to do that." I said, "Well, listen, I done what the work procedure called for." He says, "You know darn good and well that you're not supposed to go in there and throw heat on that pipe," he says. "That releases the radiation." Well, I did, but I mean, I guess it slipped my mind, you might say, but me and him had worked together long enough that he knew I was supposed to know better, but the one that checked us in, he didn't catch it either.

Why were you fired?

Evelyn Couch: Poor performance, they said. Wouldn't you think that after twenty-three years they would have found out he had poor performance before then?

What was really going on?

George: Well, I don't really know. In the early 1960s I was taken sick and my doctors told me I had a high white count, but that I had enough red cells to offset it. And this is all the information I could get. I was weak, and in an air-conditioned store or anything else, the sweat would just run off of me. I was out a little over five months and I went to nearly every doctor I could. Each one of the doctors would tell me that I had too many white cells, and enough red cells to offset it, but it wasn't leukemia. We sent off a sample every so often, and there was a time when I was having blood drawn just about twice a week. The doctor kept telling me we had to watch it, so one day I went in and he says, "Well, it showed up a high white count again," and he says, "We'll have to watch it," and then it dawned on me, and I said, "Doc, I want to ask you a question." He says, "What is it?" I says, "What are we looking for?" He looked at me and says, "I don't know." I said, "Well, how in the hell would you know it if you saw it?" And that wound up the blood tests then. So in '73 I had an automobile accident. And I rounded that up and got over that a while and then I went back to work.

In '75, after I was fired, I was talking to a friend of mine and I said, "I wish I had a doctor who would tell me what was wrong with me." He told me about this doctor about a hundred miles down in Georgia. So I went to the doctor, and the second or third trip he said, "This is crazy! How can you have a high white count and a normal differential and not have a high red count?" I said, "Doc, I don't know." He said, "Wait a minute." So he reached back and got a book and he said to my wife, "Here, read this, and remember where it's at. You've got *polycythemia vera.*" I understand that since this there have been quite a

few in this vicinity that have *polycythemia.* Although the plant claims that we don't have it.

What is polycythemia vera?

Evelyn: Well, it's too many red blood cells. And you have too many white ones too. We know very little about it yet. It is a rare blood disease.

What is usually the cause of it?

Evelyn: We have been told different things; but when George was pronounced with it they said it was brought on by either radiation or high altitude.

Do you spend a lot of time in the mountains?

George Couch

George: I was born about three miles from where I live, right here locally. And I did a stint in the Army for three years, but that was in the South Pacific. So I haven't lived in any high altitude, but I did work in radiation at the plant for twenty-two years and eight months.

Evelyn: What gets me is the way they called him in that last day. They called him in at lunch one day and sent him home as if he'd stolen something. After twenty-three years of service. When he came in he was all to pieces. I actually could have killed the man that let him drive home alone by himself in the condition he was in. They had already taken away his plant driver's license because they knew he had had a blackout or a seizure when he was in his car accident. The day they sent him home they could have at least called

someone or told him to come back the next day and they would straighten things out.

Earlier today I was out at the plant talking to the health officer for duPont, Bill Reinig, and he told me that the Savannah River Plant was the safest place in the world. For radiation.

George: I feel certain that that's the way they would tell you. I mean, he even convinced us. We thought radiation was something you could eat and it would not bother you, it was so safe. It took me a long time before I realized what it was.

Evelyn: Radiation—we don't know what it is yet, we don't know what we can do with it and we don't know what it can do with us. So I think there's a lot of studying on radiation to be done yet. And there's a lot of studying to be done on *polycythemia vera.*

George: And another thing, there is no way of telling how many people have already died from *polycythemia vera.* The only way to know would be to check your people while they're living, except they say it's very expensive. But what is the price of death? How much is a person's life worth?

33. Test Blast: Official Portrait

In the Minor Scale test blast, 4,740 tons of high explosive, ammonium nitrate, and fuel oil were detonated to mimic the blast and heat effects of an 8-kiloton nuclear bomb. This was the largest atmospheric explosion since 1963, when the Atmospheric Test Ban Treaty ended above-ground nuclear testing.

Six countries, including Germany and Sweden, as well as numerous government agencies, took advantage of the Minor Scale simulated nuclear blast to test Civil Defense hardware in a nuclear war environment.

34. Minor Scale: Unofficial Portrait

The Minor Scale observation point was 6 miles from Ground Zero. The explosion itself took place several miles from the site where Trinity, the first atomic bomb, was detonated. The principal equipment tested was the Hardened Mobile Launcher for the Midgetman missile. Also tested were Soviet tanks, U.S. missile silo covers, and Swiss fallout shelter units, which were subjected to blast pressures equivalent to those of a low-yield battlefield nuclear weapon.

35. St. George, Utah

The Mormon Temple in the center of the photograph was the first temple built after the Mormons migrated to Utah.

36. Sedan Crater

This crater began as a hole 36 inches in diameter, drilled to a depth of 635 feet. A thermonuclear device was lowered into the shaft, back-filled with sand, and detonated. Lawrence Livermore National Laboratory sponsored the test. Radiation levels at Ground Zero measured 500 rems

Sedan crater: view from the visitors' box

per hour. The Sedan fallout cloud traveled through Utah, Idaho, and along the southern border of Wyoming, then north through South Dakota, Nebraska, Iowa, Missouri, Kentucky, Tennessee, and Minnesota.

37. Judge A. Sherman Christensen—
Salt Lake City, Utah, April 26, 1987

Ordinarily a judgment after the time for appeal has expired is final and can be set aside years later only if it has been the result of fraud upon the court. Fraud upon the court is an exceedingly limited doctrine. Exceedingly limited. The Supreme Court has treated the matter on only a handful of occasions. In Sheep Case Number Two, I set aside the earlier judgment because I was convinced that fraud was practiced by the withholding of evidence and that this was of transcendent importance from the standpoint of judicial administration, trial advocacy, and the integrity of judicial proceedings.

In view of the reversal of this decision by the Court of Appeals of the Tenth Circuit, it is ironical that it continues to be one of my most discussed opinions in which there is still considerable interest. Now, here is a case in which I failed, but it teaches that failure sometimes does not mean that you have failed. I feel that perhaps it was the circuit court that failed in giving insufficient effect to the facts found by me as pointed out in the dissenting opinion of Judge McKay, and in failing to recognize the importance of the points I made in protecting the integrity of the judicial process.

I'm not going further into the reasons for this feeling because my decision spells them out the best I can.

Excerpts from Judge Christensen's 1982 decision:

"The Nevada Test Site was established on December 18, 1950, by order of President Truman . . . amid much public debate and at a time of international crises . . . which [were] widely perceived as a threat to peace and to the security of the nations of the free world. . . . Accordingly, the President committed the resources of the Atomic Energy Commission (AEC) to the rapid development of thermonuclear weapons. . . .

"During the 'Upshot-Knothole' multishot experiment of eleven atmospheric nuclear tests conducted between March 17 and June 4, 1953, at the Nevada Test Site, 252 kilotons of nuclear fission products were emitted as radioactive fallout. . . . The 14.4-kiloton "Nancy" shot [was] fired on a 300-foot water tower on March 24, 1953, and the 32.4-kiloton "Harry" shot [was] fired on a 300-foot tower on May 19, 1953. At the time . . . 11,710 sheep were grazing in an area from 40 miles north to 160 miles east of the test site. Of these sheep, 1,420 lambing ewes (12.1%) and 2,970 new lambs (25.4%) died during the spring and summer of 1953.

"After studying the conditions surrounding these deaths the AEC reported . . . that there had been no causal connection between the sheep's exposure to radioactive

available, it is evident that radioactivity from atomic tests was not responsible for the deaths and illness among sheep in areas adjacent to the Nevada Proving Grounds last spring, the U.S. Atomic Energy Commission reported today. . . .'

"In 1979 Congress and the United States Department of Health, Education and Welfare conducted independent investigations into the health effects of the Nevada nuclear tests of the 1950s and the 1960s. In connection with public hearings previously classified documents and reports were released. Testimony before the Committees tended to show that the sheep in question were in areas of above normal radioactive fallout with reference to the 'Nancy' shot on March 24 and the 'Harry' shot on May 19, 1953; . . . that government records were changed to discount evidence of a causal relationship between radiation exposure of the sheep and their deaths; that without adequate justification the AEC disregarded or discounted clinical information supportive of a conclusion that radiation was the cause of death; that the AEC had evidence which substantiated the fact that the dead sheep had received considerably more radiation than the amounts expressed in the AEC reports; that there were differences of opinion as to whether the experimentally produced lesions were comparable to those observed on the Cedar City sheep; and that the final report of the AEC was falsely presented as representing the unanimous view of those who participated in the investigation and signed the report.

Judge A. Sherman Christensen

fallout emitted during the . . . test series and their deaths. The Commission's formal conclusions, released on January 6, 1954, were introduced by the following press statement:

" 'On the basis of information now

"There are circumstances which render the case far from an easy one, not the least of which is the long interval of time with which we have had to cope. There are resulting imponderables in addition to the unavailability of a complete trial record.

There could be a temptation to treat present-day cynicism concerning the good faith of government officials as always having existed. Much has happened during the last decade or so to alter public opinion. Ideas of what conduct of investigators, witnesses and officers of the court is acceptable in the course of the judicial process may have changed, hopefully for the better, as we get further and further away from the idea of mere gamesmanship in the operation of the adversary system. The intervening years . . . have no doubt brought new perceptions in the light of which it would be unfair to nicely evaluate conduct and attitudes in the '50s, or inappropriate to assume . . . that current ethical or moral standards for litigation have always existed. . . . Judged by modern insights I took a somewhat pristine view . . . of the general integrity of government officials in the absence of evidence impugning it in specific instances. I suppose that I shall continue to do so, despite the buffetings of Watergate, these proceedings and other current disclosures. Nonetheless, I have concluded that by whatever standard or as of whatever period the circumstances found here are to be judged, they clearly and convincingly demonstrate a species of fraud upon the court for which a remedy must be granted even at this late date. . . .

"The present is not an ordinary case with mere private or even ordinary public concerns. It originated amid a transcendent chapter of world history, developing but imperfect information concerning a mysterious and awesome device as to which the AEC and those associated with them enjoyed a virtual monopoly of knowledge in comparison to that independently available to the plaintiff sheep owners, their attorneys and, indeed, the Court, and a variated and persistent program of government representatives to disclose only selectively the information fairly necessary in the prospective judicial proceedings.

"In such a setting it appears by clear and convincing evidence, much of it documented, that representations made as the result of the conduct of government agents acting in the course of their employment were intentionally false or deceptive; that improper but successful attempts to pressure witnesses not to testify as to their real opinions or to duly discount their qualifications and opinions were applied; that a vital report was intentionally withheld and information in another report was presented in such a manner as to be deceitful, misleading, or only half true; that interrogatories were deceptively answered; that there was deliberate conceal-

ment of significant facts with reference to the possible effects of radiation upon the plaintiffs' sheep; and that by these convoluted actions and in related ways the processes of the court were manipulated to the improper and unacceptable advantage of the defendant at the trial."

38.　Irma Thomas
St. George, Utah, November 7, 1982

This interview took place while the "Fallout Trials" were proceeding in Salt Lake City.

I'm so bad! I speak out so frankly, I ought to be muffled or something. But to have been duped by our own government is just beyond me. It's horrendous! I can't accept it—that's all. They asked in that meeting last night for everybody to raise their hand who no longer really trusted the government, and a lot of hands went up.

What meeting was this last night?

It was an NBC documentary that Channel 2 is doing on the down-winders' court case up at Salt Lake City, and they included a lot of the victims from around here, out at the Four Seasons Hotel. These people have been hurt, and they're not taking kindly to it from here on out. They accepted it once because they felt it was their national duty. But it's turned into something else now. We had a military president—Eisenhower—who said, "Confuse them with fission and fusion." Well, of course, thirty years ago, who knew fission from fusion? I still don't know the

difference, but I do know what it's done to us. There are now thirty-eight victims within a block of my home, and I think that's a bit much.

And I'm not the only one. It's come to where plenty of people are suing the government because of what went on. That's happening right now. Psychologists call it mass hysteria. But why wouldn't it be, when it's been mass murder? Yes, that's what you can call it. They came here and told us that nothing bad was happening, but scientists very early on informed the government what would happen from the fallout. But the government just keeps harping on this: "Well, it was low-level," you know, and "insignificant." What they don't tell us is that this low-level radiation is cumulative, it affects the genes, and it shortens life around the globe. I know that some of them have said, "Well, that was a long time ago, and we didn't really know back then." Of course they knew! I even have a 1965 government memorandum right here which says, and I quote, "In the interval from 1951 to 1962, the U.S. conducted above-ground tests in Nevada. The town of St. George, population 4,562, on one occasion recorded the highest twenty-four-hour average concentration of fallout ever measured in a populated area."

They knew, they knew. This wasn't like Hiroshima where they flattened everything, you know. A lot of Japanese people have been here and wanted to see some of the victims, and they wanted to see some disfigurements or something like that. I had to tell them, "That isn't the way it affected us. We weren't in the direct blast. It was from the fallout that we were affected." And it's a gradual thing. It's taken twenty or thirty years. And it is ongoing. Daily, I hear of first one, and then another, and then another. When I think of thirty-eight victims within a block radius of my home, I've never heard of anything like that in St. George before the testing, and I've lived in this house for forty-five years. They say the sun and old age will cause cancer—but it's not the old people who were dying. It was the young children. And the strong young men and women dying of leukemia, women dying of cancer of the brain, the breast, the stomach. The college president and many of the teachers have died of leukemia. And why were so many children being born with birth defects? Young girls were losing first babies with miscarriages and stillbirths. It was unusual, there's no two ways about it. I don't know how they can think that it's a normal situation here.

Dear, I'm giving you such a speech. You know, you can't even say hello to me—I just explode. I sat through that thing last night for three hours and I thought it would kill me dead.

Was it because you had to tell the story over again?

I didn't tell the story. It was just sitting there with all of those victims. I knew them all. And I knew which ones had lost their children and their loved ones. It's traumatic as . . . hell. Can I swear like a demon? I do sometimes. But that was the situation, and it wore me to a frazzle, I think. Because I'm consumed with it anyway. You may be able to tell that.

Well, you were one of the first to get the word out.

Yes, but it took me about eighteen years to put two and two together, and then to get up the nerve to speak against the government. I'm just sorry that I didn't get to it sooner. I don't know, maybe it would have done something for people like our sheriff, and our chamber of commerce secretary, and Beth, a schoolteacher whose doctors told her she must have walked over a uranium mine. There was even John Wayne and his entire movie crew! Of course, when it hits your own family, that's what brings you to action. When it got my family, I hit the ceiling.

What was it that happened with your family?

One of my children has muscle damage. They never did tell us anything about it. But the people who did health checks kept returning to her for more tests, and between two shows—a radio report and a television program, both of which said a survey had shown that no damage has been done—right after that I got a telephone call from her and she told me the damage that had been done to her. I really blew up, that's all. And I haven't stopped. And I'm not going to stop.

How long ago was that?

That was in '78. But she's been under doctor's care since 1965. And still is. So I see no way that I'm ever going to simmer down.

Not even if the judgment in the trial is favorable?

Well, that may tone me down a little. This whole thing has made me lose so much faith in humankind, and I resent that being done to me, because that isn't the type of person that I am, normally. It would be wonderful if Judge Jenkins rules in favor of the plaintiffs, but it won't restore any health or bring back any lives.

Industrial safety sign overlooking Frenchman's Flat, Nevada Test Site

On May 9, 1984, United States District Judge Bruce S. Jenkins ruled in favor of the plaintiffs in the "Fallout Trails." A total of 1,192 suits were filed against the federal government. Judge Jenkins agreed to hear twenty-four representative cases. The legal action began August 30, 1979. The trial transcript extended to more than 7,000 pages. Excerpts from Judge Jenkins's ruling:

". . . This case is concerned with what reasonable men in positions of decision-making in the United States government between 1951 and 1963 knew or should have known about the fundamental nature of matter. . . .

"This case is concerned with the perception and the apprehension of its political leaders of international dangers threatening the United States from 1951 to 1963. It is concerned with high-level determinations as to what to do about them and whether such determinations legally excuse the United States from being answerable to a comparatively few members of its population for injuries allegedly resulting from open-air nuclear experiments conducted in response to such perceived dangers. . . .

"It is concerned with the passage of time, the attendant diminishment of memory, the availability of contemporary information about open-air atomic testing and the application of a statute of repose.

"It is ultimately concerned with who in fairness would bear the cost in dollars of injury to those persons whose injury is demonstrated to have been caused more likely than not by nation/state–conducted open-air nuclear events. . . .

"At the core of this case is a fundamental principle—a time-honored rule of *law,* an ethical rule, a moral tenet: '[The] law imposes [a duty] on everyone to avoid acts in their nature dangerous to the lives of others' (*Thomas v. Winchester,* 6, N.Y. 397, 57 Am. Dec. 455 [1852]).

"In the pragmatic world of 'fact' the court passes judgment on the probable. Dispute resolution demands rational decision, not perfect knowledge. . . .

"FINDINGS OF ULTIMATE FACT. The court finds that defendant failed to adequately warn the plaintiffs or their predecessors of known or foreseeable long-range biological consequences to adults and to children from exposure to fallout radiation from open-air atomic testing and that such failure was negligent. . . .

"The court finds that as a direct and proximate result of such negligent failures, individually and in combination, defendant unreasonably placed plaintiffs or their predecessors at risk of injury and as a direct and proximate result of such failures that each prevailing plaintiff . . . suffered injury for which the sums set opposite their respective names should be paid."

Update: In April 1986, the Court of Appeals for the 10th Circuit reversed Judge Jenkins's decision and ruled that the U.S. government could not be sued for damage done to the population by its atomic testing program.

39.   Particle of Plutonium

An early draft of the caption under the photograph was submitted to Dr. Karl Z. Morgan for verification. The early draft read:

"The black lines in this starlike formation have been made by bursts of alpha radiation from a particle of plutonium-239 embedded in the lung tissue of an ape. These alpha particles are a form of nonpenetrating radiation. The black lines do not travel very far and their energy can be stopped by a sheet of paper. But once inside the body, the particle gives all the cells next to it a continuous and heavy dose. The amount of radiation shown here was released over a 48-hour period. Plutonium has a half-life of 24,400 years; it will remain hazardous to life for ten times as long as that."

Dr. Morgan responded to this draft with a letter to the author on May 5, 1987:

"Dear Robert:

"As I indicated last night I got interested in what you said (partly in error) about the plutonium star and did a bit of research to compile information on the caption you sent. Suggest you get a copy of the *Handbook of Experimental Pharmacology* (Heffter-Heuber, New Series XXXVI, editors Hodge, Stannard & Hirsh) if you want some better star pictures.

"I suggest your caption read something like this:

" 'The black lines in this starlike formation have been made by bursts of alpha radiation from a microscopic particle of plutonium-239 embedded in the lung tissue of an ape. These alpha particles are a form of high-energy radiation but they are relatively heavy (7,330 times that of an electron or a beta particle) and can be stopped by a single sheet of paper, while a beta particle with an energy of 2 MeV can penetrate a centimeter of soft tissue.

" 'Once inside the human body these alpha particles from the microscopic particle of Pu-239 penetrate over 10,000 body cells within their range of about 0.0044 cm. They kill most of these cells but occasionally one of these cells will survive and reproduce itself in its damaged form. After about 35 doubling times (1 to 30 years, depending on the type of cell), the clone of abortive or malignant cells is about 1 cc in volume and large enough to be detected and diagnosed as a tumor (cancer).

" 'The amount of radiation shown here was released over a 48-hour period. Pu-239 has a half-life of 24,400 years and once deposited in bone its elimination is extremely slow, requiring 200 years to remove half of it, or only 24% is removed in 80 years from the human body.

" 'A curie of Pu-239 corresponds to 16.3 grams (0.0359 lbs). After 100,000 years a curie of Pu-239 released into the environment has decayed radioactively so that only 0.0584 curies, or about 1 gram, remains. However, this 1 gram of Pu-239 is not an insignificant amount. For example, if it could be split into 3.5 billion equal parts and one part could be fixed in the body of each of 3.5 billion people, each person would get a bone dose of 25 millirems per year all the rest of his life. The 25 millirems per year is the maximum dose rate that the Environmental Protection Agency permits to members of the public from the operation of a nuclear power plant. The 3.5 billion people is about four-fifths of the present world population. The magnitude of this problem can be appreciated if we realize that thousands of persons are working with kilogram amounts of Pu-239 and about 5,000,000 grams have been released into the environment during nuclear weapons tests.'

"Sincerely, Karl Morgan

"P.S. Are you concerned about other elements similar to plutonium such as uranium and americium and curium that are becoming commonplace in our environment?"

---

40.   Dr. Alice Stewart— Birmingham, England, September 2, 1981

My only claim to fame is that I stumbled across the low-level radiation cancer risk in the following way: I was aware that there was something very peculiar happening to children after the war, with a worldwide increase in leukemia mortality. The peculiarity was that children between two and three were being much more affected than either younger or older children. I thought up the bright idea that the children's cancers might be due to prenatal influences.

Dr. Alice Stewart

What made you suspect that? Why couldn't it have been something that began after they were born?

It could have been, but prenatal life is very different from postnatal life. Therefore if you were looking for some kind of unique event, it's more likely it had something to do with that prenatal stage than with life after birth.

Some kind of event which would have gone unrecognized?

Exactly. And the thing that had gone unrecognized was, in fact, the prenatal X ray. But the effect of a prenatal X ray is so small it has never produced even a dent on vital statistics. You see, only ten percent of children are X-rayed to begin with, and half of these children who are X-rayed get cancer as a result.

So that's five percent . . .

Yes, a five-percent effect is not going to be noticed. Five percent spread over vital statistics taken in sections of five years is not perceptible.

Even by a statistician?

Well, he has to be looking for it very, very carefully. And even then you never could have found it on the basis of vital statistics alone because the group at risk from these X rays were children up to the age of four, and then you might have spotted it because individual deaths are recorded for that age, but after that they lump deaths together into five-year age groups. And the peak incidence of cancers from this occurs between the ages of five

and six. So the deaths would have been merged with the next four years, in which case there is no chance the effect could be seen. So this effect we found at first chiefly by my reasoning.

How did you know to include X rays as a factor in gathering the data?

I wanted to include everything. But also this was the mid-fifties—a time when people were very aware of the Hiroshima A-bomb findings which were just coming out. Hiroshima is built into my heart right there. You see, we started this survey in 1955, and the Atomic Bomb Casualty Commission began its project in 1950. Well, all sorts of rumors had been circulating and everybody knew that radiation was dangerous in the leukemia sense of the word. And it so happens that half of all childhood cancers are leukemias. So it was natural for anybody who was in the know to include a question on X rays in any survey they put out. The unique thing I did was to frame the question in such a way that the mother was allowed to describe what had happened to her from the moment her child was conceived. Basically you could say my study recognized that life began at conception and not at birth. But the idea of childhood cancers that were initiated before birth was totally novel. The idea that you could go to the age of ten in perfect health, while really you've been suffering from a disease since before you were born, was inconceivable to any doctor. We've since been able to show that these children, apparently in normal health, were not in normal health at all.

They've got a fatal disease.

Well, they've got a fatal disease, we all know that now, but the telling point is that when they meet with something like a bad infection on the way—they will die, and you and I won't. Now what will that do to the cancer statistics? It suppresses them, doesn't it? The children do not live long enough to realize that they are pre-cancer. So the whole story of cancer, in my mind, is the failure to realize that cancers are having an effect long before they are recognized, and the effect they're having causes these people to die easily from many natural causes. You know, once you're a year away from having leukemia, you're over 300 times more likely to die of pneumonia because your immune system is down.

Once I spotted the X-ray effect, I knew that we'd gotten onto something that was absolutely unique, because this was a cause of cancer that you could date, and it was so small that it was effectively quantified for you. And it was causing every sort of cancer known in that age range. Now there was no other cause of cancer that ran right across the board like that.

Except the X ray.

The one we'd found. Even in adults, it doesn't do this. Nobody could see my vision at the time, which was that I'd found the fixed North Star of childhood cancers, and once you've got one star in the firmament, you can fix in all the rest. But you must have time. You must be allowed to go on collecting data and collecting data and collecting data. . . .

When people speak of radiation damage, they also talk of the body repairing that damage. Can you describe how this works?

Foreign organisms in the body, if they are not recognized, will multiply. This is our friend the infection, right? But there is another form of foreign protein, and that is your own cells which have become mutant. Now they may do this accidentally, but they are much more likely to do it under the influence of radiation and other carcinogens.

Now there are lots of defenses against this. You couldn't live unless you were heavily protected, and you will understand our main defense if you understand the double helix. The helix formation of everything allows that the genes that are controlling each movement of each cell—and lots of them are silent, you're only playing the piano on certain parts of the keyboard in order to produce this and that reaction—these controlling genes are paired, and if you destroy one of them, template activities in the other will recreate it. So you've got to destroy not only one on one side and one on the other, but you've got to destroy the pair before you're in any trouble. Now every time a cell divides, the double helix stretches out. It's got to arrange for exactly equal controlling factors to the next cell, and though there's no final proof of this, there's a probability that during the full stretching-out process, if you get radiation, that's when the radiation's going to be best able to nick it.

As human beings, we are actually rather strongly defended against radiation, and I'll give you one simple reason: we've got a skin. This is the "thickness of a piece of paper" that you hear so much about, which they say can stop alpha radiation. It does in fact protect us against about fifty percent of the radioactivity around us, but we're still vulnerable to gamma radiation, neutrons, and X rays.

But if we didn't have a skin we'd be vulnerable to all kinds of other things too.

But can't you see that a unicellular organism is more vulnerable than we are? The logical argument is that single-celled organisms could not exist until background radiation fell to present levels millennia ago. And it requires just as delicate an environment for us to survive. Yet today, in the arrogance of humankind, we are raising the levels of background radiation and setting back the evolutionary clock.

Has bomb testing raised the levels?

Well, the bomb tests have had a measurable effect because you can measure it in your own bones. And if we allow every nation in this world to become dependent on nuclear energy for its electricity on the assumption that it is no longer safe to go down a coal mine, and you'd better not burn the woods—you're literally going to set the clock back. It could come to a point where biosphere development, which has taken millennia to produce human beings, will be put slowly into reverse, and humans won't be the first to go.

What will be?

Amoebae.

And then?

Then the things that feed on amoebae, and the things that feed on them, then the next, and the next, and the next . . . and then us.

Sounds like a chain reaction . . .

Well, of course it is, but it's not going to happen overnight. It's something that today is not yet numerically important—but it has no future. Nobody's ever set this clock back before. There's never been any means of doing it. If anything, the world's getting a little bit more tolerant of all living organisms. If only we'd been intelligent enough to get our energy by discovering the molecular processes that plants use, instead of splitting atoms! If we'd have put as much thought and energy into penetrating the molecular mechanism of photosynthesis as we did into cracking the secrets of fission I reckon we'd have some kind of man-made photosynthesis by now. My motto is: if plants can do it, so can we. But we'd need some Manhattan Project–sized funding to really get it going. Instead, we've pushed ahead on one side of science at the expense of the other, and we've ended up in an unbalanced situation where it looks as though we can only get our energy from the fission mechanism. And what are we doing with it? Actually

turning the Earth back. The effects are still rather puny, but imagine going on with this and extending it. Radioactive waste is bound to increase not only the population load of cancers, but much more important, the population load of congenital defects, defects of future generations of the human race. What do we think we're doing with this Earth? There are now several studies on low-dose effects, all of which are pointed in the same direction. The most important of them is a study of nuclear workers in America which is now on a sufficiently large basis to be able to show the effects of age on the risk, the effects of latency on the risk, and above all, the effects of dose level on the risk. The key finding here is that the lower the dose, which in practice means the slower the delivery of radiation to the public, the more cancer risk there is per unit dose. In other words, it does not make it safer to deliver the radiation slowly; it in fact makes it more dangerous.

By relying on the technology of fission we're going against the very processes that made life possible. Isn't it time we took the money and the pressure off this playing with matches and really pumped some funding into biological research?

41. The Parents of Sadako

Mr. Shigeo Sasaki, Mrs. Fujiko Sasaki, and **Masahiro Sasaki**— Kasuga City, Fukuoka Prefecture, Japan, October 13, 1984

On August 6, 1945, the day the atomic bomb exploded over Hiroshima, Mrs. Sasaki and her two children, Sadako (age two) and Masahiro (age four), were in Hiroshima. Mr. Sasaki was out of the city on military duty at the time.

Mrs. Sasaki, can you tell me what happened on the morning the atomic bomb fell?

Mrs. Sasaki: We were living on Kusunogi Street, a little more than one kilometer from the hypocenter. The all-clear siren had just sounded. I was getting breakfast for my children when my neighbor called out to me, "Look, up in the sky!" I stepped outside and saw something that looked like a big silvery balloon coming down.

Was the thing you saw floating?

Mrs. Sasaki: No, it was an object—it was round, a circle—and it was falling.

What did you think it was?

Mrs. Sasaki: I just thought, "Oh, it's

pretty," and went back inside where Masahiro and Sadako were still eating breakfast. Then there was a huge sound and a sharp flash, almost at the same time. I was already inside the house, so I wasn't struck by the flash, but people who were hit by it got burned. The house collapsed. Sadako was thrown into the yard and I could hear her crying *Okachan!* ["Mommy!"], but I couldn't see her because the wall had collapsed and there was dust everywhere. But she called out, "I'm here! I'm here!" and I found her and picked her up and held her. Then I found Masahiro under some tatami mats. We had all survived! I decided we should get out of the house. The factory behind our place was already on fire. I thought the river would be the only safe place to go with my children. So we climbed out of our collapsed home and went down to the river.

What did you see when you got to the river?

Mrs. Sasaki: There was an old boat and someone told me to get in. "Sasaki-san, get in here, please!" they called, because I had two children, and they knew my husband was in the army. So I got in, and we moved the boat, but we had to go very slowly because it was in bad shape. We made it out to the middle of the river then put down the anchor and waited.

How many were in the boat?

Mrs. Sasaki: There were ten other people besides me and the children, and from both sides of the river fire and sparks were flying almost out to the middle of the river. It got so hot, and there were so many sparks that I had to take water and dump it on myself and on my children. Up in the sky one or two American planes were circling. That's when the black rain fell. I thought it was oil that the airplanes were dropping from the sky. We got it all over us. I couldn't wash it out of my children's pajamas.

Were people coming to the river by this time?

Mrs. Sasaki: Yes, it got very crowded. People from both riverbanks were crying, "Please help us." But we didn't help them. We felt we would die if we moved the boat. So we pretended not to hear their voices.

Masahiro, you were four years old at the time. Do you remember anything from that day?

Masahiro: I still remember the boat. It had a big hole in it. I was sitting right next to the hole. Water kept coming in. I watched the water come in. That's what I remember the most.

Do you remember the fire?

Masahiro: Yes, I remember the fire and the black rain. But mostly I remember just being scared.

Mr. Sasaki, when did you come back to Hiroshima?

Mr. Sasaki: I came into Hiroshima the next day by truck. My orders were to help the people who could be helped. Everywhere I looked I saw bodies charred black. Corpses were lying around like garbage. Sometimes I'd get a surprise—an arm or a leg would look like a piece of burned wood, then it would move. We could not help such people. Others were walking

The Sasaki family, with Masahiro at right

around completely naked, with stiff hair, like it had been cooked. I couldn't tell if they were men or women. Our job was not to help the heavily injured people, only the ones who could climb up a ladder into the truck. I did one cleanup by truck on August 7. Four or five days later I came back to Hiroshima to help move some of the people from the riverbank to the train station.

Had the people on the riverbank gotten any food during those four or five days?

Mr. Sasaki: There was no food. The only thing people wanted was water. But if you gave them water they would die. And many of them had brain fever. They were out of their heads. Their brain functions weren't working anymore, so they were urinating and shitting. It was horrible. I also saw a lot of worms on their ears and arms. We took only the people who could walk to the platform and get into the train.

I'm wondering if we could go forward in time now, and talk more about Sadako. Ten years after the bomb she was a student in the sixth grade at the Nobori-machi Primary School in Hiroshima, is that right?

Mr. Sasaki: Yes, that is when she became ill.

I heard she had a nickname, Saru *["Monkey"]. Why was she called Monkey?*

Mrs. Sasaki: I'm not sure, but she moved and acted fast and quick.

Masahiro: She had a good sense of humor, too. And she was very clever. Everybody liked her.

When did you first find out she had a serious illness?

Mr. Sasaki: One month before her twelfth birthday, in early December, she developed a swelling on her neck, under her ear. I thought it was from a cold. I took her to the doctor in January. The doctor said it might be tuberculosis.

Then I took her to another doctor, a children's doctor, who said there was something very strange with her, and he asked me to come back again later. Sadako went to school as usual. When I went back to the doctor, he seemed to be hiding something. I said, "Tell me the truth." He told me she had three months to live, or one year at best. He said she had leukemia. That was the first time I heard the word "leukemia."

Did you tell Sadako?

Mr. Sasaki: I didn't say anything to her about leukemia because she looked fine, except for the swelling.

When did you realize her sickness was connected to the A-bomb?

Mr. Sasaki: Right away. The doctor said she had leukemia, and he told me, "Leukemia is the A-bomb disease."

They decided to send Sadako into the hospital near the end of February. When I went to get her out of school, she wasn't feeling well, so she was just watching her physical education class. I talked to the teacher first, and then we left. All of her classmates said good-bye. On the way home I took her to a kimono material shop, because I had never bought her a kimono before. I said to her, "Sadako dear, shall I buy a kimono for you?" She said, "No, thank you, please don't." But I bought her some kimono cloth in that store anyway.

Did she pick out the material herself?

Mr. Sasaki: I made the selection. It was a cherry-blossom pattern. After we got home we realized we didn't have the liner cloth. It was late, but we woke up the owner of the material shop and bought the liner cloth. I remember that night. It was very cold.

So you made the kimono for Sadako yourselves?

Mrs. Sasaki: We wanted to give it to Sadako before she went into the hospital the next day. But I didn't think I could make it by myself in one night. So we went to a relative in Mihara who was good at making kimonos. We took the whole family, and the woman and I stayed up all night to finish that kimono.

Did you give her the kimono as a way of telling her you hoped she might get better?

Mr. Sasaki: I just wanted to make her happy, that's all. I would have done anything to please her.

Sometimes when people get leukemia they get tired and lose the will to live, but I heard that Sadako was not that way in the hospital.

Mr. Sasaki: Yes, she worked very hard at folding paper cranes. I told her not to get too serious about it. It was no good for her health. In fact I tried to stop her, but I couldn't. She told me, "I'm all right. I have an idea. Don't worry, Daddy," and she just kept on folding cranes. Would you like to see some of them?

Yes, please.

(Mrs. Sasaki brings a small cellophane bag from the family shrine and puts it on the table. Mr. Sasaki pours half of its contents onto the table and continues to speak.)

She made them so small she had to use a needle to fold them. You see how tiny they are.

I read somewhere they had all been put into her coffin. . . .

Mrs. Sasaki: No, we didn't bury them with Sadako. At the funeral we gave one crane to each of Sadako's classmates, but we kept the rest.

Mr. Sasaki: I never bought her any of the special folding papers because I didn't want to encourage her. I thought she should save her strength. That is why you do not see any bright and pretty-colored papers here. She used candy wrappers and medicine wrappers and anything else she could find. She would salvage the material and smooth it out into neat squares for folding into cranes.

Is it true that paper cranes normally mean good fortune, but because of Sadako they took on a new meaning?

Mr. Sasaki: In Japan, people have always had the idea that folding a thousand paper cranes will bring good fortune. Your wish comes true if you fold a thousand of them. But Sadako was the first one to try to do it. She thought if she folded a thousand cranes she would get well. That was her wish.

How many did she fold?

Masahiro: She finished 645 of them. There are others that she started but did not finish.

Mr. Sasaki: After she died they cleaned out the hospital bed and they found something under the bedding. It was a list Sadako had been secretly keeping with the numbers of her white blood cells, red blood cells, and hemoglobin. She had been keeping a record of her cell count from the time she entered the hospital until July. This paper is in the museum now, and many people heard about it. That way, they began to find out about the A-bomb disease and leukemia. Before Sadako died hardly anyone knew about these things.

And now every year people bring cranes to her statue, especially on the anniversary of the bomb. . . .

Mr. Sasaki: Yes, they wish for world peace, or to survive a nuclear war. That is one meaning of the cranes. But for others, folding a thousand cranes might mean they hope to get into a good university.

I always thought Sadako's wish was different from an ordinary wish because she had the A-bomb disease, and it was more like hope in a situation where there is no hope.

Mr. Sasaki: Yes, hope with no hope. You are right. Sadako showed her will to live in another way too. She refused all painkillers because she knew they were no good for her life.

What kind of painkiller did they want to give her?

Mr. Sasaki: Shots of morphine.

Did they give the painkiller first before she realized it was bad, or did she never allow herself to be given any?

Mr. Sasaki: There was a fifth-grade boy in the ward next to Sadako. He cried a lot, and Sadako could hear him. When the doctor gave him a shot of painkiller he'd become quiet. But after a few hours he'd start crying again, and the doctor would give him another shot. The nurses were talking about this, and Sadako heard them say, "It's no good for his life." She used to tell me, "He'd better be patient. Painkillers are no good."

July was a bad month for her. She had blisters all over her body. The doctor said, "She's definitely in severe pain." He wanted to make her comfortable with a shot of morphine because he knew that she was dying. But she refused the injection and never spoke about the pain.

Around nine in the morning on October 25, her condition became critical. The doctor came into the room. He opened her

Paper cranes at the base of Sadako's monument

hospital gown to give her her shot of medicine, but he realized he could not help her anymore. He closed her gown and left the room. Sadako told me, "Daddy, the doctor isn't giving me the medicine anymore. Am I dying?" I ran after the doctor and asked him to give her a shot. The doctor came back and gave her the medicine, and she was very relieved.

Then I asked her what she wanted to eat. She told me she would like some of the hospital's rice. But breakfast time was over, and it was too late to get rice from the hospital kitchen. So I told somebody to get rice from outside the hospital. Sadako overheard me and said, "I don't want rice from outside the hospital. I want the hospital rice." Anyway, we got rice from somewhere and gave it to her. . . .

(Mrs. Sasaki whispers something to Mr. Sasaki.)

What did Mrs. Sasaki just say?

Mr. Sasaki: My wife reminded me that we got rice from outside the hospital and put it into a hospital rice bowl, then gave it to Sadako.

She ate two spoonfuls of it. We asked her, "Is it delicious?" She said, "Yes, it's delicious." Then she died.

Mrs. Sasaki: In the coffin she wore her cherry-blossom kimono. Many of her classmates came to the funeral.

Mr. Sasaki: And soon after that seventeen or eighteen of Sadako's classmates held a kind of memorial meeting at my barbershop. Mr. Ichiro Kawamoto suggested that they meet. People think the classmates came on their own, but it was really Kawamoto-san's idea. At this meeting they decided to write a sheet telling Sadako's story. On this sheet they brought up for the first time the idea of building a monument. Their plan was to print up copies and pass them around at a conference of junior high school principals that was going on in Hiroshima. So they went to the auditorium with Sadako's picture and passed out the sheets.

Masahiro: That meeting in the barbershop was very important. That is where Sadako's classmates decided not to waste the fact that she had died. They wanted to remind people of the tragedy of the A-bomb. So they formed the Kokeshi Group.

What does kokeshi *mean?*

Masahiro: *Kokeshi* is a kind of wooden doll with two parts, head and body. Sadako was very fond of dolls like this and collected them in the hospital. The first thing the Kokeshi Group did was pass out the sheets at the conference. Eight of the classmates from the group did that.

Do you still have one of the sheets the children wrote?

Masahiro: Oh, yes.

I'd be interested in seeing what the children wrote.

(Masahiro brings a scrapbook. He opens it and reads:)

Let's make a statue of a child of the atomic bomb.

We knew that school principals from all over Japan are gathering today, we think that we'd like you to let us announce our request.

Sadako Sasaki, who was our good friend, died of the A-bomb disease on October 25. She has been our friend since we were little, we have lived happily, playing together and studying together, but this innocent Sadako suddenly got sick in January, and she took nine long months to die.

We cannot help feeling sad about Sadako's heart which spoke about the atomic bomb and died. But it's over now, so at least we'd like to make a statue of a child of the atomic bomb and venerate the souls of children who have died in the same way.

So please tell our plan to friends of junior high schools all over Japan and get them to agree with this.

Please report this matter from the principals to the people of junior high schools.

We came here specially to ask you for this.

All the classmates of the late Sadako Sasaki, first year, Nobori-machi Junior High School.

Masahiro: So this is how the story of Sadako's death began to spread. That is how the monument got started.

Interview translated by Setsumi Del Tredici.

Sadako's monument

42. Sadako's Paper Cranes

On May 5, 1958, the Monument to the Children of the Atomic Bomb was dedicated in the Hiroshima Peace Park. On top of the 19.6-foot monument stands a life-size likeness of Sadako Sasaki supporting a large stylized crane. On the sides of the monument are the flying figures of a boy and a girl. Inside the monument is a bell and directly under it, carved in black granite, are the words of a junior high school student from Hiroshima: "This is our cry. This is our prayer. For building peace in the world."

Each year approximately 4 million paper cranes arrive in Hiroshima from children throughout Japan and from all over the world. They are strung chiefly in garlands of a thousand and placed at Sadako's shrine as well as at other monuments in the Peace Park. The park is located directly beneath the site where the atomic bomb exploded.

43. Tapered Line-of-Sight-Pipe, "N" Tunnel

In the photograph, a helium/neon laser is used for tunnel alignment. The room at the far end of the tunnel, called the Zero Room, is also referred to as the Working Point, the A-box, and Ground Zero. The two blast doors that shut to keep out the destructive blast of the nuclear detonation are located 500 feet from the Zero Room. They are made of 12-inch-thick aluminum and weigh 45 tons. They are driven shut by a high-pressure gas system that operates at 18,000 pounds per square inch. The line-of-sight pipe is part of the larger "N" tunnel complex, which contains two other tunnel systems inside Rainier Mesa. Rainier Mesa is made of volcanic tuff, or cemented volcanic ash. It is ideal for tunnel tests because it is easy to mine, and it settles in upon itself after the shock of a nuclear blast.

44. Tending to "Misty Rain"

There were approximately 500 numbered experiments in the Misty Rain test; the equipment tested was hooked up electronically through a vacu-tight seal to the outside world. Two thousand channels of primary data were fed into computers for analysis. Inside the pipe, a vacuum of less than 1 micron was created before the detonation occurred. The command post monitoring the shot was thirty miles away.

45. Trestle EMP

Dr. Gordon Soper,
Defense Nuclear Agency—
Alexandria, Virginia, June 5, 1984

Dr. Gordon Soper is an expert on the nuclear electromagnetic pulse effect.

I'm in the office of Dr.—

Gordon Soper. I'm the scientific assistant to the deputy director for science and technology at the headquarters of the Defense Nuclear Agency. Okay?

And your area of expertise is connected with—

I was a theoretical physicist but I've been dealing most of my professional career with military aspects of nuclear weapon explosions, and in particular with the electrical phenomena that are associated with all nuclear detonations.

What is EMP?

Well, that's a good question. An electromagnetic pulse accompanies all nuclear detonations. EMP is not, I think, a phenomenon that's going to turn the whole world into a fully ionized plasma. It is not a new phenomenon. It is not a recently discovered phenomenon. It is not something that hasn't been thought about and studied since the very first and early days of nuclear detonations. Indeed, in 1962, during our four high-altitude nuclear shots in the Pacific, EMP was seen, EMP was measured, and effects occurred as a result of those high-altitude nuclear detonations.

Are those when the street lights went out in Hawaii?

That was an example, and there are many other examples like that. Burglar alarms went off, different circuit breakers tripped. So there's absolutely no doubt that associated with nuclear detonations electrical things can happen, far removed from the site of the detonation. That's a concern, and one cannot at all ignore that very important fact. And within a matter of days after those nuclear detonations occurred, military theorists went to work on explaining, in detail, from laws of basic physics, what was going on, so we think the generation of EMP is well understood. How it propagates is well understood, how it couples to systems is well understood. Now, the character and the effectiveness of EMP depend upon many things. In general

we classify nuclear explosions with respect to the place where the nuclear explosion occurs. There's the high-altitude nuclear detonation, which occurs above the sensible atmosphere; then there's the nuclear detonation in the atmosphere; and third, a nuclear detonation close to or on the surface of the earth. In each one of those three separate nuclear explosions, different kinds of electromagnetic pulses will be generated. In the high-altitude nuclear detonation, a single nuclear detonation can expose the entire land or water mass to an electromagnetic pulse. Imagine yourself sitting on the nuclear detonation, and everything that you can see below you is in field of view of that nuclear detonation.

Clear out as far as you can see?

Horizon to horizon, horizon to horizon. See, you're getting right at the issue. One or a few high-altitude nuclear detonations can place at risk all military systems within that field of view. At an altitude of 60 miles above Topeka, about a third of the United States land mass would be within the field of view. If you go up to about 200 miles, then the entire continental United States would be in the field of view of that nuclear detonation. So we've got a class of nuclear detonations called high-altitude nuclear detonations that can, because of the geometry, pose a very fairly unique threat to the United States, and we've got to deal with that.

The second class of nuclear detonations, those lower down in the atmosphere at about 12 miles, produce a fairly insignificant electromagnetic pulse.

Now, the third is the Alamogordo-type test, namely those nuclear detonations that occurred close to or on the surface of the earth itself. Those are very efficient producers of EMP, but it's a different EMP, and it's not so much a geometry question as it is a point-target issue, namely, those targets, or those systems close to a groundburst that survived the effect of the heat and the blast can and will be connected to that burst somehow. For example, power lines might be close to the burst. Large amounts of energy can couple onto these power lines, or onto communication lines, or onto metal sewer pipes, or anything electrical that is connected to what we call a source region.

Anything metal, or a conductor that penetrates or connects to the source region can couple large amounts of currents and voltages onto these conductors, and these large currents and voltages can be transmitted over long distances. And as they're transmitted they branch out to subsidiary parts of the electrical system, so that way

significant amounts of energy can be transported over tens of miles away from the nuclear detonation. So you might be in another city, for example, and not even see the nuclear detonation. I hope that when you write this down you won't say that here these crazy guys at DNA are contemplating nuclear war, so I'm just—

Oh no, no—

I'm just trying to be—I wanted to speak about it in abstract terms, but when I say bombs going off in the ground I want the record to show I clearly believe that that won't happen, and I believe a strong defense will keep that from happening. But we're talking about the physical processes that occur as a result of nuclear detonations, and God forbid that any happen to occur. . . . Okay?

All right.

If that's okay, I'll proceed. . . . At any rate, with this groundburst nuclear detonation, you don't have the large area illuminated as you do on a high-altitude nuclear detonation, but you can have large currents and voltages propagated over large distances. And those energies can find their ways into protected electrical systems and cause damage if you're not careful. And when that energy eventually finds its way down to the basic piece-part level where the rubber meets the road, where the actual electrical functions are going on, it doesn't really take very much of that energy to disrupt the circuit either momentarily or permanently, which is what we call a burnout, which is a catastrophic failure where the EMP energy actually burns the circuit out, it pops it, it breaks it, and you can smell smoke. We sometimes use the word it "smokes" it.

So there you have, in a very brief nutshell, the different kinds of EMP. I hope you understand it's not a huge bolt of electricity that comes roaring out of the sky and renders everything in its path into a fully ionized plasma. EMP is very subtle, it's very worrisome because of its broad area coverage, and because we don't do nuclear testing in the atmosphere anymore, the only way we can test those systems is to build what we call EMP simulators and test our systems in a device that tends to mock up or to simulate electromagnetic phenomena.

And that's the "trestle?"

The trestle is an example of an EMP simulator. It is, as a matter of fact, the largest single EMP simulator that we have in this country today.

46. MX/Peacekeeper

The fourth stage of the MX is outside the picture frame. Photographs of it were not allowed. It contains the rotating "bus," the platform that delivers each of the missile's ten independently targetable warheads.

Total length of missile: 71 feet
Weight at launch: 193,000 pounds
Payload: 10 Mark-21 Advanced Ballistic Reentry Vehicles each carrying a W87 warhead with a yield between 300 and 475 kilotons
Range: over 7,800 miles
Targeting: The MX is designed to take out all hardened targets, including "superhard" control centers and "very hard leadership bunkers."
Accuracy: less than 400 feet Circle Error Probable
Retargeting: "automatic retargeting" capability
Cost: $55.6 billion including operations and maintenance through the year 2000

MX stands for "Missile Experimental." It was renamed "Peacekeeper" by Ronald Reagan when the missile's experimental phase was finished and deployment began.

Prayer of invocation given at dedication of MX Integrated Test Facility, Vandenberg Air Force Base, Lompoc, California, January 29, 1982

"Our Father, some may question the propriety of invoking Your blessed presence here today. We do not pray for this building, but for the men and women who will work and labor within its walls.

"We pray for them confidence in the face of stressful decision, and sagacity as they combine their efforts to ensure the common good. . . .

"We pray that all of us here gathered shall remember the freedom You have entrusted to us, and the holy obligation required of us to see that it endures.

"The affairs of this day are but a humble portion of our attempt to discharge that sacred duty. If we have failed, forgive us and enlighten us, that we might be respondent to Your divine will. For this is our quest and our prayer, now and forever. Amen."

---

47. Sam Cohen, Father of the Neutron Bomb

Sam Cohen—Beverly Hills, California, December 6, 1984

I'm in the living room of Sam Cohen. . . .

The day before Pearl Harbor.

Oh, that's right!

A vicious time—that's what led to the Bomb. Which is why we're here.

I want to begin, Sam, by asking you to introduce yourself and say what it is you've been up to, what you've accomplished, and who you are.

Nobody's ever asked me that before, so this is right off the top of my head: I'm a person, and I've led a somewhat normal life, as least as surface appearances go. Purely by accident I wound up at Los Alamos during the war. I became fascinated with it, and I've been at it ever since, which is now some forty-plus years.

What is the "it"?

Nuclear weapons. That's been my profession over all these years. And it's always been my bent to move a step or two out into the future, which is why I got interested in advanced nuclear weapons concepts right after the war. And that's what led to my concocting the neutron bomb idea and any number of other schemes, none of which have had any impact whatsoever on the shape of things, but I've thoroughly enjoyed it. Again,

Sam Cohen

trying to assess myself as a human being, I've never had any qualms. On a surface level, I've rationalized my fascination with nuclear weapons by saying it's important for the security of my country, and so there are no qualms to be had. If I went down another level in my psyche, I wouldn't know what to say—I've done it because I wanted to. So that essentially sums me up.

What did you do at Los Alamos?

I was in the Efficiency Group at Los Alamos. Our job was to figure out the yield of the bomb that was burst over Nagasaki. To do that we had to learn how neutrons multiply once the chain reaction gets started. So this was my introduction to neutrons.

Was there a sense at Los Alamos that these weapons were the beginning of something new in terms of war fighting?

On the evening of Hiroshima, when Oppenheimer was describing in very crude terms the catastrophe that had taken place over that city, the scientists who were listening to him were a bunch of howling savages, ebullient beyond imagination, as pleased as punch at what they'd accomplished. There was no consideration of what this might mean toward getting along with the Russians, or what the postwar complexion of the world might be, or anything like that. This was a fantastic day, our product had been used, apparently very successfully, and that's all they cared to know. There may have been a few who sat quietly while Oppenheimer was holding forth, but I don't recall seeing any.

I've always thought of Oppenheimer as the man who said, "We physicists have known sin."

Well, that came later, and not too long after that, either. It had a very interesting result when it did come, I might add.

Oppenheimer is rightfully called the father of the atomic bomb, but equally rightfully he could be called the father of the tactical nuclear weapon because he did the first conceptual spadework for using nuclear weapons strictly in a battlefield way instead of just decimating cities in a holocaust context.

So the father of the bomb that decimates cities is also the father of tactical nuclear warfare?

He professed to be sufficiently guilt-ridden and aghast and appalled over the bombings of Hiroshima and Nagasaki that he never wanted that to happen again. So he recommended we design lower-yield weapons that wouldn't wipe out cities but that could strictly be confined to battlefield use.

And where were you in all of this?

Well, my own personal addiction in all this has always been to tactical nuclear weapons for battlefield use.

Okay, then, let's talk about the thing you've come to be known for, Sam, the neutron bomb. You're called "the Father of the Neutron Bomb," one of those nuclear-paternity epithets. Is that an accurate description?

I invented the concept. As to whether that deserves parenthood or even knighthood, God only knows. Take your choice.

What is the concept?

The basic concept is to be able to have a battlefield nuclear weapon that won't have all these nasty side effects, like bringing down nearby cities and killing an awful lot of civilians and so on. It's something that can get at enemy personnel without causing what we call in the trade "collateral damage."

Let's talk about how a neutron bomb is different from the bombs used in Nagasaki and Hiroshima. Both those bombs were airbursts. Would a neutron bomb be an airburst?

If it's going to be used to get what we call the "separation of effects," in other words, to get rid of the blast and heat, it not only has to be air-burst, but it has to be burst high, sufficiently high above the landscape so the blast and heat will not reach the ground.

How high up does the burst need to be?

Depending on the yield, between 2,000 and 3,000 feet.

So roughly the same height as the Hiroshima and Nagasaki bombs?

Right, not too much different, but the explosive yield is ten or twenty times less, so the blast and heat won't do much, but the neutrons will.

And what's the yield of a neutron warhead?

Generally in the kiloton range, or ten to twenty times less powerful than the first atomic bombs.

Although it has ten or twenty times less explosive power than the first atomic bombs, the neutron weapon is still an H-bomb, right?

Right, it's kind of a micro-mini hydrogen bomb.

And why is it that this type of H-bomb sends out so many neutrons? I heard H-bombs normally have an outer blanket of uranium that absorbs neutrons. Is the neutron bomb missing this blanket?

Look, I can't go into too much technical detail or we'll start getting into things that are classified. But basically it has to do with the nuclear yield. The neutron weapon has this very low nuclear yield. The technology allows you to get most of the neutrons out if it is a low yield. In very large yields it doesn't allow you to do that. It's about that simple. There's no point in getting too technical.

How far do these neutrons travel in air?

Neutrons are neutral particles, which means they can go a long ways in an undense medium like air, so you can have neutrons incapacitating people perhaps a thousand yards or so from the burst.

What can a neutron do to you?

In a military sense it does two things. First, it really rips up the gastrointestinal system and causes all sorts of distressing symptoms, which the media has gone into galore, and I don't want to ruin your lunch by going into now. And then, for somewhat higher radiation doses, it affects the central nervous system and the brain.

What kind of a dose gives the gastrointestinal effect, and what kind of dose does it take to affect the nervous system and the brain?

From a dose of several hundred rads on up to, roughly, a thousand rads, you get these gastrointestinal effects. Once you start going over a thousand rads on up to, roughly, 10,000 rads, you still get these gastrointestinal effects, but you also get a deterioration of the central nervous system so that the poor victim essentially is dysfunctional. He can't operate equipment.

What is a lethal dose?

A lethal dose occurs roughly at 500 rads. At 500 rads, more than fifty percent of the people exposed will die.

Do they die on the spot, or does it take a while?

No, they won't die on the spot. To have them die on the spot, a dose on the order of 10,000 rads or so is required.

At 10,000 rads does a person die right away?

Chances are, at the 10,000-rad level, the trauma will be so great that unless medical attention is available immediately, the person will die from shock.

Is there something medicine can do for a person who has received 10,000 rads of neutron radiation?

No. Nothing.

All right, so the bomb is detonated 2,000 to 3,000 feet overhead, and its yield is about one kiloton or less. What kind of a radius are we talking about for the bomb's deadly effects?

We're talking about a radius of roughly a thousand yards where you will have these crippling effects on the central nervous system. These effects will be greater as you go toward Ground Zero. So if we had, say, several thousand rads at the periphery and we moved in toward the center, by the time we got to Ground Zero the doses could be tens of thousands of rads. Anybody in that area would be wiped out immediately.

What happens outside that area?

Radiation intensity falls off with distance. So by the time you get out to, say, 1,500 yards, you're perfectly safe from the radiation.

Is there a dose out at that distance?

Oh yeah, but it's probably less than 100 rads. And when one goes below 100 rads there are no really significant effects. You have a very small possibility that in the long run there may be an enhancement of such effects of leukemia, and other forms of cancer, but . . .

. . . but that's not militarily significant, right?

Right.

How did you come up with the idea for this weapon in the first place?

I'd had the idea for the neutron bomb about eight years before I figured out how to put it together. I put together the actual concept in the summer of 1958. It came about purely by accident when I visited the Livermore Laboratory in the spring of 1958. I asked if anybody had any new ideas going around, and they said they really didn't, though they had begun work on some peaceful nuclear explosives. And the head of the division said, "Before you go home, you ought to take a look at these," and he showed me designs for some of the peaceful devices. And there they were: the neutron bomb characteristics. One of those designs was called Dove, by the way, for "Dove of Peace."

What was it about Dove that caught your eye?

Well, there were two, Dove and Starling; both derived the major share of their energy from fusing deuterium and tritium. If the designs worked, there'd be an enormous outpouring of neutrons. But the designers weren't interested in capitalizing on them because they were bent on peaceful pursuits. I was the guy, see, with his Mars helmet on, that came up and said, "Well, what does this mean for war?" The question I asked was, "How many neutrons come out of this thing?" They made a few back-of-the-envelope calculations and the answer was: a hell of a lot. Then I took these calculations home and made my own calculations about the military effects of such a weapon, and, *voilà*, the neutron bomb! Then I put together the military concept of how to use this bomb and went off on a big sales campaign.

Was it easy to "sell" the neutron bomb idea?

At first there was enormous resistance to the concept of a radiation weapon. The United States military has never been particularly enthusiastic about battlefield nuclear weapons in the first place, and in the second place, they think of nuclear weapons in terms of kilotons of TNT. It took a long time to convince them that a nuclear weapon doesn't have to produce a huge blast to be effective.

Why is that?

Ever since day one we've patterned our nuclear war-fighting strategies after Hiroshima and Nagasaki. But when you get both sides in a conflict slugging it out with nuclear weapons, then fighting a war with classical objectives like "winning battles" or "winning wars" becomes very, very fuzzy. I'd say the notion of using a nuclear weapon on the battlefield today still throws terror into the hearts of the military. And it's out of this terror that our whole nuclear war–fighting philosophy has come.

Can you explain that more?

It's a circular argument: a nuclear war is too horrible to take place, so it won't take place, and to make sure it won't take place, we threaten that it will take place. So what we're basically proposing here to deter war is the threat of our own suicide. Now that's not a way for human beings to behave—that's lemmings! And it's all based on the premise that if we cross that nuclear threshold one more time we'll bring on the beginning of the end. So you get people like Jonathan Schell and Carl Sagan with this idea of nuclear winter and everything else. It's Armageddon. I don't find their ideas credible, and I'll tell you why: because in order to get these results from using nuclear weapons against cities, you have to have nations willing to use them that way. And I don't see any signs that either side, the United States or the Soviets, wishes to wage that kind of war.

But might not such a war happen because our thinking is so fuzzy on the subject? We've got so many of these weapons, and we're not thinking about them very straight.

We're really not thinking about them at all.

So what would be a more realistic approach?

(*Takes a long breath*) Well, now I'm going to make the most terrible statement of your entire interview by far and away. You know what the United States has to do if it wants to survive? It has to accept the fact that there will probably be a nuclear war, and it has to prepare to fight it and win it. It's a terrible, awful thing to say. But it's true, in my opinion.

What would such a nuclear war look like?

I don't have the wildest idea. But we have to take certain basic steps that will enable us to fight one.

Are you saying we are not now ready to fight a nuclear war?

If a nuclear war were to take place tomorrow morning, by tomorrow afternoon it would be all over. We'd be licked, militarily. And psychologically. The country would just fall apart at the seams.

But I thought we had enough weapons to destroy Russia a hundred times over. Or is it a thousand?

It doesn't make any difference.

Why not?

The only rational decision the president of the United States could make under such circumstances would be to throw in the towel. Unless he is going to be such a bestial, maniacal, immoral monster as to deliberately bring about the societal demise of the Soviet Union and kill tens of millions of Soviet civilians in revenge. And may God help us if we ever have a president like that. That's the fix we've gotten ourselves into!

Where does that leave our almighty Triad, the command-and-control infrastructures, and the twenty-four-hour alert we've been on since 1960?

It leaves all these things without a coherent strategy for use. If the war starts, we don't have the wildest idea of what to do. In the current predicament the best use that we can make of all these nuclear goodies is not to use them. Because the only way that we could use them would be in a morally obscene way. So our current strategy is not a strategy in the slightest. It's been U.S. national policy for more than a quarter of a century that nuclear weapons are actually unusable weapons. That's horseshit, and you can quote me on that.

The neutron bomb enables us to start a limited neutron-bomb war, but with the big ones still cocked and ready to go, that seems like a good recipe for global holocaust. . . .

If we ever had to use neutron bombs it ought to be to defend U.S. terra firma, not the soil of allies. Let the allies develop their own neutron bomb. As a matter of fact, let's sell it to them! They should have discriminate weapons for their own defense. The United States doesn't need to take on the burden of defending all the rest of the world. That is in fact the best way of getting into a nuclear war, and that'll be the end. But it doesn't have to happen that way at all. A nuclear war can still be fought for political objectives, the way wars should be fought, and not for the extermination of the human species.

Sounds like a job for the neutron bomb . . .

Well, let me put it this way: the neutron bomb offers a potential of waging far more discriminate warfare to avoid damage to the civilian fabric than any other weapon ever invented. If one wants to assume that fighting wars is basically immoral—let's assume that it is—then fighting neutron wars is considerably less immoral than fighting conventional-weapon wars, for all kinds of reasons.

And one of the reasons includes the fact that a neutron war generally stays away from a population and is intended to destroy only soldiers?

That's a primary reason, after a neutron-bomb war you don't have this aftermath of towns and cities lying in ruins, or populaces desperately trying to survive, going hungry, diseases spreading around, and so on. To me that is a moral plus.

48. Inside Cheyenne Mountain

The photograph shows the first of two 30-ton doors. Each door is made of welded steel plate and filled with concrete. The doors can close within 45 seconds. The Cheyenne Mountain Complex was designed to withstand the blast of a 5-megaton nuclear bomb.

49. Russel B. Clanahan,
public information officer, Federal Emergency Management Agency— Washington, D.C., May 19, 1982

Well, I'm Russel Clanahan, and I am a public information officer for the Federal Emergency Management Agency, which is responsible for the United States Civil Defense Program at the national level. I've been in Civil Defense since 1955.

That makes you highly qualified to compare the current fears of nuclear war with the fears that surfaced in the sixties.

The peak before now of concern and activity pertaining to Civil Defense that you are referring to took place in 1961 and 1962 and coincided with the Berlin crisis and the Cuban missile crisis. In 1961 President Kennedy kicked off the National Civil Defense Program that involved fall-out shelters. In the United States that means, basically, a lot of yellow-and-black signs. At the present time, about 90,000 shelter areas have been identified with yellow-and-black signs, and under President Reagan's proposal we would mark all of the shelters that we know to exist. In total, that is about 345,000, or space for about 240 million people.

What is the average capacity of these spaces?

They have to have place for at least fifty people before they can be considered public shelters. They must also have a protection factor against fallout radiation of at least PF40, meaning the people in the shelter could be exposed to only one-fortieth of the radiation they would get if they were out in the open.

What has your department concluded a human being can take and still be safe?

Normally, at 450 roentgens, as many people would die as would not. At 600 roentgens, most people would die.

Well, at what point do you get exposed, but you're still okay?

Normally, as I recall, anything under 100 or 150 roentgens, you're almost certain to recover.

What are some of the most up-to-date Civil Defense strategies today that are different from what was developed in the sixties?

When we had the national public fallout shelter system in 1961 there was a big problem with it. It is not a blast shelter system. To create blast shelters for the United States we're talking about the need to protect two-thirds of the population. To provide blast shelters for this number of people would cost at least $100 billion, probably more. It has never been costed out up to now, probably is not costed out now, and will not be costed out in the future.

So what do you do?

You decide to go to the next best system for lifesaving, a cost-effective system that could be done within our resources. This is the Crisis Relocation Plan. To get people

Russel B. Clanahan

out of the hazard areas and into a host area in advance of a nuclear detonation means you're talking about fallout protection rather than blast and fire protection, and this is something that can be done with the technology and resources available. And the protection that would be gained would be substantial.

Don't you need a certain amount of lead time for this plan to work?

We presume some strategic warning in order to execute the plan, yes.

How much advance time do you need?

For your smaller cities it can be from twenty-four to forty-eight hours. Most cities would probably be around seventy-two. In certain problem areas like New York or Los Angeles, it could go up to a week.

What about the time it takes for a missile to leave the Soviet Union and land in New York City?

Well, now you're starting to compare apples and oranges. No one presumes that you are going to execute a Crisis Relocation after you've learned the missile is on its way. In that case, you go to the shelters and hope for the best. That is precisely why we have Crisis Relocation: so we can do something about it in advance.

What makes you think we will get advance warning from the Soviets?

We know the nature of the Soviet Civil Defense system. They do have blast shelters for about twenty-five percent of their urban population, but about seventy-five percent of the people would have to be evacuated. And there is no way you can conceal a mass evacuation like that from our satellites.

Would we be ready to go now, if word came that the Soviets are evacuating their cities?

We have some systems in place; but we have a great deal to do yet.

I'm wondering what you say to people who are discouraged and cynical about Civil Defense for nuclear war and who say that the whole thing is a joke.

Let me address that if I might. First of all, some people suggest that having Civil Defense might even make nuclear war more thinkable. Well, people in Civil Defense are no more for nuclear war than anyone else is. I've never met a person who was for nuclear war. It would be the most horrible thing that could happen to our society, or to any other society. And I agree that the problem of mass casualty care is a horrendous problem that would exceed the medical resources. But even under our present limitations I think Civil Defense could be vitally important. If all deterrence fails and there should be a nuclear attack, then you could save tens of millions of people simply by having moved them out to dispersed host areas where they make much less inviting targets, and where only fallout is a nuclear hazard, not blast and fire. I think the government owes this to the people. And I think most people expect the government to do what it can, however imperfect, to protect them. Nobody claims Civil Defense is going to work perfectly. But what are our options, I ask. Military or diplomatic deterrents could fail; negotiations could break down. Are we simply to despair of doing anything and leave people in the cities to die?

I submit that it is better to have an imperfect insurance policy that can save tens of millions of lives that would otherwise be lost than to have no insurance policy at all. And that is, fundamentally, where Civil Defense is coming from. We have no illusions that we can provide a defense for everybody. But it is not an all-or-nothing situation. It's relative protection—either relatively more people could be saved, or relatively less people could be saved. There is no question that if we could deter a nuclear war in any reasonable way, short of national humiliation, we should do so.

---

50.   General Paul Tibbets—
Columbus, Ohio, February 25, 1985

I was notified in September 1944 that the United States was undertaking the development of the atomic bomb. My responsibility was to develop and train an Air Force organization capable of dropping the new weapon. Not too many people knew that the directive also said to be prepared to make simultaneous drops in Europe and Japan. This is what was meant when they termed it a "split operation."

The plan was to use atomic weapons on Germany and Japan at exactly the same time?

That is correct.

With only two bombs available?

At the time I'm talking about we didn't have any bombs yet. Production was only beginning. How many weapons would become available was not up to me. My job was to develop an organization and train it. I also had to work with the scientific element at Los Alamos and find out: What have we got? What does it look like? Where does it go? What do we do with it? I spent ten and a half months working with those people to get the weapon into a shape that it could be dropped with predictable accuracy from an airplane flying at 30,000 feet.

Is that what is meant by "marrying the bomb to the plane"?

Yes, that's what we called it.

What did marrying the bomb to the plane entail, exactly?

First off, we had to get an aerodynamic shape to the bomb and one that would fit within our bomb-bay limitations. Additionally, we had to keep battery-operated heaters around the bomb because we didn't want the triggering mechanism to freeze up. Then next thing was, we had a weapon in there with critical material, and we had to monitor that as we were going along to be sure it wasn't starting to get active.

Did you have to learn any unusual things as the pilot of the plane that was going to drop this bomb?

We hadn't been used to flying at 30,000 feet with our airplanes at that time. It presented a new bombing problem, because you had high-altitude winds aloft, "ballistic winds" they called them. Also, with this weapon, we knew that once it was released, we could not continue to fly forward as we did in Europe and the Pacific at that time. There was no way you could keep flying over this bomb and still

Paul Tibbets

survive. The question then became: How do you get away from it after you release it? The only answer is, you have to make a *reverse turn*—again, another flying problem at that altitude. You only had fifty seconds in which to make the turn, because that's the time it took for the bomb to fall and explode, the explosion to come to shock wave, and all of that.

And making that turn within fifty seconds was the most unusual thing?

Absolutely. The rest of it was just flying, navigating, and bombing.

The plane was called Enola Gay, *and it's generally known that this was your mother's name. At what point did you name it after your mother?*

I put the name on the airplane the afternoon before we took off the following day at two A.M.

Did you check with your mother on that?

No, no. Because obviously I couldn't talk to her, and I didn't think that was really necessary.

How did she feel about being made relatively immortal as a result of that?

Well, when I was able to get home, my father told me—he always called her "the old girl"—he said, "You ought to have seen the smile on the old girl's face when they said the airplane was *Enola Gay*."

I heard, General, that you were the one who sent the code to Washington that got the wheels rolling on the timing of the actual bombing. Can you explain how it fell to you to do this?

We had started training in September 1944. By the following April I had a good outfit of people that had been driven hard and trained well. I put myself in a position of a football coach who knows that if you overtrain, it can cause you more trouble than you can imagine. So the question was, how workable was the bomb? I approached Dr. Oppenheimer and said, "What do you think the chances are of a failure to explode?" He said, "I don't really know, but I'm looking for that possibility of one in a million that it will malfunction." I said, "One in a million! Those are terrific odds. What are the odds right now?" I told him, "I really need to know." He said, "Well, if you need to know, I'm convinced that right now we're one in ten thousand." I said, "I'll take one-in-ten-thousand odds anytime." I was afraid we'd never get over there to get on with the primary purpose of the weapon, which was to stop the war. Now at that time any organization that had trained to go overseas had to be inspected. An Air Force or a Higher Command organization would do this, but the Higher Command in this case didn't know what we were doing, and I had been told you have to do all of this yourself. They gave me a code word, which today I don't remember, and that was my word to send to Washington when we were ready to go. I, arbitrarily on my own, independently, sent that word to Washington because I wanted to get that organization moving over to the Pacific theater.

There's all this talk of training the crew for Hiroshima. What about the crew for Nagasaki?

I had fourteen separate crews. And I did the same thing with each one of the crews. It was all one organization, and I was commander of that organization. It was called the 509th Composite Group.

At what point did it become clear that you had two bombs rather than, say, one, or three?

Well, put it this way: there were three bombs that could have been used. One on the island, one en route to the island, and one at Wendover. Now how long it would have been before there would have been a fourth one I don't know, but it wouldn't have been too long. Anyway, there were three that were readily available.

I always thought it was only two. . . .

There were three. And when Japan didn't surrender after the one in Nagasaki, I flashed a code word back to Wendover, Utah, and that bomb was loaded into an airplane and headed for the Pacific but got stopped at Moffat Field because the war was over.

What type of bomb was the third bomb?

It was the Nagasaki type.

Can you describe what happened when you dropped the Hiroshima bomb?

Well, as we came into the target my mind was really on the navigation of the airplane to the target, the stability of the airplane to furnish what we call a bombing platform. I wanted it absolutely tabletop smooth. And that's the way it worked. We worked that, all the way in from the target.

We could see the city from seventy miles distant. And as we closed in on that distance we had certain procedural things we had to do. We had a check and recheck situation. First off, when the bombardier says, "I can see the city," the rule was that the navigator had to step up from his position, go up and look over the bombardier's shoulder, and say, "Yeah, I agree with you, that is—that is Hiroshima." The next thing is when we got much closer and the bombardier says, "I have the aiming point," that meant he put the cross-hairs of the Norden bomb-sight on that aiming point and the navigator then had to come up, look through the bomb-sight, say, "Yes, I agree with you, that is the assigned aiming point." I'm looking over the shoulders of both of them as they go, and, based on target study I had done trying to imprint the outline of this city in my mind, I couldn't do anything but agree also, because we had absolutely unrestricted visibility, it was just as clear as a picture.

Now as we come in, there were some things that had to be done at the last moment. We had to activate a tone which was transmitted over the radio to the other two B29's accompanying us so that they would know we were only one minute away from the bomb release point. Now this tone was silenced when the bomb departed the airplane. That was the signal for those people to release their instruments and start this turn away from the bomb that I talked about.

What kind of instruments did they release?

They were recorders to record the blast, and those recorders were attached to battery-operated radios to transmit that signal by radios to receivers back in the airplane.

Was the bomb dropped by parachute or did it just fall?

It fell. The blast gauges were floating down by parachute.

What happened when the bomb went off? What did you experience?

Well, nothing, strange as it may sound. The airplane had its back to the explosion, and it did not have a lot of windows in it. Now when the bomb exploded, the brilliance was such that even though it was a bright, sunshiny day, I could still see this silver light, it was kind of a bluish silver flash. So, fine. That is something that you didn't normally see.

And the next thing I tell everybody is that I tasted it. And they say, well, how could that happen? I say, well, years ago when I was a young fella, the dentists, when they did work on your teeth, would fill your teeth with a combination of silver and lead, and when you would accidentally touch it with a fork or a spoon you would get a feeling of a pain going through. It's commonly called electrolysis. And that's exactly what happened. It was just a momentary flash and then it was over. I knew then that the bomb had exploded.

Now at about the time I tasted it, my tailgunner, who is in the back with welder's goggles on so he wouldn't be blinded by the flash, he's looking for the shock wave. And he said, "Here it comes." He could see it coming up. A mirage like you see on the desert. Beautiful, ever-expanding circles coming right up to the airplane. We felt the first one with the force of two and a half g forces. It wasn't a scary, dramatic jolt, but it was one that positively got your attention. The second one was much lighter, and the third one wasn't strong at all.

And did you ever see the cloud from the blast?

After the bomb exploded, I was still in a partial turn, and I kept the airplane coming right around to come back because we had hand-held cameras, and we were instructed to take all the pictures that we could while we were in the air. So everybody got their cameras and they started taking pictures.

We had gone in on basically a westerly heading, and when we came out I headed to the southwest. So I passed to the left of the mushroom cloud that was going up. By the time I could turn around and look at it, the mushroom cloud was higher than we were. And we were still at about 29,000 feet. The cloud was tumbling, rolling, and boiling, and, I mean, it was obvious that there was a tremendous amount of energy contained within that cloud.

What color was it?

Well, dirty gray. That's the best color I could give you. And it was not the classic mushroom. This one was kind of strung out. Did you ever see a parachute come down that failed to open, what they call a straggler? That's what it looked like.

At what point did you see this mission from the point of view of the people on the ground? Did you ever feel that it had inflicted suffering that was beyond what anybody had experienced in a war before? Or did it seem to you similar to other kinds of bombings and simply what happens when wars start up?

Well, I think you've basically touched on my philosophy. We had a famous old southern general who said, "War is hell." Sherman. And I couldn't agree more with him. It is. When I was dropping bombs in Europe, iron bombs and such, against the Germans and so forth, I knew that people were getting hurt on the ground, and when I realized that I was understanding people were getting hurt, I said to myself, "You gotta quit thinking about this. You can't be effective if you're going to be worrying about who's getting hurt down there. You're out to destroy a target. That's the name of the game, destroy the target." And on the basis of that, I must say that I never did dwell on it. Sure, I knew that there had been terrible loss of life. I knew all kinds of damage was taking place. But again, I took it objectively, not personally.

You mentioned the name of the game was hitting the target. What was the target in Hiroshima?

The city was the target, period. We figured we'd wipe out most of the city. There was not much of a question about that. But the aiming point was a bridge right beside a Japanese temple. Don't ask me the name of the temple or the bridge, either one, but it was a positive geographical landmark that you couldn't mistake.

And how accurate was the drop?

I think we were pretty accurate. The bomb exploded within 600 feet of where we intended to explode it.

Let me ask you, Mr. Tibbets, what would you say is the lesson or legacy of Hiroshima, speaking for today?

The weapons available today make the ones we used look like miniature fire-crackers. Yes, we do have some weapons that we must do some serious thinking about. And I certainly don't advocate war. I would like to believe that nuclear weapons as such will never be used again, but I'm not that naive. I think they will be, just because we have them. The question is how to use them.

---

51. Minuteman II Missileers Lieutenants Lamb and Goetz

The Minuteman II missile is a three-stage, solid-fuel Intercontinental Ballistic Missile that can deliver a single W56 warhead with a yield of 1.6 megatons over a range of 7,000 miles at 15,000 miles per hour. First deployed in 1965, the Minuteman II is the workhorse of America's land-based deterrent force. There are three Minuteman II Strategic Missile Wings, each containing 1,500 missiles. The Wings are located at Malmstrom Air Force Base in Montana, Ellsworth Air Force Base in South Dakota, and Whiteman Air Force Base in Missouri.

Becoming a missile silo operator requires sixteen weeks of rigorous training with Vandenberg Air Force Base's 4315th Combat Crew Training Squadron. The Training Squadron's motto is "Training Quality Missileers and Talking Missiles." This unique school graduates 450 missileers a year. Since 1963, 18,000 missileers have become certified. To become a certified launch control center operator, the trainee is required to sign a Missile Combat Crew Member Personal Commitment Form on two different occasions: at the start of the training and upon the successful completion of the course.

"Initial Certification of MCCM Personal Commitment

"I fully understand as a missile combat crew member I will be assigned to nuclear weapons and weapon systems. I acknowledge that serving in this capacity, I will be in a position of high trust which requires that I maintain an unquestioned reliability at all times. Further, I understand the spirit and intent of the Personnel Reliability Program, AFR 35-99, and the qualification under its provisions is a requisite to my continued performance in nuclear-related duties. I am aware that disqualification under such program for acts or expressions which cast doubt upon my reliability or ability to execute the responsibilities of my duties will result in my removal from such duties. I also understand that the circumstances or situations that give cause for disqualification under the Air Force's Personnel Reliability Program may result in punitive action, adverse administrative action, and/or elimination from the Air Force."

"Final Certification of MCCM Personal Commitment

"I understand the responsibilities of missile combat crew member and realize what actions this duty may entail. I certify that I have no reservations over my ability and conviction to perform in such capacity."

4315th Combat Crew Training Squadron class in session

Key-turn exercise with **Lieutenants Lamb** and **Goetz**—Ellsworth Air Force Base, Rapid City, South Dakota, November 21, 1984

Goetz: What I'd like to do now is show you a tactical launch, basically give you an idea of what happens when we get the message and what our actions are. And to prepare a missile for launch, it takes three things. First off, we have to enable the missile, and that means we have to put times in the missile.

Like, we're going to launch at 3:05 P.M.?

Goetz: Well, it would be minutes from key-turn—one minute from key-turn, or two minutes—we would want it to launch. Normally, day to day, there is a special code in there, and it's no time—it's infinite hold. And even if it was key-turned on, the missile wouldn't launch.

Because it's on infinite hold?

Goetz: It's on infinite hold. So we have to put a valid time in there first, we have to prepare the missile for launch with a code, and then also to launch a sortie we would have to key-turn on it.

If you do key-turn on it, and it's got a long time, let's say twenty-three hours, can you recall it once it's been key-turned?

Goetz: There are provisions for that, but we don't have it down in the launch control center.

So it would have to be recalled from somewhere else?

Goetz: Yes, exactly. But generally there's not a twenty-three-hour time. Generally it's somewhat less. Also, I'd like to just talk about one thing, and it's what we call launch votes. To actually launch a missile it takes two launch votes. One is transmitted by two men from this capsule, and another control center does the same thing. So there are quite a few safeguards that we have to go through before we can launch a sortie. Why don't we give a demonstration of that? First off, what we're going to do—you can ask any questions after—we'll be getting the message over our primary alerting system. . . .

(Alarm sounds)

Lamb: Lima, Alpha, Uniform, November, Charlie, Hotel, Echo, November, Alpha, Bravo, Lima, Echo, Papa, Lima, Charlie, Alpha, Zero, One. Acknowledge. Out.

Goetz: Okay, I got a valid execution message. Go to the tech launch checklist. Okay, I'm on page 3-47, step one. Launch keys inserted . . .

(Each operator inserts a key into a combination lock to gain access to another key—the one used to launch the missile. Lieutenant Lamb has trouble getting his key into the lock.)

Lamb: Have they changed it?

Goetz: Not that I know of. We had to borrow this lock. . . .

Generally, he would have his own lock. He would have a combination and we would each only know the combination of our lock. In this case, we had to borrow one, and apparently they changed the combination on us. So what we'll do, we'll simulate the keys. At this time, we would open it up and we would get the keys out.

He would place his key there. I would come forward, place my key here, and we'd proceed. Okay, step two, function select switch to Off.

Lamb: Okay, function Off.

Goetz: T.E.P.

Lamb: C.P.

Goetz: P.L.C.A. launch option selector Zero One.

Lamb: Okay, Zero One.

Goetz: D.C. switch actuated . . .

Lamb: Going up. Okay, it's out.

Goetz: Five through ten. Alpha does not apply. Step eleven, program select switch to Enable. We're going to Enable.

Lamb: All right.

Goetz: Twelve, flight select switch to All. I'm going to All. Launcher select switch to All. All. Unlock code inserted. I'll read it.

Lamb: Okay.

Goetz: Echo.

Lamb: Echo.

Goetz: November.

Lamb: November.

Goetz: Alpha.

Lamb: Alpha.

Goetz: Bravo.

Lamb: Bravo.

Goetz: Lima.

Lamb: Lima.

Goetz: Echo.

(loud buzz)

Lamb: Echo . . . Echo, November, Alpha, Bravo, Lima, Echo.

Goetz: Okay . . . Code inserted. Enable. Switch to Enable.

Lamb: Down a lock.

Goetz: Light on. Light off. We have our enables, our P.L.C.M. Step fifteen—Hotel. Program select switch to Off.

(Bell rings)

Lamb: That's right.

Goetz: And step sixteen, key-turn at Commit Time. We'll key-turn in twenty seconds.

Lamb: Okay.

Goetz: And on my mark. This time we have the valid enable codes, so all the sorties are coming up and they're showing us that they're enabled. Okay, key-turn on my mark. Three, two, one, mark. *(Bell rings)* Lights on. *(Bell rings)* Lights off. Release. We'll release and we'll wait for the status. One key-turn would give us a Launch Commanded, like this. When the second key-turn goes in, it'll actually give us a Launch in Process. *(Turns key a second time)*

That's it? That's the launch?

Goetz: That's it. That is the launch. When we get Missile Away, actually that's a hot-line from the actual missile, and that would tell us that a missile has actually lifted off. So that would be it.

Then what do you do next?

Goetz: Okay. Next, we would . . . okay, our checklist—basically we would see if we need assistance from anyone. Say we need assistance from an aircraft—ah—we would compile a launch report and, um, through channels we would . . . let the command post know what actual missiles have launched, which missiles did not launch, and such.

Then what would you do?

Goetz: Well, um—then we have other, uh, procedures to go through. For example, assuming this would be our first message, we would have to, well, harden ourselves, more or less. We'd put the arms up, we'd strap in, and basically we would be monitoring any sorties that are left on the ground, and we would react to any further messages. We'd remain on alert until, well, um, basically until we're told not to be. We do remain on alert for the duration.

And how much food and air and supplies do you have down in here?

Goetz: Oh, we have, well, we don't really have any food down in a normal launch control center.

Okay. So actually, although it's hardened to be protected, you're not really meant to endure down here.

Goetz: Well . . . we could. . . . It's really hard to say. We do bring food out ourselves, but it's not stored here. So it's really hard to say how long we could. But hopefully, it would be long enough for the termination of any nuclear activity when we could make our way topside.

52. Down the Hatch

This photograph was taken inside Launch Facility LF04, which is part of the 394th ICBM Test Maintenance Squadron at Vandenberg Air Force Base. LF04 houses one Minuteman III missile.

Minuteman III has the same specifications as the Minuteman II missile except for an improved rocket motor; an increased range of 1,000 miles; a new guidance system; and a new reentry system with either two or three Multiple Independently Targetable Reentry Vehicles, each carrying either a W62/Mk-12 warhead with a 170-kiloton yield or a W78/Mk-12A warhead with a 335-to-350-kiloton yield.

A Minuteman II missile takes up to 36 hours to be retargeted; the Minuteman III can be retargeted in 25 minutes. The entire Minuteman III force of 550 missiles can be retargeted within 10 hours. Two hundred of the missiles have a backup launch control capability; that is, they can be launched from airborne launch centers should the underground launch control centers become nonoperational.

Minuteman III missiles were first deployed in 1975. They will eventually replace the Minuteman II.

53. The "Scramble"

Ellsworth Air Force Base contains two legs of the strategic land-air-sea triad: Minuteman missiles, based on land, and the air-based B-52 and B-1 bombers.

Six men make up a full strategic bombing crew. In a "scramble," the crew runs to a vehicle, drives it to the plane, and fast-starts the bomber with explosive charges to have it airborne within minutes.

Each crew member carries a pair of glasses designed to protect him from flash-blindness. The lenses of the glasses, incorporating a gold alloy, instantly darken with the onset of brilliant light. At the time of a scramble crew members are not told whether they are on an exercise or engaged in a genuine war alert.

54. Trident

The Trident can travel 400,000 miles without refueling. Its top speed is over 20 knots. It can dive to 985 feet. It has four decks, a crew of 171, and supplies for 90 days. The tuning-fork–shaped building in the left foreground is the Demagnetization Facility. Before going to sea, submarines have their "magnetic signatures" reduced here to prevent detection.

The box-shaped structure at upper left is the Explosives Handling Wharf, the largest building in Kitsap County, Washington. Here missiles are loaded into the Trident, which has 24 missile-launching tubes. Each Trident missile has a range of 4,400 miles and can carry the W76/Mk-4 MIRV weapon with 8 warheads. Each warhead has a yield of 100 kilotons. This means that one Trident can carry three times the explosive power of all the wars in history, which are estimated to have had a cumulative yield of 6 megatons. The new Trident, due in 1989, will be able to carry fifteen times the explosive power of all the wars in history.

Nuclear missiles aboard Tridents have no Permissive Action Links, or PALs—systems of electromechanical locks built into nuclear weapons. Such locks require the insertion of a code before the weapon can be used. Since the U.S. Navy maintains no PALs in its submarine-launched ballistic missiles, the captain, with a number of officers, could decide to execute a launch without higher authorization.

55. Admiral Hyman Rickover
(1900–1986), United States Navy, Director, Naval Nuclear Propulsion Program

Hyman Rickover was responsible for the design and production of the first nuclear-powered submarine engines and for the development of the USS Nautilus, *the world's first nuclear-propelled submarine (1955). As early as 1950 he proposed the idea for a nuclear aircraft carrier. He was also responsible for the establishment of the first large-scale, all-civilian atomic power reactor, in Shippingport, Pennsylvania (1957). It used a scaled-up version of the pressurized water reactor incorporated in the* Nautilus *and established at the outset a strong link between naval reactor programs and "Atoms for Peace."*

Excerpts from a hearing on defense expenditures held in the Joint Economic Committee of the United States Congress, Washington, D.C., January 28, 1982:

Senator William Proxmire: Admiral, a big issue in this country today is how much we're spending for defense. In your opinion . . . are we spending more than we need to spend on national defense? Is it possible to spend such amounts well, or is the pace of the buildup too fast?

Rickover: I think we are spending too much. I think we should be more selective in our spending. . . .

For example, take the number of nuclear submarines. I'll hit right close to home. I see no reason why we have to have just as many as the Russians do. At a certain point you get where it's sufficient. What's the difference whether we have 100 nuclear submarines or 200? I don't see what difference it makes. You can sink everything on the oceans several times over with the number we have and so can they. . . .

In general, I think we are overarming altogether because here you have a situation where weapons get more powerful, more destructive, and then you need more. And something seems to be illogical with that proposition.

Now I understand the issue of placing them in different places so they can't be all destroyed at one time . . . but I think there gets to be a point where it is meaningless, and I can't be exact with you, but I have that philosophical feeling that we are spending too much on defense. There's always scare words being used to justify defense expenditures, and the people running the military tend to get what they want. . . .

Representative Frederick Richmond: Is it true we have now twice as many senior officers in the armed forces as we did in World War II?

Rickover: I believe that's correct.

Richmond: It's a mind-boggling thought, isn't it?

Rickover: Well, you give us the money for it. You know what you're doing, don't you? It's your fault. You know what you're doing. You're on a committee that's supposed to be knowledgeable. That means you don't do your job. You know, I'm talking with brutal frankness.

Richmond: Just to change the subject, Admiral Rickover . . .

Rickover: How do you like that, Senator Proxmire? You see, I got to him. . . .

Proxmire: Admiral, civilian nuclear energy has nearly come to a standstill in this country. Will it ever become a viable source of energy in the future? . . .

Rickover: I think that ultimately we will need nuclear power because we are exhausting our nonrenewable resources; that is, coal and oil. I think they will go far more rapidly than we think they will, and the cost is already going up. I believe that nuclear power for commercial purposes shows itself to be more economic, but that's a fake line of reasoning because we do not take into account the potential damage the release of radiation may do to future generations.

Admiral Hyman Rickover at St. John the Divine Cathedral, New York City

---

I'll be philosophical. Until about two billion years ago it was impossible to have any life on earth. That is, there was so much radiation on earth you couldn't have any life—fish or anything. Gradually, about two billion years ago, the amount of radiation on this planet and probably in the entire system became reduced. That made it possible for some form of life to begin and it started in the seas, I understand from what I've read. . . .

Now when we use nuclear weapons or nuclear power we are creating something which nature has been eliminating. Now that is the philosophical aspect, whether it's nuclear power or using radiation for medical purposes or whatever. Of course, some radiation is not bad because it doesn't last long or has little effect on the surroundings, but every time you produce radiation, you produce something that has a certain half-life, in some cases for billions of

years. I think the human race is going to wreck itself, and it's important that we get control of this horrible force and try to eliminate it.

I do not believe that nuclear power is worth it if it creates radiation. Then you might ask me, why do I have nuclear-powered ships? That's a necessary evil. I would sink them all. . . . I'm not proud of the part I've played in it. I did it because it was necessary for the safety of this country. That's why I'm such a great exponent of stopping this whole nonsense of war. Unfortunately, attempts to limit war have always failed. The lesson of history is, when a war starts every nation will ultimately use whatever weapon has been available. . . .

Proxmire: What do you think is the prospect, then, of nuclear war?

Rickover: I think we will probably destroy ourselves, so what difference will it make? Some new species will come up that might be wiser. We think we are wise because we have—

Proxmire: With that knowledge, it would seem to me that we could control, limit, reduce nuclear weapons. Everybody loses.

Rickover: I think from a long-range standpoint—I'm talking about humanity—the most important thing we could do is start in having an international meeting where we first outlaw nuclear weapons to start with, then we outlaw nuclear reactors too.

Proxmire: Do you think that's realistic in a world with the Soviet Union?

Rickover: I don't know. You're asking me to think as a person who probably knows more about this and has thought more about it than anybody in the world. I think I have a reasonable mind and I can think these things through and I understand what humanity is all about and the part that human beings play on this earth. I do not believe in divine intercession. I think we are making our own bed and we have to lie in it. We can go to church every Sunday and pray, but the Lord has many demands made on him in many other worlds and in the eyes of the Lord we are not the most important thing in the universe.

---

56. Strategic Weapons Facility Pacific

---

57. Trident Christening

The Trident is an OHIO-class submarine. It is 560 feet long and 42 feet in diameter.

There are currently eight Tridents. The first Trident, the *Ohio*, entered active duty in 1981. After the *Ohio* there followed, at approximately one-year intervals, and at a cost of $1.5 billion apiece, the *Michigan*, the *Florida*, the *Georgia*, the *Rhode Island*, the *Alabama*, the *Henry Jackson*, and the *Nevada*. Six more Tridents are under construction. The Navy plans 20 to 24 Tridents by the 1990s.

58. Theodore B. Taylor —
Damascus, Maryland, October 13, 1986

I want nothing whatever to do with any more weapons development, and I've had that unwavering attitude since 1966.

What happened in 1966?

I was at the Pentagon, where I had spent almost two years. It was right in the midst of what was getting to be a very ugly situation in Vietnam. The excuse that nuclear weaponeers like myself had had was that we were making war impossible. But Korea and Vietnam showed this was obviously not so. I also became totally alarmed with the lack of understanding in Congress on nuclear weapons matters. I was present when Congress was told by the highest authorities in the Defense Department that we had no problem in terms of actually using our deterrents. And we had a very severe problem. I was the last witness at those hearings and sort of spilled a lot of beans.

Somehow that crowned the whole architecture of the new form in which I saw nuclear weaponry. At that point I said, "It's bad, it's wrong, it's immoral, it's the work of the devil, we must get rid of that."

You used a rather strong phrase, "the work of the devil." Are you speaking colloquially, or do you feel more about that?

I'm basically a person with religious beliefs, and I have a sense of some supernatural forces that are distinctly evil. I can't identify them, but sometimes things happen, people do things—I've done them—that I would call the work of an evil spirit holding control, at least for a while. I think that happens in many forms of addictions, particularly psychological addictions. For the last year or so I have been calling myself an addict with respect to nuclear weaponry. Becoming involved with it, being close to it, working on it, creates an altered state of mind. I'm convinced that the real driving force in the nuclear arms race is the weaponeers, the people who come up with the concepts. It all starts with that devilishly creative act of imagining something which is infinitely destructive. Then they go to Franklin Roosevelt or Harry Truman or Ronald Reagan and say, "Here's this thing, do you

want that?" The answer is invariably, "You bet we do!"

When you're working creatively with weapons concepts and nuclear detonations, is there any sense that somehow you're playing God, altering the structure of matter in new ways?

I don't recall any feelings of being a manipulator of nature. This wasn't a matter of a deep understanding of the laws of nature; it was engineering. Given the laws of nature, what extreme things could be done? I was always looking for extremes. I was interested in the smallest fission weapon that's conceivable, and the biggest, and the lightest, and the highest pressures that you could possibly get, and the highest temperatures. So you're going after records of one kind and another. And working with nuclear weapons can give a sense of personal power over events, like changing the nature of tactical warfare by introducing smaller, lighter things that could be fired out of a gun, or whatever.

Would it be accurate to say that the move toward miniaturization was inspired by you?

Not entirely—when I got to Los Alamos there was a group that was looking into making fission weapons about half the diameter of the Nagasaki bomb. My job was to see what improvements could be made. My contribution was to ask the question: Why stop at half—what's the smallest fission weapon you can make as a matter of principle? The answer to that question led us to results which were quite different. I was always searching for answers to the questions: Why can't you go further? What's the limit?

Maybe this is a good a place to ask you some very basic things to do with the heat, the pressures, and the speeds in the very heart of a nuclear device. My sense of it has always been that what happens there doesn't happen anywhere else on earth.

Well, it certainly doesn't happen anywhere else on earth and it probably doesn't happen in that way at all anywhere in the universe either. There are much more impressive things than nuclear explosions going on throughout the universe, but what drives this set of events, the fast critical assembly causing fission—that may be a uniquely human artifact. It gets extremely improbable that you will find material that critical connected with something that can assemble the material together the way a high explosive does. So there's a human trademark to a nuclear detonation that may not be anywhere else at all out there.

So what's going on inside this unique event?

Inside an exploding nuclear weapon are pressures that are over a thousand million—a billion—atmospheres.

One billion?

One billion atmospheres. Fifteen billion pounds per square inch or higher. And there are temperatures of 100 million degrees Centigrade. Velocities as high as 10^9 centimeters per second—that's 10,000 kilometers per second. Which is a thousand times the escape velocity from the earth.

What exactly is moving at such velocity?

Material. When the explosion takes full hold and it starts expanding and it blows apart, the outside is typically moving 200, 300, 400 kilometers a second. There's always some kind of a reflector tamper around the outside and that gets driven by the shock wave of the expanding core up to densities that are a hundred times the normal density of uranium metal—2,000 grams per cubic centimeter. In some of the thermonuclear weapons, in the very center, there are so many neutrons that the density of bare neutrons is higher than the density of molecules in water. So neutrons become sort of a bulk material, another form of matter. Neutron stars are basically that. The numbers are literally astronomical, far beyond anything in ordinary experience, so if the work you're doing involves even further increases in the really spectacular nature of the things on the blackboard, it gets very exciting.

But I'm not just talking about numbers on a blackboard. Isn't there some sense of your hand having indirectly recreated the primal stuff?

This was not a matter of understanding the laws of nature, but of making gadgets. These things were all called gadgets in the beginning. And they were gadgets that people played with, and that feeling got intensified for me when I went to my first set of atomic tests in Nevada. I saw only five explosions, all in one period.

There's a rumor that you once lit a cigarette from one of them.

It's true.

What's the story?

Well, we were waiting around, the shot had been delayed. I spotted a little parabolic reflector lying in a used-equipment heap right next to the control room. It had a little hole in the back, God knows what for. I looked at it and thought, "I wonder if I can hold that up and collect enough light from the explosion to light a cigarette?" I pointed it at the sun and got the focal point then put a Pall Mall in there, supported by some wire, right at the focus. Then I propped the mirror up on a rock and lay down on the ground right by it and aimed it at the tower. Then we had the countdown and I looked down and there was this little burning hole about a quarter of an inch from the end of the cigarette, so I pulled the cigarette out and puffed on it. It lit.

Was that Pall Mall regular or king-size?

They were all king-size in those days. Now you'd call them regular.

Theodore Taylor

What was it like being at the test site, setting up the test shots?

I'll never forget the sense of fantasy—here are all these fairly young people running around in baseball caps and short pants, setting off these huge bombs, like a bunch of kids playing with fireworks. It was fun in a very intense way. Where emotions were stirred—that was in rivalries. Everybody from Los Alamos felt much better when one of the Livermore shots failed. The only Livermore shot I ever saw was one that didn't even knock the tower over, and we were practically ready to celebrate. We weren't fighting the Russians, we were fighting Livermore.

Ted, when I think of the kind of miniature A-bombs you developed, like the Davy Crockett, it seems to make the whole

Star Wars debate look pretty silly. It's strange to me that Star Wars never addresses itself to this other end of the nuclear weapons race—the foot-based, smuggled-in, backpack nuclear explosive.

I completely agree. Star Wars and what it can turn into have nothing to do with missile defense—it really has to do with a new breed of offensive weapons, a third generation of nuclear weapons that will make the world much more dangerous than it is now.

What do you mean, a third-generation nuclear weapon?

Well, to understand that, it's useful to define what first- and second-generation weapons are. The first generation was the sort of fission weapons dropped on Hiroshima and Nagasaki. That made up most of the U.S. stockpile until the second generation came, which were hydrogen bombs, or thermonuclear explosives. In both cases the intent was to get as high an explosive yield as possible from a given weight. There was no attempt to enhance or suppress any of the several dozen types of energy that are released from an exploding nuclear weapon.

That's where third-generation weapons come in. They are a much bigger class of weapons than atomic bombs or hydrogen bombs. The intent in the third-generation weapons is to increase specific kinds of energy coming out of nuclear explosions, and then make that energy go in one direction, instead of releasing all of it in all directions at once. The transition from second-generation nuclear weapons to third-generation is analogous to the transition from gunpowder to guns.

What was the first example of aiming a nuclear explosive charge?

Well—the concept of aiming nuclear charges was developed fairly fully in connection with Project Orion, which planned to use nuclear explosives to propel spaceships. We wanted the momentum associated with the explosion to be transferred to the vehicle and not wasted by going in other directions. So in Orion the problem was to suppress neutrons and gamma rays and X rays and enhance momentum, that is, material moving toward the vehicle, so that when it struck the bottom of the vehicle it would push it.

So to do that you had to get inside the dynamics of an explosion and separate out the different effects. . . .

That's right. And in the course of doing that, it occurred to a number of people that

you could do other things as well, like designing weapons to destroy targets in space. Now I'm not saying that the Orion Project was the origin of third-generation weapons. But some of the concepts that are now being worked on did come out of that project.

Is the neutron bomb a third-generation nuclear weapon?

Yes, but its development was totally independent of Orion. It is designed to produce more neutrons released from the explosion than an ordinary fission or thermonuclear weapon. And the X-ray laser is another third-generation nuclear weapon that enhances and directs the X-ray energy of a nuclear explosion.

Are they working on an electromagnetic-pulse bomb?

I believe so. I don't know any of the details, but it is true that by careful design a lot more energy from a nuclear explosion can be converted to electromagnetic, radio, radar frequency radiation, which can cause a lot of damage at a big distance. And there are a number of other concepts that are being worked on, most of which are claimed to be for use in space. High-speed pellets is one possibility, microwaves is another. I'm especially concerned about microwaves because they'll penetrate clear through the atmosphere. High-speed pellets will not. Just a small amount of air will stop them. They only make sense for use in space.

Nuclear pellet bombs in space?

In space, pellets will move until they hit something. Some of this work is being done to see what kind of nuclear countermeasures there might be to Star Wars, because if there are countermeasures that make use of directional nuclear weapons in space, then Star Wars components would have to be protected against them.

So to protect against the possibility of third-generation–type warheads, they are designing those very warheads?

Yes, and once they are designed, Star Wars defenses may well make use of them in their own defense.

Sounds nasty. Isn't that the kind of thing Gorbachev was referring to when he insisted that we put Star Wars research and development aside because it could lead to all kinds of developments that are not in the interests of world peace?

That's right. My concern is that as people explore third-generation nuclear weapons for whatever purpose, defensive or not, offensive uses will occur to them, and although they may not make any sense, they may still be developed. New types of nuclear weapons don't necessarily have to be sensible in order for them to be built. And the best evidence of that is the insanity of our having a grand total of some 60 or 70 thousand nuclear weapons out there which make no sense, are terribly dangerous, could destroy the world. But they're still there.

One of the virtues of Star Wars is that at least it makes it obvious that the world of military activity in relation to these weapons is a pure fantasy, and a child's fantasy at that, one which has no bearing on the true nature of what Star Wars is all about, which is that factor of 10 million.

What do you mean, the factor of 10 million?

Well, you get 10 million times more energy from a nuclear explosion than you do from a chemical explosion. And that is what has fed the weaponeers with un-limited concepts for dealing with the situation defensively and offensively. I sometimes am sympathetic with people wandering around saying we should take all the scientists in the world and shoot 'em.

Would you be one of the first to go?

Well, I can understand that feeling against so-called scientists who are in fact not scientists but weaponeers. I don't think it was essentially wrong to call the work at Los Alamos scientific work. But it's not trying in some objective way to search for the truth about how nature works. We wanted to make something. What we wanted to make happened to be designed to kill as many people as possible.

So it's searching for the truth—of how a bomb works.

But searching for the truth of the implications of the existence of the bomb, that's a whole other matter.

How do you feel about where we're headed?

I think the future, if we keep going in the direction we're headed in now, is totally unattractive. If you just take the momentum of what has been happening since 1939, and extend it business-as-usual, the surprise-free world projected some time up ahead is going to be the end of the world. I think it's up to all of us together to change that course. For reasons I don't understand, I think all of us, all people on the earth, are now being put upon to put it to *them* to get something straight here. Not

with a threat, but we should do what we feel really drawn to do—and do it. This is the time for passion. Passion is what's needed to keep us off this reckless drive which has no end but death, really. I think the signal of where to get off this freeway is the receptiveness of people to expressions of good feeling and trust. We need to start looking at some of the things that we can do together where we become dependent on working together.

Take a tiny fraction of our military spending and, starting tomorrow, put it into a project to find some way to purify the aquifers in the Soviet Union and the United States that are now contaminated with pesticides. That's the way to go. I just wish we'd get on with it.

---

59. The Davy Crockett Battlefield Missile

The Davy Crockett was 30 inches long and 11 inches in diameter and weighed 51 pounds. It used a W54 warhead with a range of one-quarter kiloton.

It was first tested at the Nevada Test Site on July 17, 1962, in a test code-named "Little Feller I." Fallout from the blast traveled northeast across Nevada into Utah and Idaho. Davy Crockett was mass-produced from 1961 to 1965; in all, 400 were manufactured. The last missile was retired in 1972.

---

60. The White Train

Public attention was first drawn to the white train by Jim and Shelley Douglass. On December 8, 1982, they first saw it pass the house they had bought on the border of the Naval Submarine Base Bangor. They tracked the train back to Pantex and set up a train-watch system that has observed and followed all the comings and goings of the white train from the Pantex yard since 1983. Trains to Naval Submarine Base Bangor: December 1982, March and August 1983, February and July 1984, February 1985. Trains to Charleston, South Carolina, Naval Weapons Depot: October 1983, May and November 1984, April–May and September 1985, twice in February 1986.

Each train has a turreted guard-car at the front, in the middle, and at the rear. The white train began its deliveries in the early sixties. The Douglasses' sighting ended two decades of invisibility. Public demonstrations have accompanied all but one of the white train's deliveries since 1983. In 1984 the Department of Energy repainted the cars red, green, gray, and blue.

---

61. Nuclear-Powered Jet Airplane Engines (1957–1961)

The Nuclear-Powered Jet Airplane Engine Program was killed in 1961 by President Kennedy. By that time one billion dollars had been spent on the two engine prototypes in the photograph and on the construction of the world's largest airplane hangar to house the envisioned finished product.

62. Nuclear Jet Airplane Initial Engine-Test Facility

---

63. Perimeter Acquisition Radar Characterization System (PARCS)

PERIMETER refers to the system's location on the northern border of the country.
ACQUISITION indicates that it will be the first radar to detect an oncoming missile attack.
RADAR refers to a phased-array radar system, which has thousands of small radar transmitters and receivers that enable it to scan the sky electronically rather than mechanically.
CHARACTERIZATION refers to its ability to assess the nature of the attack. It has a 100-to-120-degree angle of coverage and a range of several thousand miles.

PARCS relays its information to the Cheyenne Mountain Complex 6 or 7 minutes before the fleet of incoming missiles reach their targets. This radar was first put into operation in 1976.

The PARCS radar system is part of the U.S. Space Command, headquartered in Colorado Springs and established in 1985 to oversee the military use of space. Space Command will control Strategic Defense Initiative systems.

64. "Star Wars" Rail Gun

A rail gun is an electromagnetic launcher. Banks of capacitors discharge 4 megajoules of energy into the gun's 10,000-volt system. A 5-meter chromium copper rail (extruded at the Ashtabula extrusion press) conducts 1.5 million amps of electricity which create the opposing magnetic fields needed to "buck" a 180-gram projectile out of the gun. To date, exit speeds have reached 2,000 meters per second. The size of the rail gun's power supply precludes it from being space-based at this time.

The rail gun is seen as part of the Strategic Defense Initiative's "Terminal Defense" program—the system's last line of defense against incoming missiles. There are four rail-gun test centers in the U.S.

---

65. Bernard Benally, Navajo uranium miner—Navajo Reservation, Red Rock (recently renamed Red Valley), Arizona, August 18, 1982

Bernard, when did you go to work in the uranium mines and how long did you work there?

I started in the mines in 1950. I was working down here at Oak Spring Mine from 1952 to 1954, when I started having problems. But before that, I worked in various mines in Colorado, like Slick Rock and Montecello. I also worked in a place by Salt Lake. It has blue water there, but I don't remember what the place is called. At Oak Spring I found out I was sick. I was bleeding from inside, from the mouth, and my supervisor told me I had to go into the hospital, where they found out there was something wrong with my lungs so they told me that I couldn't be working anymore. I stayed here for a year and was told by the nurse to go into the hospital but I didn't want to. Then they sent me to Boulder, Colorado, for some kind of

Jeanette and Bernard Benally

treatment. After I was in Boulder, I came back for another four years and I was living here again and the same thing affected me and so I was transferred down to Tucson, and that's where they found out what was really wrong with me. I had an infection on my lung so they cut some pieces out from me. I stopped working in '65, and after that I've been in various hospitals.

What kind of work did you do when you were in the mine?

I fixed the dynamite, put it in the rock. I'd put some kind of grease on and then I put a wire in the dynamite and then I set them up and then somebody came around and they'd just blast it off. After the blast there was dust because there was no ventilation of any kind. Nowadays they have ventilation, but at that time they didn't have any.

So whoever went in after the dynamite exploded got a lot of dust?

Yeah, we did the blasting sometime in mid-afternoooon and we only took a few breaks just before the blast and right after we started doing our work again.

What kind of work did you do after the blast?

I used to go in and haul the rocks out, and I guess that's where I got hurt, because there was a lot of dust after they did the blasting and we went in right away. We used to eat in there too. We used to drink water from the mine too. Even our children were playing in that water. If they had told us that those rocks were dangerous I wouldn't have made my house out of them.

What is it about the rocks that's so dangerous?

We were informed by the EPC [Environmental Policy Center] that those rocks were hot and the radiation could travel at least twenty feet. And readings were taken. They used something like a clock that went "tick-tick." We were told that this meant they were hot.

Do you feel that the companies knew things were dangerous but didn't tell?

I don't know whether it was kept from us or even if the supervisor didn't know anything. I think nobody knew because there were no signs put up saying it was dangerous. If they knew it was dangerous they would have told us. But I'm not sure. I never asked them what was all behind it.

Do you know why they're taking the uranium out of the ground?

At that time they were telling us that they really needed it for the war.

Do you know what they use the uranium for?

All I know is that they used it for something like a gun.

Interview translated by Helene Hanson.

---

66. Inside the Key Lake Mill

---

67. O.K. Liquor, Blind River

The Eldorado Blind River Uranium Refinery is the newest of the five uranium refineries in the Western world.

---

68. Uranium Turned into Gas

All of the uranium for the first atomic bombs came from the Belgian Congo and from Port Radium, in Canada's Northwest Territories. The Eldorado Port Hope plant in Ontario refined the uranium used for these bombs. At that time, the Port Hope plant was the only plant capable of refining uranium in North America.

Today Port Hope receives its uranium trioxide feedstock from Blind River and completes the refinement process begun at Blind River.

---

69. Gaseous Diffusion

Uranium enters the nuclear weapons stream when it goes into a gaseous diffusion plant. The U.S. has two operating gaseous diffusion, or "uranium enrichment," plants: the Portsmouth

plant in Ohio and the Paducah plant in Kentucky. Gaseous diffusion concentrates the small amounts of U-235 in natural uranium. U-235 is used to sustain a chain reaction in a commercial nuclear reactor when it is enriched to 3 or 4%. The standard enrichment for American nuclear weapons is 93.5%.

Inside the Paducah Gaseous Diffusion Plant

At the Paducah plant, uranium gas is enriched to approximately 2% U-235. It is then fed to the Portsmouth plant, which can enrich it up to 97.3% U-235, the amount necessary for its use as reactor fuel in nuclear submarines and ships.

Nuclear Fuel Services in Erwin, Tennessee, converts uranium enriched at Portsmouth into the chemical and physical form used in naval fuel elements.

After naval fuel is used in submarine reactors it goes to the Idaho National Engineering Laboratory, where U-235 at about 80% enrichment is recovered from it in reprocessing operations. The 80% enriched uranium is sent to the Oak Ridge Y-12 plant, where it is converted to metal for use as driver fuel in the Savannah River Plant's plutonium production reactors.

---

70. Gas into Metal

---

71. The World's First Plutonium Factory

---

72. The B Plant Reprocessing Canyon

Because of their long shape, reprocessing buildings are referred to as "canyons."

During World War II, two reprocessing canyons were built to recover plutonium from the B-Reactor's irradiated fuel: the B Plant and the T plant. Virtually identical, they were built 8 miles apart to minimize the chances of their both being attacked by Japanese bombers.

Cesium capsule—inside B Plant's Cesium Encapsulation Facility

Cesium-137 is a waste product of plutonium production operations. It is the preferred isotope for use in American commercial food irradiation. Housed in part of the old B Plant, the Cesium Encapsulation Facility packages this highly radioactive substance for shipping. A cesium capsule is leased to food irradiation plants for $400 per year, plus $3,500 shipping. Capsules are shipped in 4-foot-thick casks.

73. Hanford N-Reactor

This reactor is graphite-moderated and has no containment vessel. In these two respects it is similar to the Chernobyl reactor. The N-Reactor has been shut down since the Chernobyl accident.

74. Superphenix Breeder

75. Candu Reactor: Darlington

76. Bendix Kansas City Plant

Annual Budget: $531,800,000 (1986)

The Bendix Kansas City Plant is one of America's Weapons Production Facilities.

The U.S. nuclear weapons complex is divided into two categories of factories: Materials Production Facilities and Weapons Production Facilities. The Materials Production Facilities produce the raw materials for a nuclear explosion—uranium, plutonium, and tritium. The Weapons Production Facilities manufacture the actual parts for the bomb.

The Materials Production complex includes the Fernald Feed Materials Production Center and Reactive Metals, Incorporated, in Ohio; Y-12 at Oak Ridge in Tennessee; Hanford in Washington State; the Savannah River Plant in South Carolina; the Idaho National Engineering Laboratory; and the Paducah Gaseous Diffusion Plant in Kentucky and the Portsmouth Gaseous Diffusion Plant in Ohio.

Weapons Production Facilities include Rocky Flats in Colorado; Y-12, Oak Ridge; the Savannah River Plant in South Carolina; Mound in Ohio; Pinellas in Florida; Bendix Kansas City; and the Pantex Nuclear Weapons Final Assembly Plant near Amarillo, Texas.

Dave Jackson, chief public relations officer, Department of Energy, Albuquerque Operations Office— Albuquerque, New Mexico, August 13, 1982

Dave Jackson is the chief public relations officer for the Department of Energy's Albuquerque Operations Office, which oversees production at Rocky Flats, Savannah River, Mound, Pinellas, Bendix Kansas City, and Pantex.

What role does the Department of Energy play in the production of nuclear weapons?

The Department of Energy as a successor agency to the Atomic Energy Commission and the Energy Research and Development Administration has the statutory responsibility to design, develop, test, produce, and retire nuclear weapons for the nation's arsenal. When the weapons are produced, they are delivered to the Department of Defense, where they become part of the war research stockpile. We also have a significant responsibility in maintaining the war reserve stockpile. This is the deal we have as a whole. The Albuquerque Operations Office is the field office of the Department of Energy responsible for the weapons production complex. We actually produce the weapons.

How many different kinds of weapons are there?

We have bombs that are designed to be dropped from airplanes. There are strategic bombs, there are tactical bombs. There are atomic artillery shells, there are warheads for missiles, from the standpoint of both the strategic missiles such as the Minuteman and the tactical missiles such as the Lance. There are torpedoes and depth charges and nuclear explosives that can be carried by hand as opposed to delivered by some system.

And how do these weapons get made?

Basically, we have a manufacturing complex, which in effect is not different from General Electric, or Westinghouse, or General Motors, or Chrysler, or anything else. We have a number of plants around the country that produce specific components which are brought together into a central location for assembly. Each of these plants is run by a contractor, a major industrial firm in the United States that has developed specific expertise in a given area. We manufacture plutonium parts, for instance, at the Rocky Flats plant. We manufacture the detonation systems at Mound in Ohio. We produce neutron generators and other electronic parts at the plant in Pinellas, Florida, operated by General Electric. All of these are brought together at the Pantex plant, near Amarillo, Texas, which is operated by a firm named Mason & Hanger-Silas Mason, where the components are assembled into a weapon. So to operate this whole system, it's like any other large-scale manufacturing complex. You have to have ways of shipping things between places, and you have to establish production schedules. You have to have a very, very competent quality-assurance organization to make sure that everything is built exactly to specification and fits like a glove when it gets there. And we have an obligation to produce these on schedule and as economically as we possibly can.

While we are not, quote, making widgets that will be sold down at the local supermarket, what we are making is something that is absolutely essential for the defense of the United States, and indeed the free world. They are expected to last a long time, and we hope we never have to, but indeed if we are ever required to use them, we want to know that they will function. A great part of the deterrent is the solid knowledge that what we have will work when it is supposed to.

How long will a nuclear weapon last?

What is the shelf-life of your Pontiac automobile? If you maintain it properly and change the oil regularly, and keep it lubricated and tuned up, it might run 150,000 miles. If you really are a fanatic—there's one guy that drove his Cadillac a million miles with the same engine still in it. So, you know, part of the thing that you do is to maintain weapons. The armed forces and the Department of Energy work together to assure that the nuclear weapons in the arsenal will work as designed if needed. Period.

77. Oak Ridge Y-12
Oak Ridge Reservation
  Annual Budget: $602,000,000 (1986)

78. Mound
  Annual Budget: $216,000,000 (1986)

79. Pinellas
  Annual Budget: $138,600,000 (1986)

80. Rocky Flats
  Annual Budget: $484,900,000 (1986)

On the evening of September 11, 1957, plutonium at the Rocky Flats plant ignited into a blaze that lasted 13 hours. Fourteen to twenty kilograms of plutonium were estimated to have burned in the fire.

81. Pantex—The End of the Line

This photograph was taken on an official "window-glass" tour of the Pantex grounds. The author was driven around the inside perimeter of the site by Department of Energy officials and was permitted to take photographs of anything visible from the van. He was allowed to leave the van and photograph through the chain-link fence to obtain this shot. On the fence was posted the following notice:

"Atomic Weapons and Special Nuclear Materials Rewards Act [Public Law 84-165, as amended by Public Law 93-377]

  Sec. 2. Any person who furnishes original information to the United States

  (a) leading to the finding or other acquisition by the United States of special nuclear material or an atomic weapon which has been introduced into the United States or manufactured or acquired therein contrary to the laws of the United States, or

  (b) with respect to the introduction or attempted introduction into the United States or the manufacture or acquisition or attempted manufacture or acquisition of, or a conspiracy to introduce into the United States or to manufacture or acquire, special nuclear material or an atomic weapon contrary to the laws of the United States, or

  (c) with respect to the export or attempted export, or a conspiracy to export, special nuclear material or an atomic weapon from the United States contrary to the laws of the United States,

  shall be rewarded by the payment of an amount not to exceed $500,000.

By Order of the United States Department of Energy"

Window-glass tours are no longer given at Pantex.

82. Bishop Leroy Matthiesen—
Amarillo, Texas, August 9, 1982

I am Bishop Leroy Matthiesen. I am bishop of the Roman Catholic diocese of Amarillo. I am sixty-two years of age and have lived in the Panhandle since 1948,

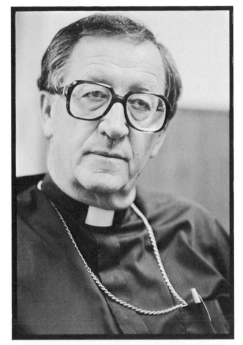
Bishop Leroy Matthiesen

when I was assigned here as a priest, and I was ordained a bishop in 1980. The Panhandle is in upper Texas; eleven miles from where I am speaking is located Pantex, the final assembly plant for all nuclear warheads manufactured in the United States.

At first I was not much concerned about what was happening at Pantex. In fact, I often used to give letters of recommendation to people who were applying for jobs there. I thought that out at Pantex they did research into the peaceful uses of nuclear energy.

What made you realize that isn't what they did there?

It started when the Carter administration went ahead with the building of the neutron bomb, or at least got the process up to the point of assembly and then

stopped, and then President Reagan announced in August of 1981 that they were going to go ahead with the final assembling.

Around that time many people were saying that the arms race is a crime against humanity and the proliferation of nuclear weapons is a tremendous danger and one ought not to continue that, and I thought, well, if that is true—and I agreed with it— then what about an individual who works in one of these plants which is contributing to the continuation of the arms race? That thought was somewhere way below the surface, but it came to the surface when a man working at the plant came to me for advice. He happened to be a deacon within our Church, and we have Church law that says that clergymen are not to engage in that kind of activity. And he was becoming aware of that. He had gone to work at the plant some years prior to his ordination as a deacon.

What was his name?

This is a man named Robert Gutierrez. He's still working at the plant. We discussed it. He said he was beginning to have problems of conscience, and what did I think, and I said I think you should not be working at a plant that exclusively assembles nuclear warheads which, if ever used, are going to be used on population centers, and which are indiscriminate in their destruction.

Was it this contact that made you focus in on the Pantex plant?

Oh, absolutely. Because now I was confronted with a direct question, and I couldn't evade the issue.

And you gave him a direct answer?

I gave him a direct answer. Now I also looked at his situation, which is that he's

Deacon Robert Gutierrez and wife

up in years, he's in his fifties, and he's had an apparent heart attack, so his chances of getting another job are not so good. And I told him he did not have to trade one bad situation for another and that he could continue to work there until he found other employment, which to this date he has not been able to find.

And he's still looking?

Still looking. That creates a problem, and it created all kinds of problems locally following a statement that I made in the fall of 1981 on the neutron bomb, which I described as an anti-life weapon, and I said it should not be assembled. On that occasion I appealed to the workers. I did not localize it to Pantex, I called on all workers engaged in the production and assembling of nuclear warheads to reflect upon the moral implications of what they're doing, and to consider whether it might not be better to go into other kinds of work. Every individual needs to make up his or her own conscience on that point. I was making an appeal to conscience.

This appeal to conscience has blossomed into the pastoral letter which now addresses the issue in great depth.

Yes, I think it was one of the factors that contributed toward the movement that culminated in the bishops' letter. But there were also other voices being raised. Archbishop Raymond Hunthausen in Seattle, Washington, described the Trident submarine as the "Auschwitz of Puget Sound." That was one of the statements that led me to consider the issue also.

The thinking is very clear in the bishops' letter, and I imagine that I hear your voice in it, so I assume you were heard and the spirit moved the bishops in the right way.

Well I think it did. I know my statement had an influence on the bishops of Texas, and they voted en bloc in favor of that letter. They issued their own statement as well. I think this indicates the value of a personal witness and of personal conviction in taking a stance. We ought not to be afraid to do that. In the wake of my public statement here I received letters locally and from other parts of the country in which people said, "I thought I was the only one who was concerned about the issue. . . ." and "Thank you for speaking out. Now this releases me to tell my story."

Of course there were people here who said they were surprised, some were shocked, some were angry. And there continues to be some anger, but anger is a good emotion. It permits you to get this out and then begin to talk to the issue.

The talk to the issue that is manifest in the bishops' statement goes directly contrary to government policy. I'm wondering if you have received any pressure from the government to go easy.

If you mean me personally, no. But there was pressure put on at the time that we had the discussion in Washington following the second draft. At that point the secretary of defense, Caspar Weinberger, had William Clarke, the special adviser to the president on defense matters, write a letter to each one of us urging us to understand that indeed the position of the government was a moral position and we ought to recognize that.

In what way was it a moral position?

Well, the thesis was that in defending our country with the possession of nuclear weapons, we were protecting innocent lives, that is, innocent American lives. It did not address the question of other people's lives. We can never directly threaten innocent people in order to protect other innocent people, as much as you would like to be able to do this. Not every means that is used can be justified.

Yes, it sounds like a classic instance of the end justifying the means.

Sure. We've often said you can't do that. And this letter calls us back to that. Yes, I think this pastoral letter is going to put the Church on a collision course with the government eventually.

I found that one of the most impressive parts of the letter was where you said that deterrent peace is not true peace.

Yes, it's peace of a sort. It's not a genuine peace. Genuine peace has got to be based on justice, not on armed might.

I spoke with a man named Reverend Pollard, who is an Anglican priest who was an early pioneer at Oak Ridge and involved in weapons development. He's now a minister. And we discussed the Christian teaching in relation to weapons, and he said we have got to learn to live with nuclear weapons forever. Human nature will not change. He says, I am not wise enough to tell you how to do that, but I know that this is so. Would you agree with that?

No, I would not. I think in one sense he may be talking about what's really going to happen. I wouldn't be prepared to quarrel with that. But the Christian imperative is always to try. We have not been able to eliminate violence from the world. And that's often pointed out to us, that that's part of human nature. We describe that as the effect of original sin. It's true. We're always going to have sin, we're always going to have people who succumb to the temptation to do evil to accomplish their own ends. But that does not absolve us from trying. If we're going to be authentic, then as followers of Jesus Christ we are probably going to end up nailed to an atomic cross. But that doesn't absolve us from trying, and if you believe, if you have faith, if you truly believe, then you will believe in a resurrection that will follow that. I have no idea what it might look like. But the other view, which is a fatalistic view, you will find very pervasive among the fundamentalists here. They say that it's inevitable and it's going to come and, if you believe, then God is going to snatch you up in the Rapture and hold you above all of this and let you back down again afterward. I don't think that's a resurrection stance. I don't believe that's a Christian stance at all.

You said you have no idea what a resurrection from an atomic crucifixion would look like. But how can we think of anything rising up out of the annihilation of matter that nuclear weapons can bring?

Yes. Well, there may come the vaporization of the whole lot. The important point is, however, that that would come not by divine will but from human will. What is so important for the Church is to be the voice that would prevent that by Faith. While recognizing the difficulties that are posed by the communist philosophy, nevertheless I don't think you deal with that in terms of material bombs, because it's an idea, it's a philosophy, and it has to be met in that way. It's terribly risky to expose oneself to that. But if we truly believe in the power of faith, what's to say we can't convert that whole system? In fact, we were promised that at Fatima in Portugal where a divine message was delivered by Mary, saying that if we pray for the conversion of Russia and fast, and do penance, then war will be avoided.

You speak of conversion of Russia, but what about conversion of America?

Well, that's the point that is always overlooked, because it says not only that we should pray, but also that we should fast and do penance. It says we *must* do penance. And for what reason am I to do penance? It implies I'm on the wrong track. Our whole thrust is we have to use prayer, conversion, communication, and dialogue, to bring about change, exporting what we have that is best, and not exporting nuclear weapons. And I think there's a judgment that we don't have that much time.

It's so easy to acquiesce in the fatalistic approach because the momentum is obvious. Yet what you're saying is that someone with faith should be able to question this armed might and challenge it. Is that presupposing some fundamental difference between an ordinary, fatalistic person and a Christian?

Yes it is.

And how would you characterize that fundamental difference?

Well, if I profess to be a follower of Jesus Christ, then I'm going to trust in him and I'm not going to trust in the bomb.

And trusting in Christ means . . . what?

Living in faith, living in the possibility of conversion of other people, even of one's enemies. Christ's most radical statement was to love your neighbor. This was not a new statement. It was already in the Old Testament. But what Jesus added to that was a definition of who my neighbor is. My neighbor includes my enemy. Christ said, your neighbor is anyone who is in need, and if it's your enemy who is in need, he is your neighbor, and you must reach out to him and you must heal him. That's the challenge of the Christian Faith. It's an ideal that perhaps will never be realized, and Christ suffered the consequences, and so have all the martyrs through the centuries.

In the preface to the bishops' letter there was a very interesting point, that the bishops are attempting to address the nuclear issue from the point of view of Christian faith, yet nowhere in the Bible does it mention nuclear arms because these were beyond the imagination of people out of whom the Bible flowed. So these weapons really are a new kind of thing, aren't they? And they force us really to do new thinking.

Yes, as Albert Einstein said, with the splitting of the atom, everything changes now, save our mode of thinking. But the bishops have changed their mode of thinking. We've got to realize that indeed the nuclear age is a qualitatively different thing. It is not just a quantitative thing that we've got so many weapons. These nuclear weapons leave a legacy into second, third, fourth, fifth generations—we don't even know how far. And that makes it qualitatively different. In order to protect our way of life, our generation, do we have the right to threaten the very existence of future generations? George Kennan, the

former ambassador to the Soviet Union, says no, we do not have that right. It is true that the Bible doesn't mention nuclear weapons, the way it doesn't mention the automobile and all kinds of things. But it does give us the principles on which to make a judgment. In the Scriptures there is talk about people being a blessing to future generations, to the second, third, fourth, fifth generations.

That people should be?

Yes, they should be a blessing. And now we are in a position of being a curse and we're about to take that option.

And there's no way to have it both ways. You can't bless with a curse?

That's right. You can't provide security with insecurity.

Can you prepare for blessings by building up a stockpile of curses, just in case?

(*Laughs*) I don't think so. No. No.

Bishop Leroy T. Matthiesen, "Statement on the Production and Stockpiling of the Neutron Bomb," *West Texas Catholic Magazine*, August 23, 1981

"The announcement of the decision to produce and stockpile neutron warheads is the latest in a series of tragic anti-life positions taken by our government. This latest decision allegedly comes as a response to the possibility of a Soviet tank attack in central Europe. . . .

"God's gifts may be used for evil or good, for war or peace. The God of Israel warned the people of ancient times that the military use of the horse is 'a vain hope for safety. Despite its power it cannot save' (Psalms 33:17). Is not the military use of nuclear energy likewise a vain hope for safety? Despite its incredible power it cannot save. . . .

"We urge individuals involved in the production and stockpiling of nuclear bombs to consider what they are doing, to resign from such activities, and to seek employment in peaceful pursuits.

"Let us educate ourselves on nuclear armaments. Let us support those who are calling for an end to the arms race. Let us join men and women everywhere in prayer that peace may reign."

---

83. Kay Gable, widow of Don Gable, plutonium worker at Rocky Flats— Arvada, Colorado, July 16, 1983

My name is Kay, I'm the widow of Don Gable, who worked out at Rocky Flats for Rockwell International as a chemical process operator. He died three years ago in September.

How long did he work at the plant?

It was ten years lacking eight months.

Kay Gable

Did you know him before he worked there?

Yes, he started working there when he was twenty one and we got married when he was eighteen. Rocky Flats was his first serious job.

What was his job exactly?

He first hired on as a janitor. After a couple of months he went on as a process operator, and he was also a chemical operator, which meant working with plutonium and other radioactive materials.

Was he happy about being more than a janitor?

He was just real happy for being hired at Rocky Flats. We were a young couple, expecting a family, and the benefits were very good. The pay was great—you get what they call "hot pay" for working with radiation, so that's why he wanted the process operator's job, because the pay's a lot better.

Did he ever talk to you about job hazards?

Not when he first started. When people are first hired there, they're told that as long as you respect the materials you're working with and obey the safety rules, there are really no hazards. They are not told what their chances of getting cancer are by working there. It took several years before he really became anxious about it.

What made him anxious?

Well, it got to be kind of a daily routine, but alarms would go off and they would

173

find out the air was contaminated so they would have to go on to supplied air. And he had several accidents where he was maybe punctured or cut, or when there was a contamination in the air and he would breathe it. It was these things combined that started to make him worry.

What does a process operator do?

From what he described to me it involved mixing different chemicals to make the end product. It meant transferring them from one machine to another. It's like a line that goes from one process to the next, and they would have to run the machinery that did it. But he never talked about his job much.

Sometimes he would be late from work and of course I'd be worried, and one time he came home with a big sore on his side that he'd gotten from some type of chemical burn, which was radioactive, and they had to scrub it with all kinds of cleaners until they got a clean count on him.

The first year, he had at least thirteen accidents. The alarms would go off and they would just automatically put their supplied air on.

And they keep working?

There were times when they would have to work all day in supplied air, which was even more pay on top of the hot pay, and they would have to scrub an area until it was free of contamination.

You said he was also a chemical operator. . . .

That's when he used to work above the machinery that purified the chemicals, I think. He would have to be on top of these tanks, turning knobs to regulate them, and his head would be six inches from an exhaust pipe, and this exhaust material that went through it was radioactive. Once he asked if that would hurt his head and the supervisor said not to worry about his head—it was internal organs he would have to worry about.

How did Don know it was radioactive there?

They have people who monitor hot areas. And they would go around and put a detector up to the pipe, and the needle would go all the way over. Rockwell keeps records of all these readings.

When did Don start having physical trouble?

In March he started having headaches and getting spacy. I thought he was just being moody. He'd forget what he was doing, and he was having headaches, so he

started taking a lot of aspirin. When he wasn't feeling well he'd go to bed early. Once I woke up and he was having a seizure. That's when we took him to the emergency room, and a week later he had surgery for a brain tumor. This was eighteen months before he died. After the first surgery, they told me he had six to eighteen months to live. Then he developed an infection and they had to operate again and they removed a piece of his skull. He never did go back to work. He got better for a while, though, after he went to Los Alamos for some experimental treatments.

What did they do at Los Alamos?

They have a new experimental treatment called pion treatment that they're trying to perfect. It's run in a half-mile-long piece of machinery. They make a body cast for the patient—they only accept terminally ill patients—and the patient lies in this body cast, and the machine is pointed toward the tumor. They calculate exactly where the tumor is and they shoot pion granules into it.

What is a pion granule?

It's a type of radioactive material and it's shot at the target, which is the tumor, and it explodes wherever the tumor is, and it just kind of chips away at the tumor until, hopefully, it's gone. When Don left, it looked like the tumor was gone, except that there was still enough left that it just took over again.

Did either of you feel the plant was to blame for Don's condition?

We both felt right away it was from working with plutonium. We asked different doctors and they wouldn't really come right out and say, "Yes, that's what happened." When we'd get up to Los Alamos we'd ask the doctors there, but you couldn't even continue a conversation with them. But I remember one night I was there late while Don was having treatment and a technician came in, he was waiting to do some experiments with some mice and I got into a conversation with him and he said, "Oh yeah, most definitely, it will cause cancer." You know, we suspected that from the very first. But we put off contacting a lawyer for a long time, and then I decided to contact Bruce Debosky and talked to him and told him exactly what was going on and he took the case. Then it went to court and Don actually did testify six months before he died.

Did you ask Rocky Flats for the records of his exposures?

We went out there and asked for all Don's medical records. I don't know that we ever got them all, but they finally did give us some medical records.

What was your impression of the place?

The security is very heavy. You can't go through the gates without getting a badge. Inside, it's like a huge community of factories. It looked pretty ominous.

Did Don ever talk to you about the fact that he was making bombs?

He never did go into that. This was a job and it was feeding and clothing his family. I guess he felt like a lot of people do.

When did he die?

He was sick for eighteen months. He died in September. After he gave his testimony he got rapidly worse. He went back into the hospital to have a plastic plate put into his head because it concerned him having his head deformed like that. And he never recuperated after that.

Did you ask for an autopsy?

Oh yes. I wanted his body tested, and the autopsy shows the amount of radiation and everything. When he actually did die, I got a phone call at the hospital and they took me to the main desk. This was within an hour after he died, and I got this phone call from a man that I don't know. He told me who he was and where he was from, I think it was Los Alamos, that's the impression I got, but I was in a state of shock so that just passed right over me, and I didn't realize it was an important call at the time. He went on to say that he wanted to do studies on Don's brain and they wanted permission to take it to do studies for the pion treatments that he'd had and the effects they'd had, and I said that's fine, but I told him also I wanted it tested for the amount of radiation in his brain, especially of plutonium, and that I wanted a written report sent to me. I specifically asked for that.

So you had your wits about you.

Yeah, I knew what I was doing, and they assured me that I would get it. So a while went by, we didn't get anything. I called Los Alamos and the most information I could get was: "We can't find any records, the doctor in charge of that isn't in right now, we'll get back to you." And no one ever got in touch with me again. Then Bruce took over and he found out from them that the brain had been momentarily lost, and that was about the gist of it, that they had just lost the brain. They didn't know where it was. It was lost. Which is hideous. Eventually they did come up with it again, but it had been used and tested so much for their own purposes that they said there wasn't enough left of it to test for plutonium anymore.

Did you have a written agreement with them about testing for plutonium?

No, this was all just over the phone. Los Alamos called me within an hour of Don's death to do tests on his brain. What really gets me, though, is how did they know he died? I mean, it was within an hour of his death and I get this phone call. There was no doctor there. The family and I are the only ones that knew.

Whatever happened about the lost brain?

Well, even if that were the only incident that happened to me it's very incriminating. But before Don died, more happened. After he testified the first time, we decided to demand all the records they had on the pipe that he worked by for the last ten years, and we also asked for all the readings of radiation that they took coming from that pipe. Don was in the hospital when they finally delivered the records, a whole thick stack of papers, all supposedly of this pipe, and I guess they were hoping that he was disoriented so that he wouldn't realize it was the right pipe but in the wrong room. So the radiation factor wasn't there yet. But Don picked that out right away and he told Bruce, "This isn't even in the right room." So Bruce takes them back and says, "What's going on?" And they go, "Oops, we made a mistake, sorry about that." Then they take another month, or maybe longer, to finally tell us that they couldn't find any documents at all to the pipe in the room where Don worked—they said the papers must be lost. And then after Don died, they secretly dismantled the pipe altogether and got rid of it.

How do you know?

Bruce found that out. When they told him they lost the papers on the pipe, Bruce said, "Well, let's get readings directly off the pipe today, since you've lost the records." That's when they told him that they couldn't find the pipe either. They had also lost the pipe.

Do you feel connected to other people who have had things like this happen to them?

That's my main objective—to help other people this has happened to—and that's what is happening, as you can tell with the other cases that are coming out. There are

about a dozen suits of Rocky Flats widows now—all since we started with Don's.

Don was the first?

Well, actually a man called Crumbach was the first, but he was quite a bit earlier. Of this group I believe that Don was the first. I'm really glad more cases are happening because this is a moral issue to me. I think people need to open their eyes and become aware of what's going on. What I really want is for Rockwell and the Department of Energy to come clean and take responsibility for what's happening.

How long will the trial last?

It'll go on for years. Even if at one point we should win, they'll appeal it.

The matter of the loss of the brain, of the records of the pipe, and of the pipe itself, is that part of the suit?

No. Right now, we're just taking one step at a time. I'd like to see something done eventually on that, though. There's not too many people that have stood up to them. That's why I'm hoping by voicing my opinion and trying to find out what's going on that more people will start saying, "Hey, this is happening to me too." I think if a person wants to work there that's his choice, but I want him to know what he's walking into.

Update: On June 4, 1987, the Colorado Court of Appeals ruled that Don Gable's death was caused by on-the-job exposure to permissible levels of radiation. Rocky flats did not appeal the ruling.

---

84. John Smitherman, atomic veteran, Operation Crossroads— Mulberry, Tennessee, July 31, 1983

John, you are suing the government for your cancer. How did it happen?

Well, the beginning of my problem started back in 1946. I was on what they call Operation Crossroads in the Marshall Islands at Bikini Atoll, and I was serving on board the USS *Allan M. Sumner*, Destroyer 692. My position at that time was fireman. This was for the first two nuclear tests that America was involved in directly after the war.

After they had dropped the first one, which was called Able, on July 1, 1946, I went aboard the carrier USS *Independence*. It was one of the test ships, and after the blast there was a fire on the back side of the ship. I went aboard the *Independence* to fight that fire.

How big was the Able blast?

I'm not sure, about the same as Hiroshima. We fought fire aboard the *Independence* one hour on and two hours off. I did that three times. And when we came on board the landing craft that was waiting for us, we had to go through and be monitored by Geiger counters.

John Smitherman

Was anybody on board the ship monitoring it?

Several men with white coats did come on—they were covered up real good and they had Geiger counters on them. Of course, at that time, we were all just a bunch of young sailors—I was just seventeen—and none of us had the slightest idea of what a Geiger counter was, or of what radiation was because this was never explained to us at any time. The only thing that I was wearing at that time was a pair of shorts, a pair of tennis shoes or sneakers or whatever you want to call them, with a turned-down sailor hat sitting on top of my head. That was the only protective type of clothing I had on.

Did you have any thoughts when you saw the people with Geiger counters coming on board all covered up?

I had no thoughts whatsoever because, well, I myself was a mountain boy. I came from the Appalachian Mountains. And nothing ever entered my mind about the dangers of radiation. Nothing was ever explained to us about it—or if it had been, it was never explained to me.

So you trusted the government when they said there wasn't a problem?

We trusted the captain of our ship. He said there was nothing to worry about.

What happened after Able?

The Baker shot was next. We watched it from a ship about nineteen miles away from the explosion, and mist from the mushroom fell on the deck of our ship and sand fell on our deck, little pieces of metal and rocks—even that far away. And while all this mess was falling we went back into the target zone. This was about ten hours later. We were ordered below deck, and we tried to wash off as much of it as we could. The mushroom cloud was still in the air when we came back in. It stayed in the air for almost two days—we could see that. The whole time we were there it was so hot we slept outside on the deck of the ship. Because of the tremendous heat in the hold of the ship we spent as much time as possible on deck. Everyone walked around in shorts and T-shirts—some went without T-shirts. To cool off we'd go swimming in the lagoon. We drank water from the lagoon too. There were no restrictions on that. You know, we were supposed to stay out there longer. They were planning to have another test. But it was canceled so we cleared out.

When did you start having health problems?

After the Baker shot I had complained of the swelling in both my feet and in my legs and was treated for it in the hospital in the islands, Honolulu. They said it was a possible kidney infection.

I have never had any problems with my kidneys—I say and maintain the swelling of my feet and legs was created and caused by the radiation fallout.

From the Medical Evaluation of Mr. John D. Smitherman, Veteran: Claim for compensation due to radiation exposure from Atomic Bomb blasts in Pacific. By Thomas F. Mancuso, M.D., Research Professor, Occupational Medicine, University of Pittsburgh, August 28, 1980

Abstracts from Medical Evaluation by Dr. Thomas Mancuso

. . . It is stated that "no records have been produced showing that the veteran received radiation exposure in the year 1946 during the nuclear testing and exposure." The basis for that statement was . . . "that there were no records for the veteran for the year 1946 concerning nuclear testing and exposure."

The implication clearly made is that since there are no records for veteran Mr. John D. Smitherman, therefore there was no exposure to radiation. The implication is definitely misleading because as stated in letter (August 9, 1979) from

Lt. Col. Edwin T. Still—to the Honorable Senator Jim Sasser—"common practice during this test was to [give a radiation exposure film] badge only to a percentage of ships' crews. Careful review of radiation dosimetry data for the ships has revealed film badge data for 26 of the 262 crew members."

Further, Mr. John R. Smitherman has stated he never was issued a film badge. . . .

The premise of denial based upon "no records of exposure" is not tenable, is not valid and should be reversed.

Dr. Karl Z. Morgan, Neely Professor of Nuclear Engineering, Georgia Institute of Technology, actually directed and carried out the radiation measurements after the Atomic Bomb Testing. . . .

In the letter of October 23, 1979, from Dr. Karl Morgan to Mr. John D. Smitherman, he makes the statement "the Navy did not have instruments to measure the Beta dose. . . ."

The importance of this absence of Beta monitoring by the Navy, and the absence therefore of any record of such radiation exposure in the veteran's records, is further emphasized by the letter of May 19, 1980, by Dr. Karl Morgan to Mr. John Smitherman. In that letter he states as follows:

"After reading over your file I am more convinced than ever that your medical problem originated from Beta exposure during your activities following shortly after weapons detonations at test Baker and possibly also after test Able in the South Pacific. As I indicated in my earlier letter of October 23, 1978, the Beta dose was very high all over the atoll after test Baker. This high Beta activity was due both to selective retention of fission product Beta emitters and to the high-energy Betas from Sodium-24 (4.17 and 1.39 MeV). The sand and small pieces of metal that fell on the ships and on the islands were very radioactive. Although some of the fission products could be washed down from top side of the ships, much of it stuck to such substances as paint, tar, rust, plastic, canvas, etc. The salt (NaCl) of the ocean spray quickly dried on the hot ship decks and the Na-24 so retained resulted in an average Beta/gamma ratio of 3 and in many cases an average of 600. These high-energy Beta rays penetrated more than a centimeter into the body tissues (the 4.17 MeV Beta has a range of 1.04 cm in muscle) causing not only the erythema you experienced, but deep tissue damage and damage to blood vessels, lymph nodes and the entire reticuloendothelial system. From the measurements my six-man team made and from information in your file, I estimate you could have received Beta doses of 1,000 to 1,800 rads to various parts of your body—especially to your feet and legs. You may wish to write to others on my six-man survey team at the Baker test. I can look up their names if you wish. The Navy took my data and I have not seen it since.". . .

There are only several conclusions that can be derived from those circumstances. . . . The Navy has to

1. acknowledge that it knowingly did not incorporate the Beta data into the radiation record of the veterans; or

2. admit that it withheld important radiation information that significant Beta radiation exposure did occur for the veterans in those particular tests; or

3. acknowledge that it misplaced the Beta radiation data, and therefore it did not get into the radiation records of the veterans.

The only interpretations that can be drawn, under these circumstances, is that in either instance the veteran is defrauded of his rights and a proper, fair hearing of his case when the information did exist and was improperly withheld by the Navy.

Conclusion

. . . I conclude that there is more than a reasonable probability that the radiation exposure, through radiation fallout, sustained by Mr. John D. Smitherman during his participation in the Atomic Bomb Blasts initiated and caused damage to the lymphatic system with resultant development of lymphedema of his extremities, which subsequently established the sequence of changes in his tissues over the years, which finally led to the amputations and has now involved the upper extremities.

I recommend that his compensation claim be approved.

Thomas F. Mancuso, M.D.

---

85. Operation Crossroads Hearing
Washington, D.C., December 11, 1985

In November 1985, the United States General Accounting Office published a report entitled "Operation Crossroads Personnel Radiation Exposure Estimates Should Be Improved." The opening page of the document states its principal findings in a memo to Senator Alan Cranston:

"The report found that certain adjustments in the calculation of Crossroads participants' radiation exposure estimates may be necessary because (1) no allowance was made for inaccuracies associated with the film badges worn by participants to measure external radiation exposure, (2) comprehensive personnel decontamination procedures were lacking or not followed, and (3) no estimates were made for radiation exposure through ingestion or open wounds and the estimate for inhalation may be in error by a factor of 5 or 10."

In Washington, D.C., on November 14 and December 11, 1985, the Committee on Veterans Affairs held hearings on the GAO report's findings. Lieutenant General John L. Pickitt, director of the Defense Nuclear Agency (DNA), was called upon to testify. He submitted a number of documents into the record. First among them:

"FACT SHEET—DNA Public Affairs Office, Washington, D.C., 20305, 3 April, 1984. Subject: Nuclear Test Personnel Review Program (NTPR)

"*Background of NTPR program.* Between 1945 and 1962, the Atomic Energy Commission carried out some 235 atmospheric nuclear tests, principally in Nevada and the Pacific Ocean. An estimated 203,000 Department of Defense (DOD) personnel, military and civilian, were involved in this testing and many received low-level ionizing radiation exposures in the performance of various activities. Almost all the exposures were well within internationally accepted radiation exposure limits. . . .

"No firm evidence exists to show that exposure to low levels of ionizing radiation would cause adverse health effects. . . ."

The second document submitted by Pickitt was an affidavit from Gerhard Dessauer:

"I, Gerhard Dessauer, being first duly cautioned and sworn, state that, during Operation CROSSROADS, I was Chief of the Photographic Dosimetry Section. I further state that:

"At Operation CROSSROADS film badges provided permanent record of the radiation doses received by personnel entering the lagoon after Test Able, and again after Test Baker. . . .

"The Photographic Dosimetry section at Operation CROSSROADS accomplished its assigned task successfully. We had no problems arising from inadequate materials, procedures, or personnel. None of the 40,000 participants accumulated a clinically significant dose of radiation during our operation in July and August 1946."

Following are excerpts from Pickitt's prepared statement to the committee:

"Mr. Chairman, members of the committee, I am Lieutenant General John L. Pickitt, director of the Defense Nuclear Agency and the executive agent for the Department of Defense Nuclear Test Personnel Review (NTPR) program. . . .

"The mission of the Nuclear Test Personnel Review program is to:

- Identify the approximately 200,000 DOD participants and determine their exposures.
- Provide assistance to veterans and the Veterans Administration on claims for compensation.
- Sponsor studies to ascertain whether test participants experienced any unusual incidences of death or illness.
- Notify veterans of Veterans Administration benefits and Department of Defense assistance.
- Declassify test-related documents and

publish historical reports covering DOD activities at the tests.

"Since the inception of the program, the Department of Defense has expended more than 1,000 man-years of effort and $54 million to ascertain the facts. . . .

"NTPR has, thus far, identified 165,000 of the estimated 200,000 DOD participants at the tests. In addition we have recovered or reconstructed radiation exposure for 160,000 of the participants. In the course of our research we discovered that, in general, the exposures were quite low. . . .

"DNA has published a 41-volume, 9,029-page personnel-oriented history of the atmospheric nuclear tests. This effort was one of the largest historical research projects ever undertaken concerning peacetime DOD activities. . . .

"Decontamination of personnel who visited the target ships is not a significant issue with respect to doses actually received. Between July 25, 1946, the date of the detonation [Baker] giving rise to the contamination, and July 31, 1946, only about 4,900 personnel boarded target ships. These personnel were scientists retrieving data from their instrumentation, damage inspections teams, and accompanying radiation safety monitors. Most of these personnel had extensive experience as a result of their previous work on the Manhattan Project and all of them were knowledgeable concerning radiation safety and decontamination procedures. . . .

"There is no reason to assume that the approximately 9,000 people (21% of the Crossroads participants) who actually boarded the target vessels received any additional exposure as a result of inadequate personal decontamination. . . . We have great sympathy for any veteran who is suffering from disease or disability. At the same time, however, we have an obligation to assure that the doses assigned to individuals reflect, as accurately as possi-

ble, both the historical facts and the best available scientific methodology. As we proceed with the NTPR program, we will continue to seek out and apply any sound suggestions or criticism which we receive.

"We will be happy to answer any questions you may have."

Senator Alan Cranston: If we were conducting Operation Crossroads again and sent in men immediately afterward on the ships, would you send them in with or without protective clothing, given what we now know?

Lieutenant General Pickitt: We would always proceed from the most cautious and protective position possible.

Cranston: You would give them protective clothing now which they were not given then?

Senator Alan Cranston at microphone

Pickitt: Sir, they were then. They were given protective clothing.

Cranston: Well, what are these photographs of people on ships that are not protected?

Pickitt: Those pictures were taken after the ships had had protected monitoring teams go on board with monitors and with detection equipment to determine if the environment was safe, so that work teams could be cleared on board. Each work team was also accompanied by an experienced and trained monitor to monitor the dosage that members of each of the teams accumulated, so that they could be evacuated from the ships before anyone accumulated excessive radiation.

Cranston: I do not think there is any evidence that the first monitors that went in wore protective clothing. But my question to you is, would you permit the people that we see photographed there without protective clothing today to go in under similar circumstances without protective clothing?

Pickitt: I think we would approach it in the same way we did then, sir.

Cranston: You would send them in

177

without protective clothing?

Pickitt: They went in with protective clothing until the environment was confirmed to be safe for people without special protective clothing.

Cranston: Well, we have photographs of people without protective clothing on those ships shortly after the tests. Would you permit them today, given our current state of knowledge, to go in without protective clothing as photographed?

Pickitt: If the environment had been checked and been deemed safe, exactly as it was done in 1946, sir . . .

Senator Jay Rockefeller: Here you are, General Pickitt, a good man, a true professional defending the honor of your nation, but in an awkward position. It would seem to me, by taking into account various reports that show that you cannot conclusively prove the relationship between radiation exposure and illnesses, one must decide what is right to do.

Now, I guess you cannot prove the origins of atomic veterans' illnesses scientifically, but is there not a moral question here? The Department of Defense ordered these things to happen, and here it is forty years later, almost, and the Department of Defense through DNA is saying, "We do not have the proof of this," or "We do not feel we have the proof of this." There are people dying, and these are people who were simply answering a call.

We can talk about clean suits, dirty suits, foam, clean ships, whatever. But here were people assigned to duties about which no one knew enough. Radiation was something that nobody understood. The servicemen, though, were doing what they were asked to do. . . .

These are your people. They were your orders, generically. It was the business of war and of preparation for war, therefore, that leads to all of this.

And I do not understand that. I am asking you a moral question of right or wrong. Why do you feel an obligation to dispute? Unless you think that these folks are trying to foist something upon the U.S. Government, which I do not believe they are doing. They have been waiting forty years.

Please feel free to generally answer my question, General.

Pickitt: . . . I am unaware of anyone in DNA that does not—could not—sign up to and share with your feelings on the moral issue, Senator. What DNA is trying to do to the best of its ability is assess exactly what happened to each individual. . . .

While morally I share your concern I think you can probably share my sense of responsibility that we need to have a substantive basis for making medical decisions. And that they should be factually as supportable as possible for our baseline.

Rockefeller: Does not the forty-year factor bother you? I mean, people are dying.

Pickitt: Yes. It bothers me that people are dying. Cancer, unfortunately, does not have only one source. It occurs as a result of many factors not associated just with atomic tests. . . .

Rockefeller: I guess the thing that bothers me is, after forty years, if the science has not produced itself, we are going to be very quickly in a situation where we are not going to need the science because the people are not going to be alive anymore. By definition, forty years plus, if you consider the age that each individual volunteered or was drafted for the military, puts the atomic veterans at least at fifty-eight years old. . . . At some point, this is going to be very academic, and are we not going to look back with a tremendous amount of regret that we relied so on science?

Chairman Frank Murkowski: Senato your ten minutes have expired, and, of course, this line of questioning is appropriate in a sense, but somewhat redundant inasmuch as it is the whole point of the hearing.

men, both of them, careful doctors and far-seeing scientists. I had to trust my life to them; I think you can trust their words.

"My primary job at Bikini, in both tests, was to fly in over the target fleet at 2,000, 1,000, and 500 feet, taking measurements of radiation coming up from the ships and the water or in the air. These measurements we radioed to the control ship. . . .

"One caveat: Not one of us is a true expert here. . . . All we can tell you is an imperfect and partial story. But that story *itself* is so astounding that it can be read without the help of experts.

"Like the one-bomb, one-city phenomenon in Japan, here is a great American naval task force, proud, sleek, beautiful, suddenly brought to a stop, run aground, dead, and ultimately sunk by—by the leftover pieces of one tiny inefficient plutonium bomb.

"It wasn't blast, it wasn't fire that killed that task force, as of course you all know. It was radiation, radiation effective beyond all expectation. On or about the 16th day post-Baker the decision had to be made to abandon the ships and the tests.

"Why? . . . Admiral Blandy, Admiral Solberg, Admiral Parsons, General Stilwell, etc. were tough, intelligent military leaders not easily spooked, not likely to be panicked by the data, the numbers Colonel Stafford Warren had assembled for them from Geiger and film badge readings all

Dr. David Bradley

Dr. David Bradley testified at the same hearings. His prepared statement reads:

"My name is David Bradley, retired surgeon and emeritus teacher at Dartmouth College. In 1946 I was one of Colonel Warren's 'Geiger Men,' the first doctors in military history to have to deal with radioactivity under field conditions. Fortunately we had received months of training from such men as Colonel Stafford Warren and Dr. Karl Z. Morgan, great

over the target area. From the gangways, from the evaporators, from food, clothes, shoes, from the hot spots on deck, from the air in the mess rooms and corridors, from the beaches, water, fish, from everywhere sailors and soldiers and scientists went.

"The numbers must have been horrendous . . . so horrendous, in fact, that I think we've been trying ever since to hide them from the veterans and from ourselves."

From Dr. Bradley's testimony to the Committee on Veterans Affairs:

Dr. Bradley: I think it must be perfectly clear to this committee that you are not going to get any science any more than you have, and it is not going to be very good science whatever you get. . . . I do not consider that we had any really satisfactory safety measures. . . . At Bikini we ran around there in shorts and skivvies and baseball hats and tennis shoes; that is what we had, and that was what everybody used, as far as I can remember. . . .

After Baker, my buddy was in a plane just ahead of me. . . . He was running into radiation back and forth across the target area of somewhere between 30 and 50 roentgens, and he did not want to continue the survey. . . . Now that would mean that at the water level . . . it would have been something like 2,500 roentgens. This was not an operation that produced a very small amount of radiation.

I have a report of one film badge that I have been able to run down from that Baker day. What do you suppose, after us running into all sorts of radiation up there, what do you suppose that film badge said, Mr. Chairman?

Chairman Murkowski: I have no idea.

Bradley: You are right. It did not, either. Zero. I do not know what the film badge was made of, tar paper or something like that. Anyway, that is what it is reported to have read. . . .

I would like to say one more thing, though, to show you how thin that safety operation was. When all the big shots went back home about the 15th of August, Colonel Warren and some others called me in and said, Bradley, you are in charge of the laboratory, that is, the water-counting laboratory, the ship survey laboratory, and urinalysis for 3,000 buckets of urine. You are in charge of the laboratory.

And I said—because orders are orders—"Colonel, can I have a book giving me some guidelines or some standards or something like that to go by so I will know what I am doing?" You know what they said? "You cannot have it." And I said, "Why not? I've got to. How can I operate?" They said, "It is secret. It is classified. We cannot leave that information out here. Do the best you can."

That is not much of a safety operation. . . .

Why is it that the atomic people, the atomic veterans, have to prove to the government that they were injured by radiation? No other veteran has to do this.

I do not understand these things. And I am ashamed, I am ashamed that this is a policy that we put on these people, good people, willing to die for the country. And that is our policy. I cannot believe it.

Mr. Chairman, I feel so strongly about this, I—I guess I will not say any more.

86. Marshallese in Washington, D.C.

Left to right: Julian Riklon, from Rongelap; John Abraham, from Einewetok; Ishmael John, senator from Einewetok; Tanaki Juda, from Bikini; Mike Jibas, from Bikini; Jijon Eknilang, from Rongelap; Edmond Billiet, from Rongelap; and Jeton Anjain, senator from Rongelap.

This delegation of Marshallese came to Judge Harkin's Courtroom Number 1 in the U.S. Court of Claims Building, Washington, to witness the legal argument over their right to proceed with a $5 billion lawsuit against the United States Government.

Jijon Eknilang, third from the right, was three years old at the time of the Bravo test. She has had eight miscarriages and/or stillbirths and has adopted two children. Edmond Billiet, second from the right, was a schoolteacher on Rongelap at the time of the Bravo test. He warned the Rongelap community not to eat the food or drink the water without having been told anything about the test.

87. ABCC, Hiroshima

Buddha in Atomic Bomb Casualty Commission shrine room, Hiroshima

The prayer in the shrine room next to the autopsy room at the ABCC (RERF) reads:

"This is a room for waiting. It stands beside the invisible bridge between the world we know and mystery. Here we wait for those we love to make their ultimate gift, to help physicians everywhere reduce pain and suffering. This is a room for thanksgiving. Here we gratefully remember our indebtedness to our loved ones for kindness, humor, love, courage. This is a room for prayer. Here we pray for the souls of the departed, for all mankind, and for ourselves, that even in our sorrow, we may be given something of the peace that passeth all understanding and strength for the tasks that lie ahead."

Carl Siebentritt, Federal Emergency Management Agency— Washington, D.C., June 5, 1984

Tell me, Carl, what is your job?

Well, the job is the research, development, and pilot production of instruments for nuclear attack preparedness and other radiological emergencies. The program is based on the Federal Civil Defense Act of 1950. That act was reinforced in 1980 by what we call Title 5, which requires that we specifically provide for an improved radiological defense and apply the resources for nuclear attack preparedness to other radiological emergency contingencies wherever possible.

In other words, if there's an attack, there's the problem of fallout, and if you develop machines to monitor fallout, you can use the same machines to monitor, say, a meltdown?

If you had the worst conceivable accident with a nuclear power plant, these instruments would be useful. But a nuclear power plant is a very forgiving device, and it's highly unlikely that it could give you an accident serious enough to require these types of instruments.

I heard FEMA is working on a new line of monitoring instruments that are almost ready, which are different from the Civil Defense types in place now.

That is right. Historically, Civil Defense only gets money when there is a national emergency. The last time we received money was at the time of the Cuban missile crisis. Then the floodgates opened and we bought $50 million worth of instruments. We acquired five million instruments at that time.

Was there a crash program to turn out those five million instruments?

There was a crash program, and soon after they were received and paid for, many thousands of the instruments were unstable, so in the interim what we've done is refurbish and repair and retrofit them to where they are now a very real national resource. But the problem is, they are over twenty years old, and we can't get certain parts for them anymore.

Is this why you're working on a new line?

That is right. We can now make instruments that will not require close maintenance and calibration, and they are better instruments.

You said you get money only when there's a national emergency. Is there some kind of new national emergency going on today that has made money available for this new line?

No, we do not have money for production today. We have just a very modest amount of money for engineering and development, and we invest this money with experts at Oak Ridge National Laboratory and with our own in-house facility, and we augment this money with monies from the Navy and the Army to do the necessary research and development.

So everybody's interested in it, but it's still in a prototype stage rather than a mass production stage?

The dosimeters are in the pilot production phase. We have a design, and it looks very, very good. Now we are in the process of scaling up the tooling. The tooling has to be mass-production tooling, which will enable precision instruments to be put together by relatively unskilled people. We feel that in a national emergency these are the only people that would be available to work on this. Another feature of the design is that it would have a long shelf-life. Still another feature is simplicity of operation. You want to be able to train citizens in the use of them real fast. Anybody that can operate a television set would be able to operate one of these instruments and get the data. This is one of the meters here.

How would you describe it?

It's a device about the length of a fountain pen. It looks like a Magic Marker. But it has a microscope in it, and it has a pocket clip, and it's made out of plastic. In use, you look through the instrument. But first you have to charge it on this charging unit.

The charging unit looks like a gun, sort of. How does it work?

It requires no batteries. We generate electricity in it by squeezing a crystal that puts out the volts when it's squeezed. It's a piezoelectric crystal. So you just squeeze the crystal and you charge the instrument until it has about 150 volts across an electrometer, then it should register zero. If you look through it you can see it's at zero now.

Oh, and the black line on the bottom tells you what the levels are?

Well, you wear it in your pocket and it will register your personal accumulated radiation exposure.

I see. And it's on a scale, it says milliroentgens, from 0 to 200. Underneath it says "RITF." What does "RITF" mean?

This is a prototype instrument made in our Radiological Instrument Test Facility in the Navy yard.

Okay. And it goes up to 200 milliroentgens?

Yes. That's what we refer to as a low-range instrument. We could easily make a high-range instrument by introducing a capacitor that controls the range. So the next one that we are already making prototypes for will be the high-range version of this. That one will become the real workhorse Civil Defense instrument.

Carl Siebentritt

And how high will the high-range workhorse go?

The high-range instruments have two scales. One goes from about 0 to 20 roentgens, and the other goes from 0 to 200 roentgens.

And those lower meters read in milliroentgens?

Yes. A milliroentgen is a thousandth of a roentgen.

So the high-range meters are higher than the low-range instruments by a thousandfold. That's quite a jump!

That's right. But these are the ranges you'll need to be monitoring when you've got real serious radiation insults happening. You're talking about life-threatening doses as a result of nuclear attack. That is the name of the game. And when I said life-threatening, you're talking about 450 roentgens or more that you could achieve if you didn't have good shelter. And if you were close to Ground Zero, but away from the blast and fire, you could achieve these kinds of doses if you are unprotected. You could be outside and you could be getting enormous dose levels of radiation downwind, early on.

What happens to a person in a field of radiation that's 200 roentgens an hour?

You could become very sick if you received an acute dose of 200 roentgens.

What happens at 20 roentgens?

At 20 you would not be sick, but 20 roentgens would be the maximum that you would like to receive in a peacetime incident. . . .

That you would like *to receive?*

No, not *like* to, but that you would ever want to receive in a peacetime incident. You wouldn't want to go above that.

For a worker in a commercial nuclear reactor, isn't it something like 5?

It's 5, yes. But the idea is that you'll be able to see 5 on a scale of 20 and maintain control.

And what is the unit called?

Well, it's two pieces. There's the cylindrical pen-shaped device that's called the dosimeter, it measures the doses, and the gun-type device is the dosimeter-charger.

What will it cost to make the complete set, the charger and the dosimeter together?

Well, for the dosimeter, the pen, the cost of the materials comes to between fifty cents and a dollar. We estimate that the labor involved in assembling it will be from ten to twenty minutes, so you add labor costs on top of that.

And the gun? The dosimeter-charger?

We don't have a real handle on the cost of materials and labor for the charger yet. But it's designed to keep these costs low.

And the people who will have to do more hazardous work will be getting the ones with the higher scale?

That may not be the case, because you need the higher scale for early on, that's when the radiation rates are high. You know, there's the good news and the bad news about radiation. The good news is that once the fallout's down it decays very rapidly. But the bad news is that it never will really ever go away; the radiation levels will always be higher than they are today. And so what you have to do is minimize the insult in the first hours after, let's say, a nuclear attack, when you know that you have fallout. And then you keep people sheltered with as much material between them and the radiation as possible, and you give them the capability of improving their shelter. And then when they are able to come out you want to minimize any further insult. So the chances are that the 20-roentgen meters would be used in post-attack recovery, whereas the 200-roentgen meter is needed up front where there's a possibility of getting up to 200 roentgens in the poorer shelters.

And what about if it's a low level of activity, not even on the low scale, but it's in the air, and you inhale it?

Well, you can easily protect against inhaling fallout particles as we understand them. Certainly you don't want to ingest them, but it would be hard to do, they're of such a size that it would be easy to screen them out with a handkerchief, or a respirator, or even without any of these. Nasal hairs would keep them out of your nose.

So we're not talking about a dust as we commonly understand that term?

That's right, we're not talking about gases and small particles that can be inhaled. In the area where you have heavy fallout, the particles are like volcanic ash or sand on the beach, beach sand.

And you don't inhale sand?

It's not like . . . if you looked at the film—oh, what was it called?—*The Day After*. They had fallout being like powder, like flour. And we don't envision it that way.

What was that, a mistake by the makeup crew?

I think it was done for effect. They knew better, but it was done to show that, you know, there would be stuff on the ground, but you couldn't really show its presence without that effect. It's kind of hard to show sand, and particularly sand on sand, and sand on grass.

Key Lake tailings dam

So, okay, you have these different monitoring instruments, some of which are near completion, and others have a way to go yet. When do you go into mass production on them?

We're hoping to get money from Congress to go into mass production. We feel that we're close enough with this dosimeter to award contracts for mass production in the private sector.

What does mass production amount to?

It means starting to produce these things so fast you can't cart them away. We hope to start a production line to produce millions of them over a period of years.

89. The Whey Train

According to the Society for Radiation and Environmental Research in Neuherberg, near Munich, the total amount of cesium-137 deposited by the Chernobyl cloud in a single day in southern Germany exceeded by five times the total cesium deposited there as fallout during 20 years of bomb tests. The total dose to the general population in southern Germany from Chernobyl fallout was between 100 and 200 millirems, the equivalent of 20 to 40 chest Xrays.

90. Stanrock Tailings Wall

Uranium mine tailings contain uranium, arsenic, ammonia, rock, sand, sulfuric acid, lime, nitrates, nickel, iron, molybdenum, copper, oxidizing agents, thorium, radium, radon gas, and all the other elements in the uranium decay chain. Radioactive and toxic waste from the Key Lake Mill is pumped into the Key Lake tailings pond; this pond employs the most advanced system of uranium tailings management available. The embankment along the horizon is made of sand and glacial till. The floor of the pond is covered with a bentonite seal. This tailings storage facility has been engineered to last many thousands of years.

91. Low-level Radioactive Burial Markers

92. Windscale

Windscale in England and Cap de la Hague near Cherbourg in France are the largest commercial reprocessing facilities in the world. Windscale was recently renamed Sellafield.

West Germany will soon complete its large-scale commercial reprocessing plant in Wackersdorf, Bavaria. The Wackersdorf facility will be able to separate out tons of plutonium per year from spent nuclear fuel. Intense public opposition has created delays in construction.

Security fence at Wackersdorf reprocessing site, West Germany

93. Windscale, Back View

"Ministry of Agriculture, Fisheries, and Food Radioactive Substances Act, 1960

"Certificate of Authorization for the Disposal of Radioactive Waste

"This is to certify that British Nuclear Fuels Limited (hereinafter called 'the Company') is authorised under section 6(1) of the Act, with effect from 1 April 1971, to dispose of liquid radioactive waste from the premises situated on a licensed site occupied by the Company known as Windscale Works, Seascale, in the County of Cumberland (hereinafter called 'the premises'), by discharging it into the sea by means of the existing pipelines constructed for this purpose. . . .

"In this Certificate . . . any reference to the sum total of curies is a reference to the sum total ascertained by measuring by any generally accepted method or, where it is not reasonably practicable to ascertain the sum total by measuring, the sum total estimated in any generally accepted manner.

"In witness whereof the Official Seal of the Minister of Agriculture, Fisheries and Food is hereunto affixed on 26 March 1971."

94. Hanford Tank Farm

The new tanks in this tank farm each hold 1.3 million gallons of highly corrosive, high-level waste from plutonium-producing reprocessing operations.

These tanks are intended for an interim storage period of fifty years. It is felt that in that time a solution will have been found for the permanent disposal of these high-level wastes.

95. Irretrievable Nuclear Waste Disposal Test Shaft

This is a diagram from the May 1984 technical report issued by the Human Interference Task Force. The report, "Reducing the Likelihood of Future Human Activities That Could Affect Geologic High-Level Waste Repositories," was prepared for the Office of Nuclear Waste Isolation, Battelle Memorial Institute, Columbus, Ohio, under contract No. DE-AC02-83CH10140 with the U.S. Department of Energy.

"*Abstract*: The disposal of radioactive wastes in deep geologic formations provides a means of isolating the waste from people until the radioactivity has decayed to safe levels. However, isolating people from the wastes is a different problem, since we do not know what the future condition of society will be. The Human Interference Task Force was convened by the U.S. Department of Energy to determine whether reasonable means exist (or could be developed) to reduce the likelihood of future humans unintentionally intruding on radioactive waste isolation systems. The task force concluded that significant reductions in the likelihood of human interference could be achieved, for perhaps thousands of years into the future, if appropriate steps are taken to communicate the existence of the repository.

Consequently, for two years the task force directed most of its study toward the area of long-term communication. Methods are discussed for achieving long-term communication by using permanent markers and widely disseminated records, with various steps taken to provide multiple levels of protection against loss, destruction, and major language/societal changes.

Also developed is the concept of a universal symbol to denote 'Caution: Biohazardous Waste Buried Here.' If used for the thousands of non-radioactive biohazardous waste sites in this country alone, a symbol could transcend generations and language change, thereby vastly improving the likelihood of successful isolation of all buried biohazardous wastes.

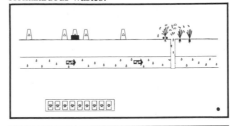

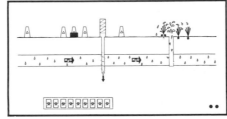

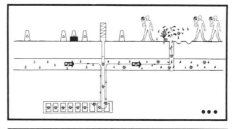

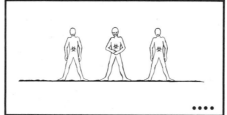

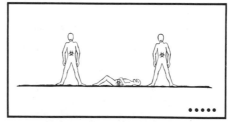

Pictographic Presentation of Biohazardous Caution Message

"The objective [of the pictograph] is to convey to the reader the sense that if the area below the markers is disturbed, toxic substances will enter the ground water and lead to severe consequences."

96. Irradiated Reactor Fuel Rods

The West Valley plant (1966–1972) was America's first—and only—attempt at commercial reprocessing.

97. Dr. Rosalie Bertell—
Toronto, Canada, March 12, 1986

Dr. Bertell, I'd like to ask you if there is something about radiation as a health hazard that is different from other industrial health issues?

Yes, the stakes are higher. There is only one set of radiation recommendations or permissible limits for workers and the general public, so you use the same set of standards whether it's a nuclear power plant, a hospital, or a bomb factory. Now, the people with the highest vested interest are the ones that are making the nuclear bombs. And it turns out they have complete control over setting the permissible levels. If you were to fix radiation limits at levels that were really protective of human health, you couldn't get anybody to make bombs.

How would you revise radiation standards to make them safe? I know for a nuclear power plant worker it's 5 rems a year.

It is 5 rems a year for the military too.

That's the level everybody talks about. Is that a safe level?

That's the magic number they decided on. But it is not safe. It should be divided by 50. That would give you .1 rem a year, which is about what you get from background. It's hazardous enough to double that—but they are actually multiplying by 50 and saying that's okay for a year.

To get the radiation limits down that low would mean retrofitting all the factories and could run into billions of dollars in capital costs and in radiation lawsuits. Doesn't that make it unworkable?

Well, the medical people could stay within that limit, and it just might be possible to redesign a nuclear commercial industry to stay within it too; but there is no way the military can handle it: Hanford, Rocky Flats, Fernald, the Nevada Test Site, the Savannah River Plant, Oak Ridge—there is no way they can do that. If you look back at who set the standards, it's the physicists on the Manhattan Project. They formed the International Commission on Radiological Protection, and they declared themselves the experts in the matter of radiation safety limits.

What did they use as the basis for setting the standards at the 5-rem level?

It was a compromise between the current British, Canadian, and American radiation standards. They set this in 1950–1951 after five years of negotiations. They had been meeting from 1946 on, and the compelling reason was that they were doing atmospheric weapons testing. These tests were blanketing countries in the northern hemisphere with radiation, and they were trying to make it legal.

Did the effects of the Hiroshima and Nagasaki bombs have anything to do with this standard?

A lot of the physicists who started the International Commission on Radiological Protection worked on the atomic bomb studies. That's why it's such an anomalous agency. It was composed of people who had to have security clearance in their own countries in order to belong. They didn't set up the commission as a professional society, they set it up as a secret club; in order to belong to the ICRP you have to be proposed by a present member and accepted by the present executive committee. So it's a self-perpetuating committee right out of the military. There has never been a woman on the commission. They have never had a public health expert on it. There has never been anyone in epidemiology on it. They've never had anyone on it who would challenge their risk estimates. They've had only three major publications, and at all of these junctures their personnel have been physicists.

Are there any medical people on it?

Someone like Alice Stewart would not be allowed to belong—her expertise doesn't fit their categories. They will only allow a medical doctor if the doctor is a radiologist. What this group is trying to do is manage the nuclear age. Because all their information is secret and classified, there is no public airing of the debate. Therefore you get a small group that reinforces one another's decisions. They are hyper about information falling into the wrong hands and about anyone undermining the military programs of the United States, which they consider to be saving the free world and preventing nuclear war.

For them, radiation safety standards are a military decision—the same kind of decision that you make when you say, "We might lose a few troops, but we will save the war." Only in this war the battlefield is the whole world and the soldiers are not named.

Have you ever met with any of the generals in this war?

I've been to several briefings at the U.S. State Department where they were discussing Strategic Arms Limitation, Intermediate Nuclear Warfare, and various other

unhappy topics. At the briefings very unemotional people discuss what we have and what they have, the throw-weights and the megatonnage, the backfire bombers, MX missiles, MIRVs and MARVs, and it goes on and on and on. It's a terribly emotional subject but was presented very dispassionately. Anyway, this one time I had been at the State Department all day— I listened for hours. Finally, at around four P.M., we were allowed to ask questions. And my question was quite simple: "How many people die every year for this program? If you count everybody from the uranium miners and millers and transport people to the ones that run the reactors, separate the plutonium, make the bombs and test them, and the people downwind, and the people that put up with the radioactive waste at every part of the cycle—how many deaths per year are required to build this number of nuclear weapons?"

Dr. Rosalie Bertell

There was great silence on the stage, and everybody just looked at the person next to him as if to say, "Who's going to answer that one?" Finally Paul Warnke came over very quietly to the microphone and he said, "That's not our department."

Up until then I had known intellectually that the military never counted the costs in dollars and cents, but that afternoon it finally hit me that when it comes to building nuclear bombs, the military doesn't count the cost in human lives. And from that time on I really started to look for the people in every part of the nuclear weapons cycle, the hidden people, for whom World War III has already started.

You talk about the testing and the people it's affected. What about the earth itself—is it possible to know how it's managing?

We've done massive damage. And we've not yet admitted that damage. We have not even been able to put together everything we're seeing. It frightens me very much that there is a whole blanket of radioactive material in the upper atmosphere, and no matter what we do it's coming down. Not all of this radioactive material has impacted on the food chain yet, so it will be coming down from the atmosphere for a long time to come, getting into the ocean and the plankton, and the fish, then onto the dinner table. This has been done on such a grand scale that it will impact no matter what, and we have no idea how to stop it.

Now we can't solve all the problems of human history, but our generation is going to have to turn around, and we're going to have do it on a fairly mammoth scale. We can't keep damaging human health and the human gene pool and at the same time damage the environment—because we make each generation physically less able to cope, while giving them more to physically cope with. We can't undermine the habitability of the planet and also undermine the gene pool at the same time. That's a death syndrome. It has no future.

I'm not sure how much more staying power the world has. Because once you tip that balance, then the whole thing will be out of whack. And we certainly don't have the knowledge or the technology to balance our air or water or the salinity of the oceans or any of these things. We don't know how to do any of these things.

So I'd say we're headed right now either to slow poison, a catastrophic reckless accident, or a nuclear war. All of which mean the demise of the planet and the demise of the human race. These arms negotiations are games. They're games with our lives, they're games with our planet. We can't afford to keep on preparing for war. The people are dying. At this point we should not be in a position of creating further damage. The time has come for us to maximize our health for what lies ahead.

98. Aggie Monica, a woman of Greenham Common—Montreal, Canada, November 20, 1983

Greenham women aren't just women who live at the Greenham Women's Peace Camp. They're every woman who feels the same as we do. Very often we feel threatened by the presence of men. The soldiers and the policemen—are always made up of men, and in any demonstration they will always go for the men first because it is much easier to incite a man to violent retaliation than it is to incite a woman. That's why Greenham Common is a woman's space. We're not angels, but we all treat each other with as much respect as we possibly can. And that's the basic thing, really.

We're not there to attack the base physically and dismantle the missiles or smash them up. We're there to recognize the strength and power that each of us has, and to join that together into a power of the will which will eventually change the physical situation in our world. We've focused on the removal of Cruise missiles because that's the most immediate threat we have. We've maintained a physical presence at the base since 1981.

Do the authorities make it hard for you to stay here?

We've had countless evictions. But when they evict, they're only allowed to take down our living structures. They aren't allowed to take our personal belongings away. So they come along and tear down our living structures, which are called benders, because they're made out of bent poles, stuck into the ground, and bent over and tied together, with some plastic over the top. And they come with rubbish-chewing machines so we can watch our shelters being destroyed. Then they go away. But we always have enough material put by so we can rebuild immediately.

What are some of the things the women have been doing at the base?

Well, last December 12, 1982, was a very special day—it was the third anniversary of the announcement that Cruise missiles were to be brought to Europe and sited at Greenham and other places. That day, altogether, we were 30,000 women, and we all joined hands and linked up, all the way around the perimeter of the fence. That was nine miles' worth of women. Actually it was more. We encircled the base and then some.

Then on January 1, forty-four women scaled the perimeter fence with ladders and penetrated the High Security Area through an open gate, then climbed up the slithery slope of an unfinished silo and danced on the top of it. They were up there for an hour before the security forces got out of bed, crawled up after them, and arrested them.

One time, several women took some spray cans with them, cut a hole in the fence, and went through. They found some of these modern technological marvels standing quite unattended, and they started spraying women's symbols on them and various other messages. They were found out and arrested. They were charged with criminal damage to the planes, and one plane in particular was singled out. The criminal damages on that came to a quarter of a million pounds. When they got to court, the prosecution withdrew the charge. They said the damage that was caused was negligible. We heard from a little bird inside the base that the plane that was sprayed had been a super spy plane with a titanium skin which made it invisible to radar. But spraying paint on it had damaged the titanium shield irreparably, so the whole plane was in fact now a write-off.

And this last summer we had an ongoing action called "snakes and ladders," which meant getting inside the base by any means. Hundreds of women cut holes in the fence and got inside and many of us were never detected.

What did you do inside?

Mostly we went in to do rituals—to reclaim the land from the forces of destruction.

So rituals are an important way of relating to things at Greenham . . .

They are. And you saw one of the bigger ones a few weeks ago. How did you find out about that? It was supposed to be a secret. We wanted to take the base by surprise, so we only told our own people, and we told them not to tell anybody.

This turned out to be our last big action before the missiles actually arrived. We put the word out, and about 3,000 women came together. We wanted the authorities to think we were going to do something similar to what we did in December, when we held hands around the fence and sang songs. But this action was going to be different. We asked women to get extra-strength industrial wire-cutters for cutting down the chain-link fence around the base. Ordinary wire-cutters aren't strong enough. The fence is made of an alloy which is very hard to cut through. So there was a run on these special cutters, and some London hardware stores were starting to get alarmed. We didn't want rumors to get out and give us away. So we recommended that people try to find the cutters in hardware stores outside London.

Why wasn't just surrounding the fence symbolic enough?

We felt that this time it would be a strong statement to open up the common ground for everyone to see. We knew the fence would be back up the next day, but the sight of that fence down, and the land opened up again, just before the missiles came in—we felt it would have a lot of meaning.

So it was primarily a visual event.

Yes, and it happened just the way we planned. We were able to do it because the guards and the police were ready for trespassers, but we didn't trespass that day. The plan was to cut down the fence and open up the space. But not trespass. The authorities didn't know how to handle it. They had no instructions for dealing with

Greenham Common fence, October 29, 1983

One of the Greens told me when I was in Bonn. He said I should keep it under my hat. I noticed that women were surprised when I showed up early that morning.

women who cut down the fence but did not trespass. After that they passed a by-law that said that touching the fence is the same as trespassing. But on October 29 we were able to do a lot of cutting because this had never happened before.

How much of the fence got cut down that day?

We worked on it from four in the afternoon till ten at night, and by the time it was over we'd cut down about four and a half miles of the fence.

Don't you think that damaging that much property is going to make people think you're a hazard to society?

Well, when is one justified in doing a certain amount of damage to protect oneself? I mean, it's only a fence that we've destroyed, after all. It wasn't the actual missiles themselves. And you know, this fence to me is a two-way thing. I was walking around the base one day and I remember feeling overwhelmed by the fear that was contained by the fence they'd built around themselves to protect themselves from us. It wasn't as though the fence was keeping us out. It was keeping them in. By cutting the fence we were liberating not only the land inside it but also the people who'd been trapped by the system into going into the army in the first place.

When the missiles came in did you feel disappointment, or did you feel that it was inevitable?

I watched it on the TV news, and we saw the carrier planes stopping, taxiing down to where the silos were, and these coffins were drawn out of their rear end. I remember thinking, this is sick. I felt really angry that this was happening. And I felt really sad that not enough people had listened to our warnings and helped prevent the missiles from being brought into the country. It seems that many people need something right under their noses before they actually start doing something about it.

---

99. Trinity: 5:30 A.M., July 16, 1945

Berlyn Brixner, official photographer for the Trinity explosion—Los Alamos, New Mexico, July 15, 1985

I'd like to ask you, Berlyn, about your work on the day the first atomic bomb went off. What was your official mission on that day?

My job was to get the motion picture record of the explosion. Whether it was the most powerful explosion that anybody estimated, or a fizzle, I was to get that record. I had a large number of cameras

with different settings so that I would be sure to get a suitable record.

How many cameras did you have, and what different speeds were they capable of?

Berlyn Brixner

I had about fifty cameras altogether. Some of them were running up to 10,000 frames per second or faster, those were called Fastax cameras, and we had other cameras running as slow as one frame per second, and all cameras in between, with different exposure settings and different lenses.

What kind of film did you use?

From 8mm to 35mm film stock.

Eight-millimeter film?

Yes, the high-speed cameras used 8mm film.

And it was all black-and-white?

Black-and-white. I selected Panatomic X film, ASA 30, and my boss concurred with that. On some of the other cameras we used Super Double-X and Plus-X.

Where were the cameras sited?

The cameras were located as close as half a mile from the target and as far as six miles away. We had two stations to the west and two stations to the north.

Did you have to protect the film from radiation?

The cameras were completely enclosed in special steel and lead bunkers that I

designed, and they looked out through lead-glass windows eight to ten inches thick.

When Trinity did go off, where was it between a fizzle and a maximum?

Well, the explosion was actually fantastic, almost unbelievable, and I couldn't even tell that it wasn't greater than they thought it might be, because when it went off I thought, "When is it going to stop growing in this great ball of fire that is coming out of there?"

Were you seized with a moment of fear that it might exceed expectations?

Well, I suppose I was, but it was such an amazing thing to see that I didn't really think about that. I was just wondering how much more it would grow.

You sound like a true photographer, taken by the visual quality of it—

Absolutely. We'd been preparing for this for months, you see, and I was just amazed. And, of course, I was sure that I got the pictures.

You knew that?

I felt that I did. My camera, which had a pan-and-tilt capability, had turned on a few seconds before Zero Time. So I thought all the other cameras were probably going properly too.

Did the other cameras have operators?

Only one other camera had an operator, and that was my boss, but it had rained the night before and apparently he hadn't covered his power supply, so when his camera came on, it immediately burned out the power supply.

Did you use your camera's pan-and-tilt capability?

Yes, I did. I was so amazed, though, initially that I just let the camera sit there. Then suddenly I realized that the ball of fire was going out of the field of view of the camera, so I grabbed the controls and started tilting the camera up to follow the ball of fire.

Does that mean that in this historic footage there's a kind of a jerky movement at that point?

There is. For the first twenty seconds on the standard-speed camera it's just sitting stationary, then suddenly you will see the field of view jump as the ball of fire is going out the top of the frame.

I guess you could call that the atomic tilt technique. . . .

Well, I guess that's it, yes. And the camera got a remarkable record for about two minutes running, just steadily purring away at twenty-four frames per second at f2.3. Every frame got an exposure. But of course the initial frames were tremendously overexposed. In fact, the first four or five frames were so badly overexposed that the emulsion was burned. Holes were burned right through the emulsion.

How long did that bright flash last? Was it an instant, or did it last several seconds?

It lasted quite a while, some thirty seconds. It was brightest at first, and then it gradually decayed. After about ten or fifteen seconds, I was able to take the filter away and look at the ball of fire without any filter at all.

Did a sound arrive from the bomb?

Yes, at about thirty seconds the shock wave reached our station with a very loud bang, and then again it was silent. If you've ever been close to a lightning bolt and heard that, that's the type of sound it made—just a tremendous bang and *crack!*

You describe the fireball, but you didn't mention the mushroom cloud.

Well, the cloud was just this black residue of material after the fireball went out. And it went up into the stratosphere, moved toward the northeast and, as I understand it, moved clear across the United States.

Let me ask you, Mr. Brixner: When you think of a nuclear weapon going off, what is the single image that comes to mind?

The image I have—well, there is this tremendously brilliant light that comes out of the initial part of the explosion, then the formation of a ball of fire, which becomes an immense ball of white-hot material. That's the image that persists in my mind, rather than the residue of dust and cloud that occurs afterward.

When you were watching all this, were you thinking of other people on the project, or was it a more private experience?

I was merely thinking of the success of the explosion itself. I didn't think about the use of the bomb or other people or anything else. But I could tell you another thing in conjunction with that, and what other people said afterward. At the station where I was located there was a loud-speaker for intercommunication between the various stations. It also had a microphone so that I could talk to all the other

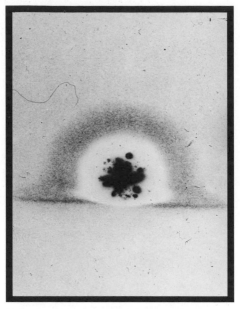
Holes burned in film emulsion: Trinity atomic blast
Photo by Brixner, Los Alamos National Laboratory

stations. As I mentioned, there was complete silence after the explosion, and for some time, possibly a minute or so, it was still silent. Then suddenly someone picked up that microphone and started talking about the explosion into the microphone because they knew other people would hear them. And then another person would grab their microphone and start talking simultaneously, and more and more people kept getting on that intercom until finally it was just a torrent of voices. And the amazing thing was the way their voices rose in frequency, as they were talking, they just got higher and higher in frequency as they were talking, and everybody that was talking had the same reaction, and it just kept on that way for several minutes.

I've never heard that story. What kinds of things were people saying?

Well, just what a marvelous thing it was and how their work had been successful. Actually I soon couldn't hear what the individuals were saying because it was just a big muttering of voices. And I was still thinking that I had to get busy and unload my cameras and get the film out of there. And pretty soon after the explosion the person monitoring radiation came over and said, "The radiation is rising here, we're going to have to evacuate."

Do you know what the levels of radiation were by the time you left?

No, I don't know what they were at all. They weren't terribly dangerous, but the cloud which had gone up was drifting to the northeast and then it dispersed a great

deal, and part of it was settling on us, and we could see it was kind of reddish in color and was coming down on us. It was very frightening just to see that. And when the monitor told us that we had to get out of there, I wasn't asking questions about how much or anything, but I was determined to get all the films that I'd exposed unloaded out of those cameras.

The trucks that you escaped on, did they have to be decontaminated after?

No, I don't think there was any problem with that. We didn't reach a high enough level. But the instruments that the radiation people had were capable of detecting almost infinitesimal levels of radioactivity. I think the meter they had hadn't been operating properly, that it was actually reading too high a level—a higher level than was actually occurring there. But I'm not sure about that. Anyway, there was no harm to the film. But of course it takes quite a bit of radiation to harm film.

Was there ever any sense of second thoughts about the work you were all doing?

I've heard that there were people who had such feelings, but I didn't come in contact with that at all. The main thing I heard was that the bombs were now being rushed to the west to be used on Japan, and we knew that that would be the end of the war. So we were pleased that things were going ahead with that actual dropping of the bombs on Japan. Of course we knew that they were disastrous as far as those cities were concerned. But that was simply the price of war. It was discussed what would have happened if we hadn't used those bombs, and the estimate was that at least a million lives, many of them Americans, would be lost if the war progressed without the bombs.

A lot of people are saying that perhaps we have too many nuclear weapons now.

Well, we let the genie out of the bottle as far as this atom bomb business is concerned, and that's too bad because it will never be put back. So now it's just a dangerous thing in the world and it seems to me it's obvious that there are far too many of these bombs all over the earth— in fact enough bombs, as I understand it, to completely destroy at least human life on the earth.

Do you think human nature has what it takes to refrain from creating such a catastrophe?

Well, it's hard to believe. I think that

fear of destruction does play a part. But if an insane person got control of these bombs, I couldn't at all hazard what might happen. We've simply got to keep these weapons under control. If we don't, it's just too bad. That's all I can say.

Okay, Mr. Brixner, I think that does it. Thank you very much.

I could tell you one more thing about the pictures. Naturally I haven't been given credit, I guess, photographically, for them. I hope that if you write a book about this photography of the Trinity explosion that you will explain that I was the cameraman on all the cameras. I did the whole job, had them all set, loaded, filters put in, stops set, speed control set—everything was my work on all fifty-some cameras. Almost all the photographs that have been distributed showing the explosion were made from the three motion picture camera films that I took there. They are all enlargements of the 35mm frames.

So it's "Photos by Brixner"?

Photos by Brixner, that's right, every one of them.

100. Hiroshima, August 6, 1945

Yoshito Matsushige, photographer— Hiroshima, Japan, September 5, 1984

At the time of the bombing I was a photographer working for the *Chugoku Shimbun* newspaper in Hiroshima. I was also an official reporter for the army.

I lived 2.7 kilometers from the hypocenter. Part of my house was a barbershop. My wife was cutting hair and running the barbershop. I was hit by the A-bomb there.

At around midnight, early August 6, an air raid sounded. I got on my bicycle and went to army headquarters. That morning at seven I returned home, took breakfast, read the newspaper, and was getting ready to go to work when the A-bomb was dropped.

What happened? What did you see from your house?

At first I saw something shining and sparkling—it was a kind of twinkling light, like you see from a sparkling electric live wire. The next instant there was this huge white flash, like a giant magnesium flashbulb. I couldn't see anything anymore after that. Then I heard a blast and when the blast hit, my body jumped in the air about one meter and I was thrown against the wall. My wife cried, "Bombing!" and ran to me. I grabbed her hand and we both got out of the house. We crossed the streetcar

Yoshito Matsushige

tracks and went out into the field across the street. I thought the bomb had landed right on my house.

I went into the field holding my wife's hand, but I couldn't see her face because of the blast and the uranium dust. Everywhere there was dust; it made a grayish darkness over everything. But I could feel the warmth of my wife's hand, and it was this that made me realize she was still alive and also that I was still alive.

What time was it?

It must have been about 8:40 A.M. A few minutes later the grayish darkness began to go up into the sky, and I thought, I am a newspaper photographer and a reporter for the army, so I have an obligation to make sure where the bomb was dropped. It was time to go to work.

When I got back to my house it was in ruins. I pulled my army uniform and my camera out from under a heap of plaster and left home at nine. I walked east down the streetcar tracks to the Miyuki-bashi Bridge. I was heading for the center of town.

Did you see anything like a mushroom cloud in the sky overhead?

No. I was just looking directly in front of me, straight ahead. But I don't think I could have seen it anyway, since I was right underneath it.

When I got to the Takano-bashi Bridge, the central part of the city was surrounded in flames. I knew then that I'd never get into that area.

Were you thinking at all about the kind of bomb that had caused such destruction?

I guessed it had not been an ordinary bomb. At army headquarters I would sometimes hear secret information, and one time a rumor was going around that

there existed bombs the size of matchboxes which could destroy large buildings. I thought this bomb must have been not exactly the same, but something like that. Military people had also been saying that the United States had invented some kind of very special small-sized bomb.

I'm surprised to hear that! I thought the atomic bomb had been a very closely kept secret.

Well, ordinary Japanese people knew nothing of this. But army headquarters was talking about it. If any of us in the military spoke out about such secret information, the police would have come and arrested us.

Where did you go when you saw the fire?

When I saw the fire I knew I had to go back and try another route if I was going to reach my office or army headquarters. That fire on August 6 was no ordinary fire; it was a fire maelstrom. And it was moving fast up the street, coming right for me. So I was forced back to the Miyuki-bashi Bridge.

When I got there I saw a crowd of people. Most of them were burned. It was at this time that I remembered, I was a professional photographer, that this was a great disaster, and that I should try to photograph it and get the pictures to the newspaper or to army headquarters.

What kind of a camera were you carrying, and how much film did you have?

I had a small 6 × 6 Mamiya viewfinder camera and two rolls of black-and-white film, 100 ASA, twelve exposures per roll. So I had enough film for twenty-four pictures. That was a lot in those days. Ordinary people had no film at all. It was because I was an army reporter that I had those two rolls. But I ended up taking only five photographs that day.

Is this photograph on the Miyuki-bashi Bridge your first photograph that day?

Yes. I took it at a little after eleven A.M. This bridge was 2.2 kilometers from the hypocenter.

What is that building?

That's a police station, the Senda-cho Station House. In front of it they had set up a temporary medical treatment center for injured persons. Two officers are putting cooking oil on burns. The oil came from the army food-storage warehouse. Injured people were everywhere. Both sidewalks of the bridge were crowded with dead and suffering victims. When I saw them I realized I had to take a picture, and I tried to push the shutter, but I couldn't. It was so terrible. These people were pathetic. I had to wait. Most of the people were students, children.

I always thought they were old people in this photograph.

No, these are mainly students from the Hiroshima Girls' Commercial High School and from the Hiroshima Prefecture Daiichi Middle School. They had been mobilized to make a fire break in case of a bombing raid.

Why did you take only five photographs on that day?

Before I became a professional cameraman I had been just an ordinary person. So when I was faced with a terrible scene like this, I found it difficult to push the shutter. I was standing on the Miyuki-bashi Bridge for about twenty minutes before I could do it. Finally I thought, I am a professional cameraman so I have to take pictures. Then I managed to push the shutter.

Soon after, I took a second picture, but I couldn't push the shutter a second time without crying, because it was a really terrible scene. It was just like something out of hell, and I didn't feel like taking many pictures. I was just dumbfounded.

My viewfinder was fogged because of my tears. I understand why you ask me why I did not take more pictures, but in reality it was very difficult. When I set my camera at somebody who was asking for help I could not really push the shutter.

Does that mean several times you thought of taking a picture and then decided not to do it?

Yes—there was one time. It happened when I left the Miyuki-bashi Bridge at around two, when the flames were more subdued.

I went to my newspaper office downtown. The way was very difficult. I could find no street. Everything was gutted, a few fires were still burning here and there, roof tiles were everywhere. It was hard not to walk on the dead bodies. I tried not to, but I had to. On the way I passed Hiroshima University. There is a swimming pool at the university. The previous day it had been full of water, but when I passed by in the afternoon there was almost none. It must have evaporated because of the fire. All that was left was a little water in the bottom of the pool, and people had jumped in to get to the water, but it must have been almost boiling, and the people couldn't get back out of the pool, so they died in the hot water. There were seven or eight people like boiled fish at the bottom of this pool.

Was this a scene you tried to take a picture of?

It was such a terrible situation I didn't think of my camera at all. I felt I was going crazy. So I just kept trying to get to

the newspaper company. When I finally got there I tried to enter the building but I walked only a few steps into it. I couldn't go in farther because of the heat.

When I couldn't get into my building I walked back into the street. Several dead bodies were lying in front of the building. I went to the corner, and there was a streetcar. I went up to it and looked inside. It was jammed with people. They were all in normal positions, holding onto streetcar straps, sitting down or standing still, just the way they would have been before the bomb went off. Except that all of them were leaning in the same direction—away from the center of the blast. And they were all burned black, a reddish black, and they were stiff. It was about twenty people in all. They had all died instantly. I felt that they had their eyes open even though they were all burned.

This was the scene I tried to take a picture of. I put one foot up on the streetcar and looked into it. I put my finger on the shutter for one or two minutes, but I could not push it. I refrained from taking the picture. It was too terrible to take a picture of. This was the only scene I was going to take a picture of but did not.

How close was this to the center of the bomb?

This was very close—about 300 meters from the hypocenter.

Where did you go after that?

I went back to my house, and there I took the third and fourth photographs. My house was 2.7 kilometers south-southeast from the hypocenter. The fire did not reach this part of the city, but the damage from the blast was terrible. I got home at around two P.M.

The third picture is of the barbershop chairs. That is my wife in the background. She is looking after our valuables.

The fourth picture is the view out our barbershop window, with the streetcar tracks and a man walking by. The destroyed building is the Kaimi branch of the Nishi Fire Station. It was a three-story wooden building with a watchtower. The blast from the bomb made the building collapse. One fireman was in the watchtower when it collapsed. Fire trucks and

several firemen on the first floor were buried. One of them was seriously wounded and several were injured. The injured firemen were treated in my house for about one week, beginning that evening. My wife nursed them.

Later in the afternoon I went back to the area of the Miyuki-bashi Bridge, where I took my final photograph, the one of the bandaged soldier writing at a table. That

was about four in the afternoon, near the other end of the bridge, on the curve of the trolley-car tracks on the Ujina line.

Who is the soldier? What is he doing?

He is a policeman. He is writing a certificate for people who were hit by the disaster. With a certificate a person could be given a little bread.

Why did you take a picture of this activity?

I don't know. I didn't think, "This is important."

And this was your last picture?

In the evening I was in the vicinity of the present A-bomb hospital and there was a fire. I took two or three pictures of that, but the film at that time was not as sensitive as it is today and none of them came out. I threw the negatives away. If only I knew that those pictures would turn out to be so valuable I might have preserved them. But I had no way of knowing this at the time.

I think if the situation had been different, and it had been Japan that had dropped the atomic bomb on America and I went to the United States to take pictures of the effects of the bomb, then I might have taken lots more pictures. But here in Hiroshima those who were dying were all my fellow countrymen, my fellow Hiroshimans, and I had never fought with them, so I couldn't take pictures of so many terrible scenes.

You know, if the situation today were different, if the world were not so full of nuclear weapons, these photographs would have been forgotten, or remembered only as relics from the past. But the situation today makes these pictures very important. These views are very meaningful because they are not just about something that happened a long time ago.

There should never be war in which nuclear weapons are used. So I hope that you listen to as many people as possible in Hiroshima, and that you make as many people as possible know how terrible the A-bomb is. That is my wish.

Interview translated by Mieko Yamashita.

---

101. Hiroshima Peace Park

This cenotaph currently contains the names of over 125,000 victims of the Hiroshima bomb. Each year the list grows by 4,000-5,000.

---

102. Moscow Hospital Number 6

The enormous cost of the cleanup of the Chernobyl reactor and the resettlement of its evacuees has been borne in part by Soviet citizens who volunteer their labors in nationwide "free Saturday" work campaigns. Moneys that would normally have been paid in wages are donated to defray costs of the accident. Bank account number 904 was also established throughout the country so that people in the Soviet Union can enter any bank and contribute toward the Chernobyl relief effort by putting money into this account.

103. Tsue Hayashi, age 84—Sakura-baba, Nagasaki, Japan, August 14, 1985

Tsue Hayashi's only child was named Kayoko. In August 1945, Kayoko was fifteen years old. Like many her age, she had been mobilized for the war effort. She worked at the Shiroyama Primary School, which had been converted into a torpedo-assembly plant. The school was located in Nagasaki's Urakami district, 3.5 kilometers from her home.

The story of Kayoko's cherry trees is well known in Nagasaki, but outside Nagasaki not many people have heard of it. . . .

That is right. It is not known. I never meant it to be famous. I'd prefer people to leave Kayoko's cherry trees alone. The story came from my desire to pray for Kayoko's spirit and for everyone who died in the bomb.

How does it begin?

On the morning of August 9, I gave Kayoko her lunch box, and she went out of the house to go to work at the Shiroyama Primary School. A few minutes later she came back and put her lunch box down. I asked her, "What is wrong?" She said, "I don't feel like going to work today." This was unusual. Kayoko was a very serious girl. She always worked hard. This was the first time she had said something like this. I wanted to tell her, "Please take a day off," but I didn't. Her birthday was coming in two days, and I wanted her to take a day off then. If she took a day off now that would make two days in one week. So I told her to go to work, and in two days she would have a holiday. She picked up her lunch box and went to work. I am the one who sent her away. I regret and regret and regret this.

Later that morning the bomb fell. At first I did not realize it was an atomic bomb. I just noticed something bright and flashing, like sparks from a trolley car, and I heard thunder. I ran out of the house without my shoes on and saw the sky over Urakami full of black smoke. It was unusual. My first thought was to get Kayoko. I started making my way toward Urakami, but the chief of my block saw me and called out, "Where are you going?" I told him, "Kayoko is in Urakami!" He grabbed me and said, "You'll die if you go there!" I stood there for a long time. The smoke began to turn into flames. I went home. People with burns on their faces and backs started going past my house. Some had skin hanging down like rags. I asked them, "How is Urakami?" and, "Have you seen Kayoko? She was working at the Shiroyama Primary School." They told me that a big bomb had been dropped and that Urakami had been destroyed.

The whole night I waited for Kayoko on the front porch. I kept praying for her to be alive. The morning after the bomb, and every day after that, from early morning until evening, I walked all over the city looking for Kayoko. I saw many people suffering and dying. It was very sad. I felt deeply the severe power of the A-bomb. I cannot remember seeing a single other person walking. Maybe that is because of the rumor that you will die sooner if you go into Urakami. There were no trees there, no grass, no houses, only a lot of broken roof tiles. And many corpses. I thought, "I've heard of hell. It must be like this." Some of the people were still dying. When I walked past them they would say, "Give me water, please. Please help me." I could only say, "I'm sorry. I have no water. I can't help you. Forgive me. I have to look for my child."

When I was looking for my child I kept thinking about the wisdom of mankind. I wondered, "What on earth is this wisdom of mankind?" Whatever it was, I hated it. It wasn't the bad people who were killed. The A-bomb killed everybody. Even condemned criminals have a better death than the people I saw suffering. I couldn't help them at all, I had to walk right through them. My feet were hurt and bleeding, but I kept thinking stubbornly about the wisdom of mankind. Who invented this bomb? If they had such great brains, why couldn't they also invent a way to help the victims recover? I knew there would be no answer to my questions. I think mankind opened the lid of the box that God said not to open in the Bible. I hope mankind never uses the A-bomb again.

Day after day, for twenty-one days, I wandered, seeking my Kayoko. It was the middle of summer and the days were very hot. One time I was looking for Kayoko in the mountains and I saw a young woman with a cotton shawl over her head, nursing her baby. I was frightened and wondered if she was a real human being. I went closer. I found out she was not a person in this world anymore. It was a corpse. When I saw that, I thought, "How miserable!" Maybe only women will understand the feeling of nursing a baby. It is a very pure and innocent time. It is like heaven in this world. The A-bomb killed this woman in that pure and innocent moment.

At first I was looking for a live child, but about halfway through my search I started looking for her among the corpses.

But the corpses were so burned you could recognize only the shape of the skull. I decided to look at the corpses' teeth. My child had a row of teeth that was different from others'. Her front bottom teeth came out a little farther than usual. She was also starting treatment on a back tooth. So I opened the mouths of corpses to look at their teeth. Some of the corpses' mouths were closed very tightly. I had to pry them open.

One day I found a corpse whose teeth looked like my child's. I wasn't sure, though, because Kayoko's back tooth had not received a real filling yet, but the corpse whose teeth were like Kayoko's looked like it had a filling. Still I thought, "It's Kayoko," and I brought the remains back home. I held a funeral ceremony with my neighbors.

Tsue Hayashi

When I finished the funeral, my heart would not become calm. I had a dream at that time. In the dream I saw Kayoko wandering in the ruins. That made me think, "Kayoko is still waiting for me out there. Maybe she is even still alive, just barely breathing, and can't call out." So I kept looking for my child every day, even after the funeral.

At last I found my real child. It finally happened twenty-one days after the bomb exploded. I found her on the top floor of the Shiroyama Primary School. This was the third time I had gone up there to look for her. To get to the third floor, I had to crawl, because the stairway had been destroyed.

How did you know it was the real Kayoko this time?

During the war I made an air-raid hood for Kayoko out of my cotton kimono. I heard cotton did not burn easily. I sewed a small notebook into the top part of the hood. In the notebook I had written my last will and testament. I told Kayoko: If I die, you should live in such-and-such a way. I have left your belongings under my parents' place in the country. When the war is over, get them. Your home's economical condition is such-and-such. Learn this condition and live according to it. You should never commit suicide, even if I die and you become very sad. Keep living firmly. You were born with the ability to survive.

When I went upstairs this time at the Shiroyama Primary School, I noticed a piece of that air-raid hood. I said, "What's that?" and ran over to it. There I found the upper part of my child's body. It was half burned. There was no lower part remaining. Everything else on the third floor had been burned completely. Other people's bones were burned and had become like pieces of small gravel. But my child's bones remained intact, even though there was no meat on them. And the shape of my child's open mouth formed an "ah" sound, as if she was saying "Ka-a-a-a-a." When I saw that, I thought my child must have been calling *O-ka-cha-ma* ["Mommy"] before she died.

Was the notebook still in the cotton hood?

Yes, it hadn't been burned. I was very sad to pick up my last will and testament again in this place. I wrapped up my child's bones in cloth. To get down to the ground floor I had to slide down on my bottom, pulling the cloth bundle behind me. On the ground, I cremated my child. When I got home I came down with a very high fever, and I had to stay in bed.

What happened with the remains of the other child?

I buried her in the same grave as Kayoko's. So the unknown girl was enshrined as one of my family's deceased. When the Festival of the Dead comes I have the priest pray for the unknown girl, too. Do you know what *Ta-mu-ke* is? It means to offer something to dead people, like flowers or cookies. I still offer cooked rice and tea every day.

For Kayoko?

Yes, but I saw many dead people everywhere. I walked through them, crying. When the war was over, I eagerly wanted to make some kind of offering. I thought about it over and over. I decided

I'd like to plant cherry trees to go around the school. I wanted to do this for their souls.

For the souls of . . .

For the souls of everyone. If it were only for Kayoko I wouldn't have dared to ask for permission to plant the trees. Thousands of people died—there were so many corpses it was hard not to step on them. I wanted to offer something to all those people. The cherry trees were for everybody. Do you understand?

The Shiroyama teachers said, "All right, you may plant cherry trees." But there were no young cherry trees in Nagasaki at that time. A gardener told me, "There's not even food here, not to mention young cherry trees!" I asked the gardener and his son to go around the bay to Kurume to buy them. They planted the cherry trees around the school. Those trees were beautiful when they bloomed.

Thank you for telling your story. I learned today that Kayoko's cherry trees were not only for Kayoko, but for everyone.

Do you know something? I never named them "Kayoko's Cherry Trees." The school named them that. I would have called them just something like *"Ta-mu-ke no sakura"* ["Cherry Tree Offering for the Dead"]. I didn't build the monument either. The school put it in. This whole thing has become more and more famous, and I am somewhat embarrassed by it.

Interview translated by Setsumi Del Tredici.

104. Dr. Edward Teller, Hoover Institute— Palo Alto, California, December 14, 1984

Dr. Teller, my first question to you regards something you wrote in a book called The Legacy of Hiroshima. *You stated there that we entered the atomic age with dirty hands. This was in reference to the fact that we bombed Hiroshima and Nagasaki without prior warning. How has this particular lesson of Hiroshima influenced our subsequent nuclear-war thinking?*

I think it is truly regrettable that a suggestion to demonstrate the atomic bomb before using it has not been put into practice. Imagine that we might have carried out such a demonstration, for instance, dropping a nuclear explosive over Tokyo without warning, but at such altitude that it would have lit up the evening sky for many miles and not done any damage whatsoever. In the end we dropped the

bomb on Hiroshima, and the Japanese leaders were completely undecided what to do about it. The war was ended only by the personal and illegal intervention of Emperor Hirohito, who was God, and was not supposed to interfere with any military decisions. But I believe there was a very real chance that the demonstration over Tokyo with a subsequent demonstration of what it was, a demonstration that Hirohito would have seen, might have led to the same consequence. We could then have followed up with an actual bomb in two weeks if they did not surrender. But I think the chances are they would have surrendered. If we could have started the atomic age by having demonstrated the power of technology to end a dreadful war without killing a single person, I think we all would have a better conscience, we would

Dr. Edward Teller

be able to think more calmly about nuclear explosives, we would be more safe, and war would be less likely today.

Is there some way out of where we are today?

What was done cannot be undone. But at least we can promote initiatives to use nuclear explosives in a defensive way. We should consider, as well, using all other means which in many cases may be more efficient and more appropriate, and not make distinctions between nuclear and non-nuclear weapons, but make a strong distinction between aggression and defense. That, I think, would lead us out.

You once stated, "For as long as I could remember I have wanted to do one thing: to play with ideas and find out how the

world is put together." Could you describe, in your career, the role that playfulness, imagination, and curiosity have had in terms of your own major scientific breakthroughs?

To apply imagination to pure science was what I wanted, and that's what I did. It is something wonderful in its day-to-day execution, and it brings people together. But as soon as the practical element enters, serious differences will unavoidably appear. Unfortunately, when the Second World War started we had reason to believe that the Nazis would work on an atomic weapon, and I was persuaded that we had to do likewise. And this needed an entirely different style of work. No more could we enjoy a completely free exercise of the imagination. That was not the kind of work I like. It's the kind of work I pursued because I understood it to be my duty. After the passage of almost half a century I still believe, unfortunately, that it is my duty, because the simple idea that technology must be developed and applied wherever it can be, but it must be applied by reason and limited by the decisions of a democratic society that straightforward point of view is not accepted by the scientific community.

Most scientists imagine they create weapons which then become independent of man, and, whether man wants it or not, these weapons will work destruction. Too few understand that technology for peace, technology for defense, cannot be separated in its technical origins from technology for destruction. These important differentiations have to be made, *not* by scientists, but by the public, which decides in a democratic society how technical advances should be used. There are too few spokesmen who continue to insist on the development of technology for defense and the welfare of the people, and not excluding arms because arms cannot be excluded in the present unstable political situation. Arms instability is caused by deep historical and ideological differences, and not by the arms race. This point of view needs people to defend it, and I happened to acquire at least an opportunity to be heard, which for me also is an obligation. From my own personal point of view, nothing would be more wonderful than if I could return to pure science, which I still am trying to do in my few free moments. That I'm not doing it full-time is simply due to the fact that among my colleagues the majority happen to look at nuclear war from exaggerated points of view. I find that the point of view which is for technology but also insists on its right application is underrepresented.

I'd like to ask you a question, Doctor, about the arms race. One disquieting aspect of it for many people is its mirrorlike quality. It goes like this: if we can think of it, so can they, and we may as well build it, because if we don't they will. Yet if you have two parties who both think this way, it seems you have a situation that will never end. Is there a way out of such a mirrorlike condition?

You have mixed up in a most unusual and yet ingenious fashion what is correct and what makes no sense. If we can think of it, so can they—of course! The point is that one year before the hydrogen bomb debate started, before most people in our scientific community said, "If we don't do it, neither will the Russians," a year before that, Sakharov had already decided to work on the hydrogen bomb. The simple fact is true: we can think of it, they can think of it, but this does not need to lead to an impasse, because if we could work on defensive weapons, and we can prove, as I hope we can prove, that they are more effective than offense, then that will lead to two armed camps facing each other armed not with swords but primarily with shields. And that will be a much less dangerous situation than the present horrible balance of terror. Therefore, there is a way out. It seems to me to be a thoroughly worthwhile objective, and it should not be condemned as an element of the arms race. One should understand that any new development in technology can be applied to thoroughly peaceful purposes or to war and within war it can be applied to defense or attack. These distinctions will have to be made, quite obviously, by the public. But the technology must be made available to the public because otherwise the technology of attack, or of world domination, will develop in that country—Russia—which has applied suppression and pursued expansion for hundreds of years. That is why the situation is not mirrorlike. The mirror does not exist.

Is weapons development in America a democratic process?

The arms race is not a purely democratic process, as long as secrecy excludes the full participation of the public. But the arms race is deeply influenced by public opinion. To that extent it is a democratic process.

A final question, Dr. Teller, about what I sense is an underlying assumption throughout your writing. I would put it this way: man is here to stay, the human race shall survive. Today many people are full of fear and trembling over whether man shall be here to stay and whether the human race shall survive. Could you comment on this?

I am afraid I have to contradict you, just in a flat and complete manner. That the human race will survive was never my basic assumption. It was my conclusion in every case where the question arose. I did not begin with any conclusion during the fallout scare, the scare connected with the depletion of the ozone layer, and now the scare connected with nuclear winter. In each case many of us, including me, have taken a careful look and tried to separate exaggeration and propaganda from fact. And in each case we came to the conclusion that the human race will survive as certainly as could certainly be stated at any time in the past. Without exception, those who object to war like to find additional reasons why war should be excluded. So we frequently are led to exaggeration, like picturing the end of the human race.

Let me tell you, I am afraid that we may not survive. I am not *very* much afraid of this; I am *somewhat* afraid of it, in connection with biological warfare, which might get out of control. In nuclear warfare the extinction of the human race is much less likely. A nuclear winter is already an exaggeration, because the probabilities are for only a limited effect on temperature. It might get big enough to influence crops in the hemisphere, but it is practically certain not to lead to the extremely serious consequences that have been discussed. Actually, I believe that fallout, ozone depletion, nuclear winter—or, more properly expressed, nuclear temperature change—will cause possibly great additional suffering, but, with practical certainty, not as great as the suffering or slaughter that will occur in the nations that participate in the nuclear conflict. Nuclear war could result in probably more than a hundred million deaths, perhaps a thousand million deaths. Still—survival. But together with survival, the probability not only of immense suffering in the nations participating in the conflict, but destruction of all human ideals. German science, which used to be something really splendid before Hitler, never yet has recovered from what the Nazis did. A nuclear war will leave behind, I am afraid, no matter how it works out, some sort of madness, and some of my friends say that madness may turn out to be incurable. Of that I am much more afraid than of the end of the human race.

The wish to avoid nuclear war need not be strengthened by fairy tales of the end of the human race. What is really to be expected should be sufficient to make us strongly determined to keep our ideals without a nuclear war. And I think it can be done, and the most hopeful approach today is the development of defensive weapons, non-nuclear or nuclear, as long as they defend the innocent. The way out of the present difficulties exists through increased emphasis on defense. I think a peaceful future can be secured only if those who want peace also develop technology to its limits.

105. The Becquerel Reindeer

Soon after the Chernobyl accident the Swedish government announced that it would purchase contaminated reindeer meat from Lapp herdsmen at a price slightly higher than the standard rate. Reindeer meat unfit for human consumption is not destroyed but is sent to mink farms where it is used to feed mink.

106. All the Warheads in the U.S. Nuclear Arsenal

The *Amber Waves of Grain* ceramic installation was created by Denver artist Barbara Donachy. It currently contains a total of 33,561 pieces (representing 31,500 warheads; 1,700 ballistic missiles; 324 intercontinental bombers; and 37 submarines). The installation has been displayed in New York, West Berlin, Washington, San Francisco, Detroit, and other cities. An exhibit is planned for Hiroshima in late 1987.

According to the *Nuclear Weapons Data Book*, (Volume 2, *U.S. Nuclear Warhead Production*, by Cochran, Arkin, Norris, and Hoenig of the Natural Resources Defense Council; Ballinger Publishing Company, 1987), the United States has been engaged in the design, testing, and manufacture of nuclear warheads since 1940. Four agencies or departments have overseen these activities—the Manhattan Engineer District (1942–46), the Atomic Energy Commission (1947–74), the Energy Research and Development Administration (1974–77), and the Department of Energy (1977–). Together, they have spent approximately $89 billion ($230 billion in 1986 dollars). Meanwhile, the Department of Defense (DOD) has spent an estimated $700 billion ($1.85 trillion in 1986 dollars) on the nuclear delivery systems (aircraft, missiles, ships) and other support costs.

From 1945 to 1986 the nuclear weapons production complex has manufactured approximately 60,000 warheads of 71 types for 116 kinds of weapons systems. Forty-two types have been fully retired, leaving 29 in the current stockpile.

The warheads are designed, tested, and manufactured in a U.S. government–owned, contractor-operated (GO-CO) complex. The complex spreads over thirteen states, covers a land area of 3,900 square miles, and employs some 90,000 people.